THE ABUNDANT LIFE
BIBLE
AMPLIFIER

DANIEL
7–12

WILLIAM H. SHEA

THE ABUNDANT LIFE
BIBLE
AMPLIFIER

DANIEL
7–12

Prophecies of the End Time

GEORGE R. KNIGHT
General Editor

Pacific Press Publishing Association
Boise, Idaho
Oshawa, Ontario, Canada

Edited by B. Russell Holt
Designed by Tim Larson
Typeset in 11/14 Janson Text

Maps on pages 87, 91, 99, and 129 taken from Zondervan NIV Atlas
of the Bible by Carl Rasmussen. Copyright © 1989 by Carta, Jerusalem. Used by permission of Zondervan Publishing House.

Unless otherwise mentioned, all Bible quotations in this book are
from the New International Version, and all emphasis in Bible quotations is supplied by the author.

ISBN 0-8163-1340-7 (paper)·
ISBN 0-8163-1341-5 (hard)

96 97 98 99 00 • 5 4 3 2 1

CONTENTS

MAPS

To

Josie, Ted, and Becky

GENERAL PREFACE

The Abundant Life Bible Amplifier series is aimed at helping readers understand the Bible better. Rather than merely offering comments on or about the Bible, each volume seeks to enable people to study their Bibles with fuller understanding.

To accomplish that task, scholars who are also proven communicators have been selected to author each volume. The basic idea underlying this combination is that scholarship and the ability to communicate on a popular level are compatible skills.

While the Bible Amplifier is written with the needs and abilities of laypeople in mind, it will also prove helpful to pastors and teachers. Beyond individual readers, the series will be useful in church study groups and as guides to enrich participation in the weekly prayer meeting.

Rather than focusing on the details of each verse, the Bible Amplifier series seeks to give readers an understanding of the themes and patterns of each biblical book as a whole and how each passage fits into that context. As a result, the series does not seek to solve all the problems or answer all the questions that may be related to a given text. In the process of accomplishing the goal for the series, both inductive and explanatory methodologies are used.

Each volume in this series presents its author's understanding of the biblical book being studied. As such, it does not necessarily represent the "official" position of the Seventh-day Adventist Church.

It should be noted that the Bible Amplifier series utilizes the New International Version of the Bible as its basic text. *Every reader should read the "How to Use This Book" section to get the fullest benefit from the Bible Amplifier study volumes.*

Dr. William H. Shea is an associate director of the Biblical Research Institute in Silver Spring, Maryland. Before coming to his present position, Dr. Shea served as a professor of Old Testament at the Seventh-day Adventist Theological Seminary at Andrews University. He holds doctoral degrees in both medicine and Near Eastern studies. A prolific author, Dr. Shea has written scores of articles and reviews for both scholarly and popular journals. He has taken a special interest in the book of Daniel. Many readers of this volume will be familiar with his *Selected Studies on Prophetic Interpretation.* He has also authored *Daniel 1–7: Prophecy as History* in the Bible Amplifier series.

George R. Knight
Berrien Springs, Michigan

AUTHOR'S PREFACE

In terms of subject matter, Daniel's book is divided almost equally, with the first half being mostly history and the second half being mostly prophecy. Of course, we find elements of prophecy in the historical chapters, and there are, likewise, some historical elements in the prophetic chapters. But the general division of the book into roughly equal sections of history and prophecy is an accurate and helpful distinction.

My own studies into Daniel began with the historical portion of the book. I was interested in establishing the authenticity of the Neo-Babylonian setting for the book and its author. From that study, an interest emerged in God's divine foreknowledge as clearly indicated in the prophecies of Daniel—especially given the lengthy time periods they cover.

I began my research into Daniel's prophecies by looking at the close connection between chapters 8 and 9. In the early 1980s, about the time I had completed my initial study, controversy broke out in the Seventh-day Adventist Church regarding these particular prophetic chapters. As a result, my work with the Biblical Research Institute of the General Conference required me to give more detailed attention to the prophetic portions of Daniel. This study resulted in an unpublished manuscript, "Daniel and the Judgment." Eventually, the Biblical Research Institute published certain chapters from this manuscript as volume one of the Daniel and Revelation Committee Series, under the title, *Selected Studies in Prophetic Interpretation*. As the title suggests, this work was not a chapter-by-chapter commentary on Daniel's prophecies, but dealt rather with certain topics only.

In contrast, this second Bible Amplifier volume on Daniel does deal with the entire sweep of the prophetic chapters. This enables the reader to study the text in a more orderly fashion. However, I have chosen to deal with the text of Daniel in a way that does not strictly follow the original order as given in the book itself. For example, in examining chapters 7, 8, and 9, I have reversed the order—taking up chapter 9 first, then chapter 8, followed by chapter 7. I have done so because I believe the text becomes more meaningful if viewed in this order. I have also followed this "reverse" order based on insights that have come from studying the literary structure of various Old Testament texts—especially the Psalms. In the introduction to this volume, as well as in the various chapters that cover these prophecies, I have provided further justification for altering the order of the chapters for the purpose of studying them.

The history presented in the earlier portions of Daniel's book flows quite naturally into the prophetic sections. There is a sense in which prophecy is merely history written from the divine viewpoint before it happens. Some elements of history provide a basis for reviewing the fulfillment of prophecies after the events have happened. Thus, we will not find a sharp separation in Daniel's book between history and prophecy. The great outline prophecies in Daniel begin quite naturally with Babylon and Medo-Persia—the kingdoms that existed in the prophet's own time. They go on to point to kingdoms yet to come—Greece and Rome. Finally, they come down to our own time and beyond—until God's kingdom makes its appearance. God's eternal kingdom is the great goal of history. It is also the great goal of prophecy, and it should be the great goal of our own personal, spiritual journey as well.

Therefore, as we see the unfolding of history and prophecy in Daniel, we see God's hand guiding that history by His mighty acts on behalf of His people—national Israel in the Old Testament, and the church in the New Testament. As surely as He has guided that history in the past, just so surely will He eventually bring about its culmination in His glorious kingdom. That was Daniel's inspired focus, and it should be ours as well. Our own spiritual experience with God should have as its goal living with Him forever in the kingdom He has promised to set up at the end of time. It is my hope that this volume in the Bible Amplifier series will contribute in some measure toward that end.

William H. Shea
Silver Spring, Maryland

How to Use This Book

The Abundant Life Amplifier series treats each major portion of each Bible book in five main sections.

The first section is called "Getting Into the Word." The purpose of this section is to encourage readers to study their own Bibles. For that reason, the text of the Bible has not been printed in the volumes in this series.

You will get the most out of your study if you work through the exercises in each of the "Getting Into the Word" sections. This will not only aid you in learning more about the Bible but will also increase your skill in using Bible tools and in asking (and answering) meaningful questions about the Bible.

It will be helpful if you write out the answers and keep them in a notebook or file folder for each biblical book. Writing out your thoughts will enhance your understanding. The benefit derived from such study, of course, will be proportionate to the amount of effort expended.

The "Getting Into the Word" sections assume that the reader has certain minimal tools available. Among these are a concordance and a Bible with maps and marginal cross-references. If you don't have a New International Version of the Bible, we recommend that you obtain one for use with this series, since all the Bible Amplifier authors are using the NIV as their basic text. For the same reason, your best choice of a concordance is the *NIV Exhaustive Concordance,* edited by E. W. Goodrick and J. R. Kohlenberger. Strong's *Exhaustive Concordance of the Bible* and Young's *Analytical Concordance to the Bible* are also useful. However, even if all you have is Cruden's *Concordance*, you will be able to do all of the "Getting Into the Word" exercises and most of the "Researching the Word" exercises.

The "Getting Into the Word" sections also assume that the reader has a Bible dictionary. The *Seventh-day Adventist Bible Dictionary* is quite helpful, but those interested in greater depth may want to acquire the four-volume *International Standard Bible Encyclopedia* (1974-1988 edition) or the six-volume *Anchor Bible Dictionary*.

The second section in the treatment of the biblical passages is called "Exploring the Word." The purpose of this section is to discuss the major themes in each biblical book. Thus the comments will typically deal with fairly large portions of Scripture (often an entire chapter) rather than providing a verse-by-verse treatment, such as is found in the *Seventh-day Adventist Bible Commentary*. In fact, many verses and perhaps whole passages in some biblical books may be treated minimally or passed over altogether.

Another thing that should be noted is that the purpose of the "Exploring the Word" sections is not to respond to all the problems or answer all the questions that might arise in each passage. Rather, as stated above, the "Exploring the Word" sections are to develop the Bible writers' major themes. In the process, the author of each volume will bring the best of modern scholarship into the discussion and thus enrich the reader's understanding of the biblical passage at hand. The "Exploring the Word" sections will also develop and provide insight into many of the issues first raised in the "Getting Into the Word" exercises.

The third section in the treatment of the biblical passage is "Applying the Word." This section is aimed at bringing the lessons of each passage into daily life. Once again, you may want to write out a response to these questions and keep them in your notebook or file folder on the biblical book being studied.

The fourth section, "Researching the Word," is for those students who want to delve more deeply into the Bible passage under study or into the history behind it. It is recognized that not everyone will have the research tools for this section. Those expecting to use the research sections should have an exhaustive Bible concordance, the *Seventh-day Adventist Bible Commentary*, a good Bible dictionary, and a Bible atlas. It will also be helpful to have several versions of the Bible.

The final component in each chapter of this book will be a list of recommendations for "Further Study of the Word." While most readers will not have all of these works, many of them may be available in local libraries. Others can be purchased through your local book dealer. It is assumed that many users of this series will already own the seven-volume *Seventh-day Adventist Bible Commentary* and the one-volume *Seventh-day Adventist Bible Dictionary*.

In closing, it should be noted that while a reader will learn much about the Bible from a *reading* of the books in the Bible Amplifier series, he or she will gain infinitely more by *studying* the Bible in connection with that reading.

The Book of Daniel

One of the best ways to study a book of the Bible is to read it thoughtfully and prayerfully from beginning to end in as short a time as possible. The following suggestions will help you to get the most out of a thoughtful reading of Daniel.

1. **As you read Daniel, what major themes do you find in each chapter? List those themes in your Daniel notebook. How do they fit into the overall content of the book?**
2. **Write down two or three texts in each chapter that especially speak to you at this point in your Christian experience. Why are these texts meaningful? What can they teach you for your life in the present?**

Daniel and His Book

This survey of the book of Daniel began in the first volume of this commentary with a brief review of the author's personal biography. We needed to become acquainted with Daniel the man before we came to the subject of Daniel the prophet.

Daniel was born in the late seventh century B.C. and lived his early years in Jerusalem or its vicinity. By the time he had grown to manhood, political and military struggles in the great nations of his time altered the fate of little Judah in which he lived. From the time of Daniel's birth until 605 B.C., Judah was nominally under the control of Egypt. In that year, however, a major battle took place; Egypt was defeated, and Babylon came to exercise control over Judah and Jerusalem. Nebuchadnezzar II, commander of the Babylonian army, led his troops to the gates of Jerusalem and demanded the payment of tribute and a selection of choice hostages. Daniel was among those chosen. He was selected, along with the others, because of his future potential as a civil servant in Babylon—a task he fulfilled, after the requisite training period, for more than sixty years.

But God had something more in mind for Daniel than mere service at the court of Babylon. God called him to the office of prophet and gave him dreams and visions. Some of these dreams, visions, and prophetic statements were addressed to the people of his time. On three different occasions, Daniel was given prophecies which dealt with, or were delivered to, kings at the royal court in Babylon. This type of prophecy—dealing with contemporary persons and issues—is sometimes called *classical* prophecy. Daniel spoke with prophetic voice to the kings of Babylon just as Jeremiah spoke to the kings in Jerusalem.

On other occasions, he was given prophecies which involved a longer range of vision, looking into the future history of the nations. This second type of prophecy is commonly called *apocalyptic* prophecy because it deals more specifically with revealing the future. It is also called outline prophecy because it outlines the history of nations in advance.

Thus in Daniel's book we find these two different types of prophecies—classical and apocalyptic. We also find another distinct type of narrative—history. Different sections of the book clearly contain these different types of literature. In general, the book of Daniel divides in half; the first half is history, and the second half is prophecy. It is in the first half of the book—in the context of history—that we find the classical prophecies that deal with contemporary persons and events. The prophecies of the second half of the book are more apocalyptic in character.

The languages used in Daniel's book also emphasize the distinction between the two main sections. Most of the historical chapters were written in Aramaic, while most of the prophetic chapters were written in Hebrew. Hebrew was Daniel's native tongue, and Aramaic was a related language that was used for part of the official correspondence of the Neo-Babylonian and Persian Empires. More than any other book in the Bible, Daniel is bilingual. Ezra was also written in both Hebrew and Aramaic, but only a small part of Ezra—the royal decrees—is in Aramaic.

This twofold nature of Daniel provides a convenient outline with which to study the book. In this Bible Amplifier series, the study of Daniel is presented in two volumes. Volume 1 deals with the historical chapters, and volume 2 focuses on the prophetic chapters. Because of the different types of material in Daniel, both the historical and prophetic volumes contain their own introductory chapters, dealing in detail with historical and prophetic issues respectively. The introduction to the historical chapters takes up some issues regarding the date of the composition of the book. Some commentaries on Daniel hold that this book was not written by a single individual, Daniel, who lived in sixth-century B.C. Babylon, but rather by an unknown, anonymous author who lived in Judea in the second century B.C. The nature of the materials found in the historical chapters bear upon this question, which is explored in the introduction to the historical section.

The prophecies of Daniel also have been interpreted in very different ways. Three main schools of thought exist on the interpretation of Daniel's prophecies. *(1) Preterist.* This method of interpretation places all the emphasis on the past and sees the fulfillment of portions of the prophecies as past. *(2) Futurist.* This school of thought places the fulfillment of portions of Daniel in the future. *(3) Historicist.* This view of the prophecies emphasizes a flow and continuity from the past through the present and into the as-yet-unfulfilled future. It is sometimes called the continuous historical view, because it sees the prophecies as part of a continuum from the past to the future. The introductory chapter to the prophetic section of Daniel's book explores the strengths and weaknesses of each of these schools of interpretation. The approach taken in the two volumes in this Bible Amplifier series falls in the category of the historicist view.

Daniel's experience included more than just being a historical figure. There was even more to Daniel than his experience as a prophet. There was also the matter of his own personal spiritual experience with God. This side of his experience and his book should not be neglected or overwhelmed by the other elements. The last chapter of volume 2 considers the important matter of Daniel's own spiritual experience as a chosen instrument of God.

So that will be the order of march in the two volumes covering Daniel: history, prophecy, and spiritual experience.

A Note on the Order of Treatment

The reader will notice that the order in which these volumes on Daniel take up the different aspects of his book varies somewhat from the standard and canonical order of the chapters in the book itself. However, if one looks carefully at the datelines of the biblical chapters—when they are given—it is apparent that Daniel does not present his material in strict chronological order either. For example, the prophecies of Daniel, chapters 7 and 8, were actually given *before* the historical events of chapters 5 and 6. Although all of the events recorded in Daniel are historical in the sense that they actually happened, they have been arranged in a certain way for a certain purpose. *To a degree, this study on Daniel has endeavored to follow the thought order rather than the written order. For that reason, the reader will find some irregularity in the order in which the chapters are presented.*

In volume 1, the historical section, the chapters studied follow an altered order. Chapters 2 and 7 have been grouped together because they are concerned with prophecies about the nations. Chapters 3 and 6 have been grouped together because they deal with persecution of the Jews in exile, Daniel and his three friends in particular. Chapters 4 and 5 have been grouped together because they deal with Nebuchadnezzar and Belshazzar, the kings of Babylon. This type of order is sometimes known as a *chiasm* (from the Greek letter *chi* which looks like an X). That something like this was intended by the original author is evident from the fact that it is precisely these six historical chapters that were written in the Aramaic language.

When we come to the prophetic chapters, the order is reversed. Thus we have chosen to study the three main prophetic chapters in the heart of the book of Daniel in reverse order; beginning with chapter 9, then going on to chapter 8, followed by chapter 7, and finally concluding that section with a summary of these three chapters. The reason for this order of study has to do with thought order, not chronological or historical order. In terms of the events to which these prophecies refer, chapter 9 comes first because it focuses especially upon the Messiah. The contents of chapter 8 go on well beyond that point into the Christian Era. But it is Daniel 7 which carries the prophecy on into the final kingdom of God and pictures the saints of the Most High as entering and possessing it.

There is a reason for following this thought order; it is not the arbitrary selection of a modern commentator who simply wants to do something different. In modern western-European thought, we reason from cause to effect. We collect all the data and then synthesize it into a hypothesis. Finally, we refine that hypothesis to a theory. That is the procedure of the modern scientific method.

But the ancients were not moderns nor were they scientists, so they worked out things in their own way. While they were quite capable of working through things in chronological order as we do, they also utilized an approach that involved reasoning from effect back to cause. The prophets could depict a scene in such a way that their listeners were led to inquire, "Why did this happen?" This question led them back to the cause. An inspired prophet could say, "This land will be destroyed and left desolate," leading back to the natural question, "Why will this land be destroyed?" The answer to that question commonly lay in the fact that the people to whom the prophet was sent were a wicked and rebellious people who had broken their covenant with God. For an example of this approach, see Jeremiah, chapters 4 through 7, and Micah, chapter 1. Wickedness was the cause, and desolation was the result—but the prophet gave the result first in order to lead his readers to a discussion of the cause.

That is the kind of thought order followed in these three prophecies at the heart of Daniel. If Daniel were presenting these prophecies to a modern audience today, he would naturally give chapter 9 first, because that chapter deals with the first events to happen. He would follow with chapter 8 because that prophecy presents the next events to happen. Finally, he would give chapter 7 because that prophecy presents the grand climax to the series. Only when these prophecies are put in this thought order does the modern reader appreciate fully their great sweep and connection with each other—something that would have come more naturally to an ancient listener or reader because of the way in which his or her thought processes had been conditioned. By reversing Daniel's original order of presentation, we have attempted to unveil the full beauty of the way in which these prophecies were first presented.

The final major line of prophecy in Daniel's book is found in chapters 10–12. Chapter 10 presents the introduction, or prologue, to this prophecy, and chapter 12 contains its epilogue, or conclusion. The body of the prophecy in chapter 11 is very detailed and follows a historical and chronological order.

There are four major apocalyptic, or outline, prophecies in the book of Daniel. They are found in chapters 2, 7, 8, and 11. Outline prophecies cover the rise and fall of nations from the prophet's day to the end of time.

The other major prophecy in Daniel's book is found at the end of chapter 9. While the four major outline prophecies deal with the rise and fall of nations, chapter 9 deals more exclusively with the people of Daniel's city and country—Jerusalem and Judah. Although the events of this prophecy run parallel to those of the major outline prophecies, they focus upon a particular part of that world not covered in the other prophecies—the history of the Jewish people in Judea down to the time of the Messiah. The fact that the four major lines of prophecy in this book go over the same outline of nations is called *recapitulation*, or *parallelism*. Just as the four Gospels go over the same events from different perspectives, so these four lines of complementary prophecies go over the same territory, filling in more details each time. The presentation starts out on the broadest scale in chapter 2, with the nations represented by different metals in an image. By the time we reach chapter 11, we are down to the individual kings of each nation and their personal actions. Chapter 2 starts out with the use of the telescope, while chapter 11 ends up with the use of the microscope.

The final chapter of volume 2 on Daniel in the Bible Amplifier series ends on the theme of spiritual relationship. This element is found not so much in the prophecy itself as in the experience of the prophet. That is where I feel it should also end up for the reader of this book.

Outline of the Book of Daniel

A standard outline of the contents of the book of Daniel is organized something like this:

    I. Daniel's exile (1:1-21)
   II. Nebuchadnezzar's dream: an outline prophecy (2:1-49)
  III. The great image: Daniel's friends vindicated (3:1-30)
  IV. The king is mad: Nebuchadnezzar's illness (4:1-37)
   V. The night that Babylon fell: Belshazzar's end (5:1-31)
  VI. Daniel in and out of the lions' den (6:1-28)
 VII. Daniel's dream: an outline prophecy (7:1-28)
VIII. Daniel's vision: an outline prophecy (8:1-27)
  IX. The seventy weeks: Gabriel's prophecy about the Jews (9:1-27)
   X. The appearance of God to Daniel (10:1-21)
  XI. Gabriel's prophecy: an outline prophecy (11:1-45)
 XII. Epilogue: dates for the previous prophecy (12:1-13)

Because we have chosen to follow a more literary and thematic order in this study of Daniel, these chapters have been rearranged in the following order:

    I. Exiled (1:1-21)
   II. Fallen kings (4:1–5:31)
  III. Persecution (3:1-30; 6:1-28)
  IV. Fallen kingdoms (2:1-49; 7:1-28)
   V. Christ as sacrifice (9:1-27)
  VI. Christ as priest (8:1-27)
 VII. Christ as king (7:1-28)
VIII. The final message (10:1–12:13)

For Further Reading

1. For a general survey of how Daniel has been interpreted through the years, see the article, "History of the Interpretation of Daniel," in F. D. Nichol, ed., *The Seventh-day Adventist Bible Commentary*, 4:39-78.

2. For a more contemporary and popularized exposition of Daniel's prophecies, see C. Mervyn Maxwell, *God Cares*, vol. 1.

3. For a more dated, but detailed, treatment of the entire book of Daniel, see Uriah Smith, *Thoughts on Daniel*.

LIST OF WORKS CITED

Blenkinsopp, Joseph. *A History of Prophecy in Israel.* Philadelphia: Westminster, 1983.

Chiera, Edward. *They Wrote on Clay.* Phoenix paperback ed. Chicago: University of Chicago, 1956.

Comba, Emilio. *History of the Waldenses in Italy.* London: Truslove and Shirley, 1889.

de Liguori, Alphonses. *Dignity and Duties of the Priest; or, Selva.* Brooklyn, N.Y.: Redemptionist Fathers, 1927.

Froom, Leroy Edwin. *The Prophetic Faith of Our Fathers.* 4 vols. Hagerstown, Md.: Review and Herald, 1946-1954.

Geiermann, Peter. *Convert's Catechism of Catholic Doctrine.* St. Louis: Herder, 1957.

Hasel, Gerhard F. "Interpretations of the Chronology of the Seventy Weeks." In *The Seventy Weeks, Leviticus, and the Nature of Prophecy,* edited by Frank Holbrook, Daniel and Revelation Committee Series, vol. 3. Silver Spring, Md.: General Conference of Seventh-day Adventists, 1986.

Herodotus. *The Histories.* Loeb Classical Library. 4 vols. Translated by A. D. Godley. Cambridge: Harvard University, 1920-1925.

Heschel, Abraham J. *The Prophets.* 2 vols. New York: Harper, 1962.

Holbrook, Frank, ed. *Symposium on Daniel.* Daniel and Revelation Committee Series, vol. 2. Silver Spring, Md.: General Conference of Seventh-day Adventists, Biblical Research Institute, 1986.

Holbrook, Frank, ed. *The Seventy Weeks, Leviticus, and the Nature of Prophecy.* Daniel and Revelation Committee Series, vol. 3. Silver Spring, Md.: Bibilical Research Institute, General Conference of Seventh-day Adventists, 1986.

Horn, Siegfried H. *The Spade Confirms the Book.* Hagerstown, Md.: Review and Herald, 1957.

———. "New Light on Nebuchadnezzar's Madness." In *Ministry,*

April 1978, 38-40.

————., et al. *Seventh-day Adventist Bible Dictionary.* Rev. ed., edited by Raymond H. Woolsey. Hagerstown, Md.: Review and Herald, 1979.

Horn, Siegfried H., and Lynn H. Wood. *The Chronology of Ezra 7.* Hagerstown, Md.: Review and Herald, 1953.

James, Edward. *The Franks.* Oxford: Basil-Blackwell, 1988.

Jerome's Commentary on Daniel. Translated by Gleason L. Archer. Grand Rapids, Mich.: Baker, 1958.

Kelly, V. J. *Forbidden Sunday and Feast-Day Occupations.* Washington, D.C.: Catholic University of America, 1943.

Kenyon, Kathleen. *Royal Cities of the Old Testament.* London: Barrie and Jenkins, *1971.*

Kingdom, Robert M. *Myths About the St. Bartholomew's Day Massacres, 1572-1576.* Cambridge: Harvard University, 1988.

Ladurie, Emmanuel LeRoy. *Montaillou: The Promised Land of Terror.* Translated by Barbara Bray. New York: Vintage, 1979.

Lecky, W. E. H. *History of the Rise and Influence of the Spirit of Rationalism in Europe.* Reprint ed. New York: G. Braziller, 1955.

McHugh, J. A., and C. J. Callan. *Catechism of the Council of Trent for Parish Priests.* New York: Wagner, 1958.

Maxwell, C. Mervyn. *God Cares,* vol. 1. Boise, Idaho: Pacific Press, 1981.

Mayer, Hans E. *The Crusades.* 2nd ed. Oxford: Oxford University, 1988.

Neugebauer, Otto. *The Exact Sciences in Antiquity.* Paperback ed. New York: Dover, 1969.

Nichol, Francis D., ed. *Seventh-day Adventist Bible Commentary.* Rev. ed., 7 vols. Hagerstown, Md.: Review and Herald, 1976-1980.

O'Brien, John A. *The Faith of Millions: The Credentials of the Catholic Religion.* Huntington, Ind.: Our Sunday Visitor, 1963.

Polybius. *The Histories.* Loeb Classical Library. Cambridge: Harvard University.

Roux, Georges. *Ancient Iraq.* 3rd ed. New York: Viking Penguin, 1993.

Saggs, H. W. F. *The Greatness That Was Babylon.* New York: Hawthorn, 1962.

Seilhammer, F. H. *Prophets and Prophecy*. Philadelphia: Fortress, 1977.

Shea, William H. "Daniel 3: Extra-Biblical Texts and the Convocation on the Plain of Dura." *Andrews University Seminary Studies*, Vol. 20 (1982). 1:29-52.

———. "Darius the Mede: An Update." *Andrews University Seminary Studies*. Vol. 20 (1982) 3:229-248.

———. "Darius the Mede in His Persian-Babylonian Setting." *Andrews University Seminary Studies*, Vol. 29 (1991). 3:235-257.

———. *Daniel 1–7: Prophecy as History*. Boise, Idaho: Pacific Press, 1996.

———. *Selected Studies in Prophetic Interpretation*. 2nd ed. Daniel and Revelation Committee Series, vol. 1. Silver Spring, Md.: Biblical Research Institute, General Conference of Seventh-day Adventists, 1992.

Smith, Uriah. *Thoughts on Daniel*. Nashville: Southern Publishing Association, 1944.

Strand, Kenneth. *Interpreting the Book of Revelation*. 2nd ed. Naples, Fla.: Ann Arbor Publishers, 1979.

Wiseman, Donald J. *Chronicles of Chaldean Kings*. London: British Museum, 1956.

———., et al. *Notes on Some Problems in the Book of Daniel*. London: Tyndale, 1965.

Whitcomb, John C. *Darius the Mede*. Grand Rapids, Mich.: Eerdmans, 1959.

White, Ellen G. *The Great Controversy*. Boise, Idaho: Pacific Press, 1950.

———. *Patriarchs and Prophets*. Boise, Idaho: Pacific Press, 1958.

———. *Prophets and Kings*. Boise, Idaho: Pacific Press, 1943.

Xenophon. *Cyropaedia*. Loeb Classical Library. 2 vols. Translated by Walter Miller. Cambridge: Harvard University, 1914.

VOLUME TWO

Daniel 7–12

Prophecies
of the
End Time

CHAPTER SIX

The Interpretation of Prophecy

Among the interpreters of Daniel's prophecies there is considerable disagreement about how the task of interpreting prophecy should be carried out. Three basic schools of thought exist.

The *preterist* view wants to put the fulfillment of all of Daniel's prophecies in the past, ending with the second century B.C. In this case, none of the prophecies would extend to Rome or beyond.

The *futurist* view considers much of Daniel's prophetic section as still future and as yet unfulfilled. Futurist interpreters begin in the past, starting Daniel's prophecies with the historical sequence of Babylon, Medo-Persia, Greece, and Rome. But then they jump over the entire Christian era and place the main fulfillment of most of these prophecies in the last seven years of earth's history.

The *historicist* view sees the prophecies of Daniel as being fulfilled throughout history, extending from the past through the present to the future. Because of the flow of history that is involved in this view, it is sometimes called the "continuous historical" view.

As an example of how these different methods handle the prophecies of Daniel, let's look briefly at what each does with the prophetic symbol of the little horn of Daniel 7 and 8. For the preterist, the little horn refers to the Seleucid king, Antiochus Epiphanes. Antiochus ruled Syria from Antioch during the Hellenistic period of history from 175-163 B.C. He was noted for his persecution of the Jews.

The futurist also concentrates on one central figure when inter-

33

preting the symbol of the little horn. But instead of the historical figure of Antiochus Epiphanes, the futurist identifies the little horn with a personal antichrist who will arise in Israel at the end of time and who will persecute the Jewish people. The Christian church, however, will have been raptured out of the world and will not have to endure this persecution, according to this view.

The historicist takes Daniel's symbol of the little horn to be corporate, not individual. The historicist view is that the little horn stands for an institution, the religious phase of Rome, that is, the papacy. This institution stands at the end of a series of nations outlined by the prophecy and, according to the time specification, was to be a central prophetic figure through the medieval period.

Obviously, these three schools of thought—preterist, futurist, and historicist—must be using widely differing rules of interpretation in order to reach such widely differing conclusions. Let's look at some of the more important of these rules of interpretation, known technically as *hermeneutics*, and see how they stand up against the biblical text and the rules which it proposes for interpreting itself.

When interpreting the prophecies of Daniel, we need to ask four basic questions:

•What is a symbol, and when does it operate?
•What is the basic outline of the nations involved in these prophecies?
•How prominent a place should be given in these prophecies to the role of Antiochus Epiphanes?
•How should prophetic time in Daniel be understood?

Symbols

The prophecies of Daniel contain numerous symbols. In fact, this is one prominent characteristic of apocalyptic prophecy such as we find in Daniel and Revelation. Symbols are also used in classical prophecy such as is found in the books of Isaiah, Jeremiah, Hosea, and others. (For a discussion of the differences between apocalyptic prophecy and classical prophecy, see the Introduction to this volume, page 20). However, apocalyptic prophecy employs symbols to a much greater degree than does classical prophecy. That is why we find such a large cast of symbols in Daniel—metals, beasts, horns, winds, seas, etc.

It is a relatively simple task to sort out what is literal and what is symbolic in chapters 2, 7, and 8 of Daniel. The text itself makes sharp distinctions between the two. Daniel clearly tells us when he was in vision and what he saw in those visions. Here we find the symbolic elements. Following the vision, the prophet also clearly lets us know when he is literally talking with an angel interpreter and the content of that conversation. These divisions are straightforward and clear. In chapter 7, for example, the vision ends with verse 14, and the explanation begins with verse 15. In Daniel 8 the vision also ends with verse 14, and the angel's explanation takes up the rest of the chapter. Even in chapter 2 these divisions are clear. Although Daniel himself recites the dream (vss. 31-35) and also gives the interpretation (vss. 36-45), the transition between the symbolic dream and its explanation in chapter 2 is quite distinct.

The situation is somewhat different in chapters 9 and 11. In these two prophecies, no symbolic vision precedes the explanation. Rather, these two chapters consist of further prophetic information given to Daniel by the angel Gabriel, based on the earlier vision given in chapter 8. Gabriel makes this connection clear in Daniel 9:23, and Daniel himself notes this relationship in Daniel 10:1. So in chapters 2, 7, and 8 we have symbolic visions followed immediately by their explanations, while in chapters 9 and 11 we have only explanations referring back to a previously given symbolic vision in chapter 8.

The distinction made here between symbolic visions and literal interpretations should not be understood as meaning that, in Daniel, the visions are 100 percent symbolic and the explanations are 100 percent literal. There is some overlap. For example, Daniel's vision of the heavenly court scene (7:9-14) is essentially literal, although it is part of the vision. The beings Daniel sees there—God the Father ("the Ancient of Days"), God the Son ("the Son of man"), and the angels—are all literal beings. There is no need to make them into symbols. Likewise, occasional symbolic elements may occur in the more literal interpretations of a vision. An example would be the time elements appearing in both the symbolic visions (8:14) and their interpretations (7:25), where they still retain their symbolic value. Thus we should say that the visions are *predominantly* symbolic and the interpretations are *predominantly* literalistic, but they are not exclusively so.

Kingdoms

The commentaries on Daniel generally agree on what is symbolic and what is literal in the book, largely because the book of Daniel itself makes a rather clear distinction between the two. However, there is no general agreement at all on how these symbols should be interpreted. For example, interpreters have significant differences of opinion regarding the identity even of such a major symbolic element in Daniel as the four-nation sequence of chapters 2 and 7. Yet, if we cannot correctly interpret such basic prophetic symbols in Daniel, there is little hope that we will be able to correctly interpret lesser symbols. If we cannot identify the kingdoms involved, how can we understand the prophetic details given regarding these kingdoms?

Here is how the different schools of prophetic interpretation have identified the four kingdoms outlined in Daniel 2 and 7:

School of Interpretation	Gold/ Lion	Silver/ Bear	Bronze/ Leopard	Iron/ nondescript beast
Preterist	Babylon	Media	Persia	Greece
Historicist	Babylon	Medo-Persia	Greece	Rome
Futurist	Babylon	Medo-Persia	Greece	Rome

There is general agreement that the first kingdom represents Babylon. The golden head of the image in chapter 2 is specifically said to be the kingdom of Babylon (vs. 38), and all the different interpretive schools of thought accept this identification.

The major difference of interpretation involves the identity of the second kingdom. Preterists identify the silver in the image of Daniel 2 and the bear in the vision of Daniel 7 as the Median kingdom alone; historicists and futurists see these symbols as representing the combined kingdom of Medo-Persia. The effect of this different view of the second beast is to upset the identification of the rest of the sequence. As the diagram indicates, preterists conclude the four-nation sequence with Greece, but futurists and historicists see the sequence ending with Rome. Thus, three of the four kingdoms listed are given different identities, with the result that their individual characteristics are identified differently as well.

The biblical symbols for the second kingdom clearly favor identifying it with the dual kingdom of Medo-Persia, rather than with the kingdom of Media alone. For example, in chapter 7, the second kingdom is represented by a bear that is raised up on one side (vs. 5). The bear's bi-form nature is of major importance in properly identifying the kingdom represented because it establishes a parallel with the symbol of the ram in chapter 8. The bear raised up on one side in chapter 7 is mirrored in chapter 8 by the symbol of a ram with two horns, one of which is higher—some Bible versions say "longer"—than the other (vs. 3). Verse 20 clearly identifies this ram as representing the dual kingdom of Media *and* Persia. Thus the bear of chapter 7 also represents the combined, Medo-Persian kingdom.

With this clear identification, why do preterist interpreters divide these two kingdoms, identifying the second kingdom in the sequence with Media and the third with Persia?

The answer is that they feel the book of Daniel itself makes a distinction between Media and Persia in chapter 5 when it identifies the king mentioned there as Darius *the Mede* (vs. 30). This indicates, they argue, the existence of a separate Median kingdom in Daniel's thinking.

We have already mentioned briefly the special historical problem of identifying Darius the Mede and have cited some specialized literature on the subject (see chapter four of the first volume on Daniel in this series). Beyond that, however, there is further evidence in Daniel 5 and 6 that the author considered Medo-Persia to be a single, combined kingdom. Daniel 5:28 indicates that Babylon was to be conquered contemporaneously by the Medes *and* the Persians, and 6:8 indicates that Darius was under the law of the Medes *and* the Persians. These two chapters, describing events contemporaneous to the fall of Babylon, give direct evidence in harmony with 8:20 that the writer knew the power that overthrew Babylon was the combined kingdom of the Medes and Persians. The internal evidence of the book of Daniel invalidates the preterists' attempt to divide the second kingdom in the series into separate Median and Persian kingdoms, symbolized by different metals and beasts.

Preterists have interpreted this major symbol—and thus the entire series of kingdoms—incorrectly. Historicists and futurists have correctly interpreted the sequence of kingdoms as Babylon, Medo-Persia, Greece, and Rome.

The Little Horn

The little horn is another major symbol to interpret in Daniel 7 and 8. It is described as "little" only in its formative stage; it quickly grew and became great. All three schools of prophetic interpretation—preterist, futurist, and historicist—agree that this horn is a symbol, but they disagree about what it represents. The preterist school holds that the little horn should be identified with Antiochus Epiphanes (175–163 B.C.), a Greek king who ruled Syria and Judea from Antioch. Historicist interpreters since the Reformation have identified this power as the papacy, the religious power to emerge supreme from the breakup of the Roman Empire. Futurist interpreters see the little horn as representing an individual person who will arise in Israel and persecute the Jews in the last days. Thus for futurists, there is a gap in the prophecy from Imperial Rome down to these future, final events—an intermediate period not covered by any elements present in the prophecy.

Since Antiochus Epiphanes has played such a large part in the history of the interpretation of the little horn, we need to examine his historical career in the light of the characteristics of the little horn as given in the prophecy. How well does Antiochus fit the prophetic details?

Since the little horn emerges from the fourth beast (7:7, 8), it is clear that the little horn's identity depends upon the identity we give to the fourth beast. That actually is the preterist's motivation for shortening this series to end with Greece, not Rome. Since Antiochus emerged from the breakup of Alexander's Greek kingdom, the preterist can identify the little horn with Antiochus only by identifying the fourth kingdom with Greece. But as we saw above, preterists are in error to identify the fourth beast as Greece. The fourth beast is Rome, not Greece. And since preterists have misidentified the fourth beast in the series, they have also gotten the identification of the little horn wrong. Clearly, the Greek king Antiochus cannot come out of Rome!

Another consideration militates against the little horn being Antiochus. In Daniel 8, we see a progression in the power of the kingdoms pictured. The ram (Medo-Persia) magnified himself (vs. 4). Then came the goat (Greece) who magnified himself exceedingly (vs. 8), followed by the little horn that magnified itself to heaven (vss. 9, 10, 11). Such a progression fits much better if the little horn is seen as Rome rather than Antiochus. Rome's power was greater than that of Greece. But if we identify the little horn as Antiochus, the progression does not match, because the power of Antiochus was far less than that of Alexander the Great, represented by the first great horn on the goat (vss. 5, 21).

Verse 9 states that the little horn pushed its conquests "to the south and to the east and toward the Beautiful Land." These directions fit Rome perfectly as it picked off the four main pieces of the Greek Empire—Macedonia and Pergamum to the east in 168 and 133 B.C., the "Beautiful Land" of Judea in 60 B.C., and Egypt to the south in 33 B.C.

Antiochus, on the other hand, did rather poorly in these three directions. He had some success to the south in 169 B.C., capturing the eastern half of the Egyptian delta. But when he returned the next year, the Roman ambassador drew a line in the sand and threatened Antiochus with the power of Rome if he did not turn back. Antiochus turned around and went back to Syria without firing an arrow, which shows where the real power of the time was located.

Antiochus had some initial success on his eastern campaign but then died during the expedition. His record was even worse with the "Beautiful Land" of Judea. Not only did he not conquer it, he was the one who was responsible for losing it. Chafing under his persecutions, the Jews rose up and liberated Judea from Syria! Thus Rome fits this specification of the prophecy far better than does Antiochus.

A final point regarding the identification of the little horn has to do with prophetic time in Daniel's book. None of the prophetic time periods in Daniel—the 2300 days (8:14), the three and a half times (7:25; 12:7), the 1290 days (12:11), or the 1335 days (12:12)—fit Antiochus Epiphanes. The book of I Maccabees says that Antiochus' desecration of the temple in Jerusalem lasted exactly three years to the day. Even if measured in literal, not symbolic, years, it's obvious that all the prophetic time periods in Daniel exceed three years.

Preterist commentators are aware of this difficulty and have endeavored to resolve it by dividing the 2300 days, literally 2300 "evening-mornings" in half to arrive at 1150 days, or symbolic years. However, this does not solve the problem because three complete luni-solar years equal 1092 days (354 + 354 + 384).

Thus we should reject the interpretation that sees Antiochus Epiphanes as the fulfillment of the little horn symbol. In chapter 7, the little horn represents the religious phase of Rome, which came up after the divisions of Imperial Rome (vss. 7, 8; cf vs. 24). And in chapter 8, the little horn initially represents the imperial phase of Rome that came on the scene of action after the division of Greece (vss. 9, 23). These identifications fit the historical facts far better than does the view that sees Antiochus Epiphanes as the fulfillment of the little horn.

Prophetic Time

How shall we understand the time periods brought to view in the prophecies of Daniel? When the prophecy speaks of "2,300 evenings and mornings" (8:14) or "1,290 days" (12:11), should we understand that to be literal days or symbolic time?

One clue lies in the point just made that the little horn is best identified with Rome. If this identification is correct, then the prophetic times associated with the little horn's activity should also fit with the time periods covered by Rome. Imperial Rome lasted a number of centuries, and Papal Rome continued on through the Middle Ages. Taken in terms of literal time, the prophetic periods of Daniel would not span even a small portion of that history. This correlation indicates that the prophetic periods should be understood as symbolic time in harmony with their contexts.

Preterist and futurist commentators, however, hold that these periods of time should be taken as literal time—with the exception of some references in Daniel 9. Preterists, of course, place that literal time in the past, while futurists place it in the future. Historicists, on the other hand, understand these prophetic periods as symbolic time, fulfilled, like the larger content of the prophecies in which they occur, through the course of centuries of history.

What evidence is there that these prophetic times should be understood symbolically? And if they are to be so interpreted, what rules of interpretation should be followed?

The first feature of these time periods which points to their symbolic nature is their symbolic context. For example, the 2300 evenings and mornings are found in the vision of Daniel 8 in a setting containing various other symbols such as a ram, a goat, four horns, and a little horn.

In Daniel 7:21, the prophet says, "As I watched, this horn [the little horn] was waging war against the saints and defeating them." This is clearly symbolic imagery. Verse 25 indicates how long ["a time, times, and half a time"] this persecution of God's people would continue. Since the entire context of what is said about this persecuting power is symbolic, it seems logical that the time periods given would likewise be symbolic.

The fact that these prophetic time periods should be understood symbolically is also indicated by the symbolic nature of the units in which they are given. Daniel 8:14 uses "evenings and mornings" which is not a normal unit of expressing time in the Old Testament. Similarly, the "time, times and half a time" of Daniel 7:25; 12:7 is not the word for "years." These times have to be interpreted as years through 4:16, 23, 25, 32 along with Revelation 12:6, 14; 13:5. Again, in chapter 9, the time unit is "weeks" or "sevens" (vss. 24-27), even though as the content of the prophecy shows, these are not normal weeks of seven twenty-four hour days.

Another point to note is that the time periods are expressed in quantities that emphasize their symbolic nature. A Hebrew would not normally date some event as being 2300 days in the future. He would say six years and four months. Nor would he date something by referring to seventy weeks. Instead, he would say one year and four and a half months. The 1260 days, the 1290 days, and the 1335 days would have more commonly been spoken of as three and a half years, three years and seven months, or three years and eight and a half months.

All these considerations indicate that we are not dealing with literal time in the prophetic portions of Daniel, but with symbolic time.

If so, by what standard should we evaluate these symbolic times in terms of actual historical time? This brings up the day-for-a-year rule in prophecy. It is found first of all in Numbers 14:34 and Ezekiel 4:6—two classical, not apocalyptic, prophecies. Numbers 14:34 sets forth a rule to be utilized as a basis for the future judgment of Israel. The forty days spent scouting the land by the spies who brought back a bad report provided a scale for the forty years during which the Israelites would wander in the wilderness.

In Ezekiel 4:6, the prophet was to symbolize the past years of iniquity in Israel and Judah by lying on his side for a corresponding number of days on the basis of the year-for-a-day rule. Thus Ezekiel, who prophesied at the same time as Daniel, knew and used this rule regarding prophetic time.

There is also evidence right in Daniel's book that this day-for-a-year rule should be utilized in his time prophecies. Daniel 9:24-27 refers to a prophetic period of seventy weeks. Because of all the events that were to occur within these seventy weeks, it is clear that they must be understood symbolically. Within these seventy weeks, Judah was to return to its own land and rebuild Jerusalem and the temple. Then, sometime later within this time period, the Messiah would come and minister to the people, but he would be cut off, or killed. Obviously, all of this could not have been accomplished in a literal year and a half. These "weeks" must be symbolic.

The pragmatic test of history shows that the symbolic unit of one week is equivalent to seven literal years—a day for a year. Using this standard, the events of this prophecy work out correctly. The period was to begin with "the issuing of the decree to restore and rebuild Jerusalem" (vs. 25) and end with the Messiah confirming the covenant with many (see vs. 27). Jerusalem was to be restored at the end of seven "sevens" or weeks (vs. 25), and Messiah was to come sixty-two "sevens" later (vs. 26). If we use the rule of a day for a year and begin the seventy weeks (or 490 years) in 457 B.C. when Artaxerxes issued a decree which resulted in the rebuilding of Jerusalem, the predicted dates all fall into place with the time period ending in A.D. 34. We will be examining the details of this precisely fulfilled prophecy in the next chapter.

Although both preterists and futurists believe the prophetic time periods of Daniel are literal rather than symbolic, they implicitly acknowledge the validity of the year-for-a-day rule when it comes to the seventy weeks in chapter 9. They do not use the precise dates given above (457 B.C. and A.D. 34), but neither do they try to fit the prophecy into a literal seventy weeks—or about a year and a half. Futurists often date the beginning of the period around 444 B.C. and end the sixty-ninth week with a date for Christ's crucifixion of A.D. 33 or 34. Preterists often begin the seventy weeks in 593 B.C. and bring it down to the time of Antiochus Epiphanes c. 165 B.C. But despite such variations, both futurists and preterists commonly see the seventy weeks in Daniel 9 as referring to a period of time that clearly extends far beyond a literal "seventy weeks," thus implicitly admitting that the year-for-a-day rule has value for this prophetic time period at least.

Earlier in this chapter, we made the point that chapter 11 consists of further prophetic information given to Daniel by the angel Gabriel, based on the earlier vision given in chapter 8. Chapter 8 provides the symbols, and chapter 11 provides their literal interpretation. This fact gives us an additional reason for seeing the prophetic time periods in Daniel as symbolic.

For example, in chapter 8 Daniel sees symbolic entities (kingdoms), but in chapter 11 these are presented as literal persons (individual kings). In chapter 8, Daniel sees symbolic actions taking place (casting down stars, etc.); in chapter 11, we have literal actions (recognizable battles). And in chapter 8, Daniel is given symbolic time periods (evenings-mornings); in chapter 11, we find literal time (years).

For example, in chapter 11, verses 6, 8, and 13 refer to "years." In each case, these years measure (although without specifying a particular number) some of the activities of the Greek kings in Egypt (the Ptolemies) or in Syria (the Seleucids). These Greek kings belong to the time period covered by the four horns that came out of the head of the goat (8:22). That same time period of the goat and its four horns is also covered by some of the 2300 evening-mornings (8:14). Thus when we utilize chapter 11 to interpret chapter 8, we find that the evening-mornings in chapter 8 correspond to literal, historical years in chapter 11. It is clear, then, that the time period in chapter 8, the 2300 evening-mornings, must be symbolic. If they were literal time, they would extend only for less than six and a half years—not nearly enough time to encompass the activities presented as their counterpart in chapter 11. Thus the book of Daniel itself teaches the year-for-a-day principle.

Summary

The book of Daniel contains a type of specialized prophecy known for its intense use of symbols. In Daniel, the symbols are found mainly in the recorded visions, while their literal, historical equivalents are found mainly in the interpretations given by the angel. The distinctions between the symbols and the interpretation is fairly sharp in chapters 2, 7, and 8. But in chapters 9 and 11 there is no symbolic vision. Rather, these chapters refer back to the symbolic vision in chapter 8 and provide interpretations of certain aspects of that vision.

Foundational to the prophetic portions of Daniel is the outline of successive world powers found in chapters 2, 7, 8, and 11. The basic work of interpretation involves identifying the kingdoms presented by the symbols in these chapters. Using correlations found within the book of Daniel itself, I have taken the position in this volume that the sequence should be identified as Babylon, Medo-Persia, Greece, and Rome. The little horn of Daniel 7 and 8 follows the fourth of these kingdoms, indicating that it comes on the scene of action as a new phase of Rome, a religious phase. Thus the position taken in this book is that the little horn represents the papacy, not Antiochus Epiphanes. The events of recorded history confirm this identification.

Several of the prophecies of Daniel include time periods, raising the question of whether these should be understood as literal or symbolic. The context, the units of time measurement used, and the numbers themselves all indicate that these prophetic time periods should be understood symbolically and that they stand for long periods of actual, historical time. Numbers 14:34; Ezekiel 4:6; Daniel 9:24-27; and Daniel 8:14, compared with Daniel 11:6, 8, 13, demonstrate that the rule for interpreting prophetic time in apocalyptic prophecies should be the day-for-a-year principle.

These are the basic interpretive principles that we will apply to the book of Daniel as we examine its prophecies. Others will be presented as the need arises in the context of specific prophecies.

For Further Study

1. For more on the topics covered in this chapter, see W. H. Shea, *Selected Studies in Prophetic Interpretation*. Especially valuable are chapter 2, "Why Antiochus Epiphanes is Not the Little Horn of Daniel 8," and chapter 3, "The Year-Day Principle."

2. For a discussion of the rules of interpreting apocalyptic, see K. Strand, *Interpreting the Revelation*. Unfortunately, a similar treatment of Daniel is not available, but much of the material from Revelation applies here too. Various commentaries on Daniel have introductory chapters which deal with some of the principles of prophetic interpretation.

3. For the history of interpretation of Daniel and Revelation, see L. E. Froom, *The Prophetic Faith of Our Fathers*.

4. Other helpful works dealing with the interpretation of prophecy in Daniel are F. Holbrook, ed., *Symposium on Daniel*; F. Holbrook, ed., *The Seventy Weeks, Leviticus, and the Nature of Prophecy*; and those sections of M. Maxwell, *God Cares* and F. D. Nichol, ed., *Seventh-day Adventist Bible Commentary* that discuss issues related to prophetic interpretation.

CHAPTER SEVEN

Christ As Sacrifice

Daniel 9

The prophecy of Daniel 9 begins with one of the longest prayers recorded in the Bible. It is also a beautiful prayer because it is so unselfish. Daniel prays—not for blessings for himself, but for his people. He intercedes with God for the remnant of Judah which is still living in exile in Babylon.

As he prayed, Daniel had the scroll of the prophet Jeremiah in mind, especially the portion we call chapter 25. There Daniel read Jeremiah's prophecy that the exile of Judah in Babylon would last seventy years (see Jeremiah 25:10-14; Daniel 9:1-3). He knew those seventy years were almost over.

Three different times Nebuchadnezzar of Babylon had besieged Jerusalem—first in 605 B.C., then again in 597, and finally in 589-586. Each time, he took captives back to Babylon. Daniel went with the first group in 605 B.C. By the time Babylon fell to the Persians, Daniel himself had been in Babylon almost seventy years. No wonder his prayers took on a note of urgency as he saw the predicted time period drawing rapidly to a close.

In response to Daniel's prayer, the angel Gabriel was sent to reassure the prophet that God's answer was Yes! "Yes," Gabriel promised Daniel, "your people will go home to their own land. Yes, they will rebuild Jerusalem and its temple."

But God's answer to Daniel went beyond the immediate future. "God is telling you more," Gabriel continued. He wants to tell you what is going to happen to your people a long time after that restoration. He wants to tell you about the Messiah—when He will come, what He will do, and what will happen to Him. God wants to tell you how your people will respond to the Messiah who will come and what will happen to them as a result."

All this God made known to His prophet Daniel, and that revelation is the content of the prophecy of chapter 9.

■ Getting Into the Word

Daniel 9:1-24

Read chapter 9 through twice. During the second reading, begin to think about answers to the following questions.

1. What light does Jeremiah's book shed on Daniel's prayer in chapter 9:4-19? (Note especially Jeremiah 25:10-14). Use the marginal references in your Bible to gain a better understanding of what Daniel found to be of special interest in the book of Jeremiah.

2. Outline Daniel's prayer in 9:4-19. What does it say about the covenant? What does it say about the reason for the Babylonian captivity? What does it say about God? What does it teach about the sanctuary and God's special city? For background on the Jewish captivity, read the article, "Captivity," in the *Seventh-day Adventist Bible Dictionary*.

3. What are the "seventy 'sevens' " of verse 24? List any evidence you can find in Daniel 9:24-27 that (a) these are symbolic time periods, and (b) they should be interpreted as a day representing a year of actual time.

4. Verse 24 contains six infinitives ("to" plus a verb) that express what is to be accomplished during the "seventy 'sevens.' " List those six infinitives in your notebook, and for each, write down who is to accomplish that action, and summarize what that activity is and what it might mean.

■ Exploring the Word

A Prayer for Understanding (9:1-19)

Daniel dates his prayer as taking place in the first year of Darius and then goes on to identify Darius by his father, his ethnic affiliation, and his political office (vs. 1). Then he repeats the date (vs. 2). What are we to make of this?

It should tell us that prayer ought to be tied to specific, concrete situations in our lives. It is not something vague and unconnected to the real events that are taking place in our experience. Like Daniel, we need to pray about things that deeply concern us. With Babylon's conquest by the Medes and Persians, exciting changes had taken place. This was the first full calendar year under the new government, and Daniel was eagerly anticipating coming events as he prayed.

He knew from the prophecy of Jeremiah (25:10-14) that the Jewish captivity in Babylon was to last for seventy years. He also knew the end of that period was drawing near; he himself had lived in Babylon almost seventy years. He had come to Babylon in 605 B.C., and now it was 538/537 B.C. Daniel was praying over an open Bible (vs. 2), as he thought about these things. This is an example we would do well to follow. We find precious promises in God's Word; it's fitting, then, for us to take these to Him in prayer, pleading for their fulfillment in our lives and in the church.

Daniel began his prayer by addressing God as "the great and awesome God, who keeps his covenant of love with all who love him and obey his commands" (vs. 4). This introduction says much about Daniel's understanding of God and the experiences he had had with Him during his long life. In our prayers, we, too, should express our feelings about God, based on the experiences we have had with Him and our understanding of Him. Daniel's description of God as "great and awesome" expresses God's transcendence. His very nature is deserving of reverential awe—an appreciation of His holiness and almighty power. This is what the Bible means when it speaks of "fearing" God.

Daniel's reference to God as a covenant-keeping God emphasizes the fact that God is faithful to keep His promises to us. As surely as did ancient Israel, we today have likewise entered into a covenant agreement with Him. This covenant imposes certain obligations on us and on God, but on neither side are the obligations carried out merely from a sense of obligation. As Daniel points out, love is the motive that both originates the covenant and sustains it. It is based on love—God's love expressed toward us, and our love for Him. The Hebrew word used for this idea of covenant love is *chesed.* This is a word rich in meanings that are difficult to translate adequately. It contains the idea of faithfulness—that God will always fulfill His part of the covenant. But it also conveys the idea of the deep love from which that faithfulness stems. The English Bible sometimes translates these concepts as "lovingkindness." It reminds us here that we can approach God in prayer expecting that He will hear and answer us because He loves us.

The idea of God's lovingkindness is particularly startling in the context of Daniel's prayer. After nearly seventy years of exile in a foreign land, the natural question would be, "Where are You, God?" Was God really working through all the calamities that had overtaken them? The natural inclination would be to feel that God had abandoned His people. But Daniel says otherwise. "God," he prays, "You have not abandoned us; rather, we have abandoned You." That perception is just as valid today as it was in Daniel's time.

In his prayer, Daniel goes right to the heart of the matter. Verses 5 and 6 repeat one central idea many times—"We have sinned." "You gave us good laws," Daniel says, "but we broke them. You sent your servants to us, but we would not listen to them." Daniel had the book of one of these prophets open before him. The people had refused to listen to Jeremiah; if they had been willing to pay attention to him, they could have saved themselves, the city of Jerusalem, and their nation.

We marvel today at their stubborn refusal to listen to God through His prophets. But do we act any differently? How carefully do we listen to God's voice through His modern-day servants and through His written Word? If we had lived in Jeremiah's time, would we have listened to him any more than did the people of Jerusalem then?

Daniel reaffirms the view of God as unchangingly righteous. "You are righteous" (vs. 7). The people are not righteous, but God is. Even when the people persist in their unrighteousness, God continues to be righteous. He changes not. Today, we have to do with the same unchanging, ever-righteous God. Like Daniel, then, we should serve Him in righteousness. We should ask Him for the gift of His righteousness through Jesus Christ.

According to verse 7, the result of the people's unrighteousness was clearly evident. They had been scattered in exile throughout the nations of the ancient world. And worse, the inhabitants of these pagan lands knew why God's people had been scattered. The Hebrews and their God had become a byword for shame in the ancient world.

Our failures and sins have repercussions as well—on ourselves and on our God. We have to face that reality. But there is a remedy. Daniel shows us the way. We need to surrender to God our waywardness and the sad results it has produced. He is the great Restorer. He can forgive and bring us back to our original state. Just as God could restore the sanctuary, He can restore our lives to righteousness if we are willing to have Him do so.

More so than people do today, persons in ancient times identified quite directly with their ancestors. This is what Daniel is talking about in verse 8. "O Lord, we and our kings, our princes and our fathers are covered with shame because we have sinned against you." Daniel felt the need for a forgiveness that would cover the collective sins of himself and his countrymen, wiping out the shame of the past and restoring God's favor to His people. For this, he relied, again, on God's "merciful and forgiving" character (vs. 9). He freely admits that neither he nor the people nor their forefathers deserve mercy. But he trusts a God who forgives, even when we don't deserve to be forgiven.

In verses 10 and 11, Daniel once more goes over the list of sins, summarizing them by saying, "All Israel has transgressed your law" (vs. 11). This is similar to Paul's summary of the human condition, "There is no one righteous, not even one" (Romans 3:10).

The next element in Daniel's prayer (vss. 11, 12) is an acknowledgment of a more specific reason why the exile came upon the people of Judah. Their unfaithfulness had laid them open to receive the curses contained in the law of Moses for those who fail to obey. These are found especially in Deuteronomy, chapters 26 through 33. Moses pointed out that the people would be blessed in obedience to these laws but that the curses would fall upon them as a result of disobedience. This is the outworking of the principle that there are natural consequences that result from disobedience. But it is also a function of God's judgment against sin. Daniel saw the inexorable outworking of these principles in the fate of the people of Judah as they suffered exile in foreign lands.

We, too, receive the results of our disobedience today. As an example, lung cancer can be traced directly to smoking in the vast majority of cases. By smoking, one runs the risk of developing cancer because he or she is introducing a carcinogen into the bronchial tree. Similar effects operate in the spiritual realm as well. In other cases, such as Job's, no direct cause can be determined for calamities that befall us. But regardless of the situation, we can know that a loving and forgiving God waits for us to return to Him in repentance.

It was clear to Daniel where the spiritual cause for the exile lay. It lay with the disobedience of the people themselves. In this intercessory prayer, he seeks forgiveness for them. As their intercessor, Daniel once again draws on God's mighty acts as the ground for his appeal (vss. 15, 16). He reflects back on the experience of the Exodus from Egypt in which God brought His people out with a mighty hand. Covenant making in the ancient world always began with an introduction that recounted the story of past relations between the two covenanting parties. Following this structure, Daniel "reminds" God of these events. He admits that such gracious acts by God in the past should have motivated the people to loving obedience. He admits their ingratitude and faithlessness in the light of God's great love for them and their fathers.

As we look back on the loving, gracious way God has led us in our personal lives, we should be motivated as well to serve Him and love

Him. We need to express in our prayers a recognition of all that God has done for us and admit how often we have failed to respond in love.

Daniel's final appeal to God is based on the honor of His name (vss. 17-19). By forgiving the unworthy, undeserving people of Judah, God would cause His name to be honored among all the nations of the world. People everywhere would realize how great and merciful He really is.

The honor of God is at stake in the world in our day as well as in Daniel's. We all play a part in the great controversy, and we have an obligation to bring praise and glory to our heavenly Father. It is difficult to avoid selfish prayers, but we need to have a larger view, praying not just for ourselves and our families, but for the honor of God. Jesus put it this way in His Sermon on the Mount: "Let your light shine before men, that they may see your good deeds and praise your Father in heaven" (Matt. 5:16). Our lives should be lived in such a way that God's name is praised.

The language with which Daniel closes his prayer indicates the earnestness of his feelings. His words breathe with the intensity of his desire. "O Lord, listen! O Lord, forgive! O Lord, hear and act! For your sake, O my God, do not delay, because your city and your people bear your Name" (vs. 19). Too often our prayers are offered up in a listless fashion with much repetition and hackneyed phrases. Like Daniel's prayer, they ought to breathe with an intensity of interest. Daniel's prayer was no sleepy repetition of standard, trite phrases. This was a prayer into which Daniel immersed himself with emotional intensity. If we prayed in a similar way, we would no doubt see more answers to our prayers because we would be demonstrating to God that we are serious about what we are praying for.

Finally, in response to Daniel's earnest prayer, God's initial response was to send Gabriel to the aged prophet. Gabriel brought God's answer to Daniel, and that answer relates to the prophecy given in chapter 8 and discussed further in the following chapters.

We can see from Daniel's prayer something of what Daniel thought about God. But what did God think about Daniel? We get an idea in some of Gabriel's introductory words to the prophet. "You are highly esteemed" (vs. 23), he told Daniel, addressing him in terms of respect and endearment. "You are greatly beloved" is how it is translated in the RSV, which conveys more emotion.

Daniel was an aged warrior for God. He was almost ninety years old at this time. One might think he was of little usefulness to God at such an age. On the contrary, he was still "highly esteemed." This should give encouragement to those who are advanced in years. God still takes note of the elderly and cares for them. He holds us each in high esteem; we are greatly beloved by the God of the universe!

Gabriel Sent to Answer Daniel's Prayer

In answer to this earnest prayer regarding the captivity of Daniel's countrymen and the desolation of their city and sanctuary, God sent the angel Gabriel to give Daniel an answer (9:21). This answer is contained in verses 24-27. Basically, Gabriel assured Daniel that his prayer for the deliverance of the people would be answered. The Hebrews would return to their land. They would rebuild the temple, and they would reconstruct the city.

But Gabriel went on to tell Daniel more about the future of God's people beyond these initial events. The prophecy looked to events beyond with a special focus—the Messiah. Verses 25 and 26 specifically mention the Messiah, and verse 27 describes further Messianic activities. Gabriel's prophecy (vss. 24-27) basically revolves around two poles: one pole is the people, the city, and the sanctuary; the other is the Messiah. And a considerable part of the story here is the working out of the relationship between the two.

A third party intrudes into the picture, however, bringing storm clouds that darken the sky over this picture. That third party is known as the Desolater (vss. 26, 27). The Desolater brings desolation to the city of Jerusalem and to its temple. This we know was historically accomplished by the power of Imperial Rome, the forces of which eventually conquered and destroyed Jerusalem in A.D. 70. Thus, despite the bright spots of this prophecy—the restoration of the people and the coming of the Messiah—it ends with the somber note of another destruction.

Daniel 9:24—The Preliminary Answer

For modern readers, the prophecy begins in a somewhat unusual way. It begins with a summary or conclusion (vs. 24). Then it goes on to give the details that fill in or support that conclusion (vss. 25-27). Modern thought, influenced by the scientific method, would first collect the data, or details, and then work out a summary. Gabriel did it the other way around because people in Daniel's time commonly reasoned from the effect back to the cause. Daniel and other Old Testament books contain other examples of this approach.

The opening phrase of verse 24 specifies the time element involved and the special focus of that time element—the people: "Seventy 'sevens' are decreed for your people and your holy city." In the margin, the NIV gives "weeks" as an alternate reading for the word translated "sevens." Most other English versions of the Bible also prefer some variation of the word *weeks* instead of "sevens." Although the word for "week," *shabua*, was built upon the root word for "seven," *sheba*, it was given different vowels so that there is no mistaking the difference between the two. Nor should we add the word *years*, (weeks of years) here as does the RSV, because that word is not in the original text. The word used here should simply be translated "weeks"—that, and nothing more.

Obviously, however, the use of the word *weeks* brings with it the clear idea that symbolic time is involved here. No commentator holds that all of the predicted events could have taken place in a literal year and a half. That was hardly time enough to rebuild the altar of the temple, much less the rest of the temple and the city (Ezra 3). Clearly, we are dealing here with symbolic time. Seventy weeks of seven days each equals 490 days. If each day stands for a year of actual time (Numbers 14:34; Ezekiel 4:6), this prophecy spans almost five centuries—a long-range prophecy indeed!

Basically, all commentators agree that some form of the year-for-a-day principle must be employed in chapter 9 because it is impossible to squeeze all of the predicted events into a literal seventy weeks—approximately a year and a half. This matter becomes even more acute in the time prophecies of chapters 7, 8, and 11 to 12.

Arguments for the application of this principle can be drawn from Old Testament passages outside of Daniel, but a comparison of the symbolic time unit "evening-mornings" of Daniel 8:14 with the literal "years" of Daniel 11:6, 8, 18 indicates that the former should be interpreted by the latter. This connection is supported by the fact that Daniel 11 is the closest and most direct explanation of the symbolic prophecy of Daniel 8. (Some specialized reading on the subject of the year-day principle has been suggested at the end of this chapter. See also chapter 6 for further discussion of this topic.)

The time-range of this prophecy was extensive, yet its geographical focus was narrow. It focused especially upon "your people and your holy city" (vs. 24), that is, Jerusalem and the people of Judah. This is a very different focus from that of the other major lines of prophecy in the book of Daniel. The prophecies in Daniel 2, 7, 8, and 11 outline the rise and fall of world nations and their rulers as they come on the scene of action and disappear. But in Daniel 9 we do not see the onward march of Babylon, Medo-Persia, Greece, and Rome. Some of these nations formed the historical backdrop against which the fate of Judea played out, but Daniel 9 focuses more specifically upon the people of God.

The verb in the phrase "seventy 'sevens' are decreed for your people" (vs. 24) is also commonly translated "determined." More literally, it means "to be cut off." This meaning forms a definite connection with the prophecy of Daniel 8. That connection is discussed further at the end of the next chapter.

The opening phrase of this prophecy proceeds to list a series of six events, or actions, that are to be accomplished by the end of the specified seventy weeks allotted to the Jewish people. It does not yet say precisely when each of these events is to be accomplished; that awaits the more detailed portion of the text. Remember, this is only the opening summary, which will be given more substance in subsequent verses.

These six actions come in three pairs. The first pair is addressed especially to the people of Judah and describes what they were to accomplish within this time frame of seventy weeks. The second pair describes actions that God would take upon Himself as His own responsibility. The final pair points to the results that would flow from the combination of the previous four actions.

The two actions that were the responsibility of God's people were "to finish transgression, [and] to put an end to sin" (9:24). The Hebrew language has quite a few words for sin, each with its own shade of meaning. The meaning of "transgression" (in the phrase "to finish transgression") is sin as rebellion against God. The second phrase ("to put an end to sin") uses the common word for sin, meaning to miss the mark, the goal, or standard which God has set up. Thus, Gabriel charges the Jewish people with the responsibility of putting away sin and developing a righteous society. Like ancient Israel in the wilderness, they were to purify the camp in order to prepare conditions which would be right for the Messiah to come.

God's responsibility, as reflected in the second pair of actions in verse 24, was "to atone for wickedness, [and] to bring in everlasting righteousness." Atonement was a central feature of the sacrificial system in the Hebrew sanctuary (Leviticus 4 and 16). But the atonement mentioned here goes beyond what that system could accomplish. As the book of Hebrews points out, there was a problem with the old system. The problem was that the atonement provided was temporary. A sin was dealt with by offering a sacrifice, but when another sin was committed, it required another sacrifice. Round and round the system went (Heb. 7:11; 10:4). But what Daniel 9:24 looked forward to was *one great final atonement*. That was provided for us by Jesus Christ in His death on the cross. Since that great all-encompassing sacrifice has taken place once for all people, no more ongoing round of sacrifices is necessary (Heb. 7:27; 9:12, 25; 10:10, 12, 14).

This marks the transition from a temporary, transitory righteousness to one that is permanent and everlasting. And that is exactly the next action referred to in Daniel 9:24—"to bring in everlasting righteousness." The righteousness that flows from Christ's death continues until today, almost 2,000 years later, and it will continue to flow unabated into eternity.

The final pair of events in verse 24 are results of the first four actions. The first was "to seal up vision and prophecy." The word translated *prophecy* here is actually the word for "prophet." There would come a time when both vision and prophet would be sealed up. This is in the context of what would happen to the people of Judah. This prophecy would be dramatically fulfilled with the stoning of Stephen (Acts 7). One may reasonably ask what there is there about Stephen's martyrdom that makes it more special than others. Several features show it to be especially significant in a spiritual sense.

First, there is the setting of Stephen's speech. He gave his defense before the Sanhedrin, the highest religious body of the people and the religious representatives of the nation (Acts 6:15). Second, there is the nature of Stephen's speech. To a modern reader, it is rather long and not very interesting, because it goes through a lot of history. It starts with Abraham (7:2); it continues with Isaac, Jacob (vs. 8), and Joseph (vs. 9) to explain how the Israelites happened to be in Egypt. Then it takes up the story of the deliverance under Moses (vs. 20) and the rebellion under Aaron at Sinai (vs. 40). Joshua brings the people into the land of Canaan (vs. 45). Then Stephen mentions David (vs. 45) and Solomon (vs. 46) who built the temple. At that point, Stephen breaks off his speech to accuse the religious leaders of resisting the Holy Spirit and the prophets and of crucifying the Righteous One, the Messiah.

Why this long historical speech?

When God made a covenant with His people in the Old Testament, there was a historical prologue which showed how gracious God had been to His people. This served to motivate them to give Him loving obedience.

When the Old Testament prophets brought God's messages to the people, they commonly started right where the original covenant did—with a historical prologue, showing how gracious God had been to His people and how ungrateful they had been to God. There is a technical term for this kind of prophetic speech—a "covenant lawsuit" in which the prophet serves as the prosecuting attorney from the heavenly court. A good example of this kind of speech can be found in Micah 6. Stephen was giving an inspired "covenant lawsuit" speech before the religious leaders of the nation in the Sanhedrin.

But they did not like it. As a result they dragged him outside of the city and stoned him (Acts 7:58). Just before this happened, however, Stephen, "full of the Holy Spirit, looked up to heaven and saw the glory of God, and Jesus standing at the right hand of God" (vs. 55). And he witnessed to what he saw before the assembled group.

When a person looks into heaven and sees God sitting on His throne and Jesus standing at His right hand, that person is having a vision. People who have visions are, by definition, prophets. At that moment, technically speaking, Stephen was a prophet. But his audience would not hear or accept his vision; they rejected him and stoned him, sealing his lips in death. When Stephen died, *the last prophetic voice had spoken to Israel as the elect people of God.*

Of course, there are other prophets in the New Testament after Stephen—Paul and John, along with others. But the prophets who followed Stephen were prophets *to the Christian church,* not to the nation of Israel. A profound shift had taken place from prophecy directed to national Israel to prophecy directed to the Christian church. "Vision and prophet" had been sealed up to "your people and your holy city" (Daniel 9:24).

The second half of the final pair of events in verse 24 is the matter of anointing "the most holy." From the time of the early church, there have been two main opinions about this action. One school of thought has seen this as a reference to the anointing of the Messiah. There is a problem with this interpretation, however, as the phrase is not normally applied to persons. It is normally used in connection with the sanctuary. It can be used for the holy place, the most holy place, or the sanctuary as a whole. It can also be connected with the vessels in the sanctuary. In any case, it is a sanctuary phrase and should be seen as such in this verse. Besides, the anointing of the Messiah is referred to in the next verse (vs. 25), so we lose nothing by applying the phrase in verse 24 to the sanctuary.

The question then is, to which sanctuary does this anointing refer?

The tabernacle in the wilderness had long since gone out of use, and the first temple lay in ruins in Daniel's time. The soon-to-be-rebuilt second temple is not a very good candidate either, because Daniel 9:26 says of it: "The people of the ruler who will come will destroy the city and the sanctuary." This very prophecy contains a prediction of the destruction of the second temple. So by a process of elimination, we are left with only one other biblical sanctuary to which verse 24 could be referring—the heavenly sanctuary.

In ancient times, sanctuaries were anointed as part of the ceremony that commenced their ministry. A good example of this is found in Exodus 40 where the tabernacle and everything in it was anointed with oil to initiate its ministry. Parallel with this action, the anointing of the heavenly sanctuary should have taken place when Christ was inaugurated there as our great high priest. The earthly sign of this heavenly anointing was the falling of the Holy Spirit on the day of Pentecost.

This final event of the six listed in verse 24 is the one place in the prophecy of chapter 9 where earth and heaven are connected. The rest of the prophecy concerns events on earth. This link is, therefore, very precious, for it shows us that heaven and earth are very close.

◼ Getting Into the Word

Daniel 9:25

Read Daniel 9:24-27 several times. Then respond to the following items.

1. **What is the relationship of the decree to rebuild Jerusalem (vs. 25) to the seventy weeks (vs. 24)?**
2. **Where is that decree found? Read Ezra 1:1-4; 6:1-12; 7:11-26; Nehemiah 1, 2. Summarize the authority granted in each of these four decrees.**
3. **What is the significance of the words "times of trouble" in 9:25? How do the books of Ezra and Nehemiah help us understand those words? (See, for example, Ezra 4.)**
4. **According to 9:25, what is to happen at the end of the first sixty-nine weeks (483 prophetic days)?**

■ Exploring the Word

Verse 25 begins the detailed part of this prophecy. It marks off two significant points in the prophecy's time frame—the starting point and the time when the Messiah would come.

The Starting Point for the Seventy-Week Prophecy

The prophecy identifies the starting point as beginning with the word or decree that would lead to the rebuilding of the city of Jerusalem. It specifically names Jerusalem, so rebuilding only the temple would not fulfill this specification. Usually, ancient history is filled with gaps because a large number of original documents have been lost. Here, however, the problem is not a lack of original documents, but just the reverse. Four different decrees in Ezra and Nehemiah relate in one way or another to the rebuilding of Jerusalem. The problem is to sort them out and see which one best fits the specification of the prophecy.

Four Decrees

The book of Ezra begins with a decree from Cyrus (1:2-4) issued in 538 B.C. and giving the Jews permission to return to their homeland of Judah. It authorized them to rebuild the temple and allowed them to take financial assistance with them. A temple is not a city, however, so this is not the desired decree.

The returnees erected the altar in the temple courtyard before opposition from the Samaritans prevented them from carrying out the rest of the planned reconstruction. Not until 520 B.C., when Darius I issued a second decree for the rebuilding of the temple (Ezra 6:1-12), did work resume. The temple was finished and dedicated four years later in 516 B.C. (vss. 15-18). Neither of these decrees affected the ruined city of Jerusalem. Further decrees were necessary to accomplish its reconstruction.

The next decree was given to Ezra himself (Ezra 7:12-26). It bestowed extensive authority upon him to install public officials, requisition funds from the royal treasuries, and even teach God's law to non-Jews. This decree did not specifically mention rebuilding Jerusalem, but it is obvious that Ezra felt authority was granted him to do so, for upon his return to Judah in the summer of 457 B.C., he promptly rallied the people and started work on the city.

Because the book of Ezra does not follow a strict chronological sequence in relating these events, the order in which all this happened can become somewhat confusing. The decree under which Ezra operated to begin the rebuilding of Jerusalem is given in chapter 7. But the story of his doing so is given in chapter 4! Ezra 4 contains what might be called a topical parenthesis. The first 23 verses depart from the chronological sequence in order to treat the various oppositions the Jews encountered in rebuilding the temple and the city. Verses 1 to 5 recount the opposition in the time of Cyrus. Verse 6 relates the opposition in the time of Xerxes, and verses 7 to 23 deal with the opposition Ezra himself experienced in the time of Artaxerxes. Then the narrative comes back to the time of Darius in verse 24 and takes up the story of the successes of the Jews. The NIV does a nice job here by separating verses 23 and 24 into different paragraphs, showing that they belong to different times.

In Ezra 4, the account of the opposition Ezra faced in his rebuilding project is given in the form of a letter. The heading of the letter reads, "To King Artaxerxes, From your servants, the men of Trans-Euphrates" (verse 11). The men of Trans-Euphrates were the western governors of the Persian Empire. We have here both the name of the addressee (King Artaxerxes) and the return address of the writers (the western governors), so there is no doubt about the identity of the recipient of the letter. In spite of the fact that Ezra does not relate the events in strict chronological order, the letter is definitely addressed to the same King Artaxerxes who had authorized Ezra to return to Jerusalem.

What did the western governors report? The king, the report indicates, should know that "the Jews who came up to us from you have gone to Jerusalem and are rebuilding that rebellious and wicked city. They are restoring the walls and repairing the foundations" (vss. 11, 12). Two important facts emerge here. First, there was clearly another return of the Jews to Jerusalem in the time of Artaxerxes, after the main return in the time of Cyrus. Second, it was this second group of Jewish returnees, under the leadership of Ezra, which supplied the stimulus to start rebuilding the city. Ezra 7 recounts that Ezra led this new group of returnees to Judah after receiving a decree from Artaxerxes authorizing him to do so, and the list of those who went with him is given in chapter 8.

Unfortunately, the Jewish building project was stopped once again. This time it was not the Samaritans who opposed their efforts; it was the western governors. They threatened the king with the loss of tax revenues if he let the city of Jerusalem be built. That argument was persuasive enough to Artaxerxes so that he told the governors to stop the building until he gave further word. The governors were quite happy to do so (Ezra 4:13-23).

This sad state of affairs continued for thirteen years. Nothing further was done on the construction of the city of Jerusalem until Nehemiah, King Artaxerxes' Jewish cupbearer, intervened with the king. The king relented and sent Nehemiah as the governor of Judah with permission and responsibility to rebuild the city (Nehemiah 1, 2). Much of the rest of Nehemiah's book is taken up with the story of how he led out in the reconstruction of the walls of the city, the opposition he received, and the celebration when the construction of the walls was finished. Once the walls were in place, the buildings within the city could be built at a more leisurely pace and under better protection.

Thus the decree of Darius I led to the completion of the work on the temple started under the decree of Cyrus. Likewise, Nehemiah's completion of the walls of the city under Artaxerxes' decree completed the first phase of the work started by Ezra. The letter that Artaxerxes gave to Nehemiah helped to fulfill the work started under the decree that the same king had earlier given to Ezra. So if we are looking for the decree which authorized the reconstruction of the city of Jerusalem, we should look to the decree Artaxerxes gave to Ezra (Ezra 7:12-26). Nehemiah's letter of authorization merely served to complement the decree given to Ezra, enabling the work to be carried out.

Thus Artaxerxes' decree to Ezra is the one that best fits the specification of the prophecy in Daniel 9:25. This was the initial decree that went forth leading to the reconstruction and rebuilding of the city of Jerusalem.

Dating the Decree

Two more questions remain about this decree. When was it given, and according to which calendar should it be figured?

Because the seventy-week prophecy of Daniel 9:24-27 begins with the issuing of Artaxerxes' decree as recorded in Ezra 7, the date of that decree becomes important. The key to the date of the decree is tied to Artaxerxes' seventh year. Ezra 7:8 tells us that "Ezra arrived in Jerusalem in the fifth month of the seventh year of the king." Under conditions of a forced march, the Babylonian army could cover the 400 miles from Babylon to Jerusalem in one month. Ezra had a large body of slow-moving people with him, and it took them five months to cover the same distance.

Fortunately, the dates for Artaxerxes' reign are well known and historically secure. They are based on several sources. First, Greek historians such as Herodotus preserved some of these dates in terms of their own dating system of Olympiads. Second, the astronomer Ptolemy who lived in Alexandria, Egypt, in the second century A.D. provided a table correlating the regnal years of certain rulers of the ancient world (the years that they reigned) with astronomical eclipses. This list is called Ptolemy's Canon, and it goes all the way back to the eighth century B.C. Some of those eclipses occurred during the reign of Artaxerxes and help to fix his dates. More recent archaeological discoveries have helped to refine the system provided by the Greek historians and the astronomer Ptolemy.

Third, the highest regnal dates on business tablets from Babylonia have been compiled from cuneiform texts; these extend from the seventh century B.C. to the first century A.D. Dates for the reign of Artaxerxes can be located in these tables. Finally, a series of papyri have been found in Egypt which bear two sets of dates—one using the Egyptian calendar and the other the Persian-Babylonian calendar. These papyri are letters and business documents written in Aramaic by Jews serving in the Persian army on the island of Elephantine in the Nile where they manned a Persian fort on Egypt's southern border. Since the Egyptian and the Persian-Babylonian calendars operated in different ways, these double dates serve as a check on each other and help to fix the regnal years of the kings during whose reigns they were written. Some of these documents come from the time Artaxerxes reigned and are an aid to confirming his regnal dates.

Thus there are four main lines of evidence which guide us in establishing the dates for Artaxerxes' reign—(1) the Greek historians, (2) Ptolemy's Canon, (3) the Babylonian business tablets, and (4) the Elephantine papyri from Egypt. All four lines of evidence point to the same chronological conclusion: Xerxes died in 465 B.C., and Artaxerxes came to the throne in the latter part of that same year. Under the Persian and Babylonian system of counting regnal years, the remainder of the year in which a king died was considered to be year 0 of the new king who succeeded him. It was called his "accession year." The new king's first official year began with the next new year which commenced in the spring. According to this reckoning, Artaxerxes' seventh year began in the spring of 458 B.C. and ended in the spring of 457 B.C. Thus by the Persian calendar, Ezra would have begun his journey from Babylon in the spring of 458 B.C. and arrived in Jerusalem in the summer of that same year.

The Jews, however, considered the new year to begin in the fall, according to the civil calendar by which they kept track of the reigns of their kings and those of other nations. (The Jews also used a religious calendar which began the year at a different time, much like our modern fiscal year often begins in July, while the regular calendar year begins in January.) Thus by the Jewish civil calendar, Artaxerxes' seventh year would have begun in the fall of 458 B.C. and ended in the fall of 457 B.C. By this reckoning, Ezra would have begun his journey to Jerusalem in the spring of 457 B.C., arriving there in the summer of the same year. Since Ezra used the Jewish civil calendar, not the Persian calendar, we should apply his date—457 B.C.—to the decree Artaxerxes made regarding the rebuilding of Jerusalem rather than 458 B.C. as the Persians would have considered it. This date, 457 B.C., gives us the starting point for the prophecy of the seventy weeks given in Daniel 9:24.

To recap, this is how we arrive at the starting date for Daniel's seventy weeks which was to begin with a decree to rebuild Jerusalem:

•Of the four decrees mentioned in the books of Ezra and Nehemiah regarding the return of the Jews to Jerusalem, the third one, the one Artaxerxes gave to Ezra, is the one that fulfills most closely the specification of the prophecy in Daniel.

•Ezra 7:8 ties this decree to Artaxerxes' seventh year.

•From a variety of ancient documents, we can date Artaxerxes' seventh year to the year that overlaps what we know as 458 and 457 B.C.

•We then apply the Jewish calendar to that date and see that Ezra's journey occurred in 457 B.C. This process gives us the date of 457 B.C. for the commencement of the seventy prophetic weeks of Daniel 9.

The First 69 Weeks and the Anointing of the Messiah

Daniel's prophecy divides the seventy weeks into different portions. The first time period covers sixty-nine weeks (seven weeks + sixty-two weeks) at which time the Messiah, "the Anointed One" (Daniel 9:25), is to come. The noun, *Messiah*, comes from a verb which means "to anoint." Thus, literally, a "Messiah" was an Anointed One. Gabriel tells Daniel, "Know and understand this: From the issuing of the decree to restore and rebuild Jerusalem until the Anointed One, the ruler, comes, there will be seven 'sevens,' and sixty-two 'sevens' " (vs. 25). Sixty-nine weeks is 483 days (7 x 69 = 483). According to the year-for-a-day principle discussed above, each of those days should be understood as a literal year of actual time. Beginning the 483 years in 457 B.C. with the commencement of the seventy weeks brings us down to A.D. 27 for their ending point (there is no year 0 in calculating dates from B.C. to A.D.). At this time "the

Anointed One, the ruler," is to come.

What does it mean for the Messiah, the Anointed One, to come? What event are we to look for in A.D. 27? Messiah's birth? His death? Something else?

When did Jesus of Nazareth become the Messiah? Since *Messiah* means "the Anointed One," Jesus became the Messiah, technically speaking, when He was anointed. When was this? He did not have oil poured over His head like the Old Testament kings and priests in Jerusalem. But was there a specific occasion when He was anointed and formally began His public ministry? Yes. This occurred at His baptism by John in the Jordan River when He was anointed by the Holy Spirit (Matt. 3:13-17). God the Father was present on that occasion and marked it by His own pronouncement, "This is my Son, whom I love; with him I am well pleased" (vs. 17).

Luke tells us that John the Baptist began his ministry in the fifteenth year of Tiberius Caesar (Luke 3:1). Augustus, Tiberius' adoptive father, died in A.D. 14. Adding fifteen years to this date, we arrive at A.D. 29, not A.D. 27—two years too late for Daniel's prophecy. But there is a further factor here. Two years before Augustus died, the Roman Senate voted Tiberius co-ruler of the provinces with his father Augustus. Such an arrangement is called a co-regency and is similar to the situation when King David put Solomon on the throne with him before his own death (1 Kings 1).

Judea was among the provinces that came under the joint rule of Tiberius with Augustus in A.D. 12. Thus the events involving Jesus of Nazareth as the Messiah, which occurred in the Roman province of Judea, can reasonably be dated according to this arrangement by which Tiberius began to rule with his father in A.D. 12. Adding Luke's fifteen years of Tiberius' reign to this date brings us to the year A.D. 27 for the Messiah's public inauguration as Daniel's prophecy predicted.

Thus the prophetic details as we have seen them so far (we will discuss the seven weeks, or forty-nine years, later in this chapter) can be illustrated by the following chart:

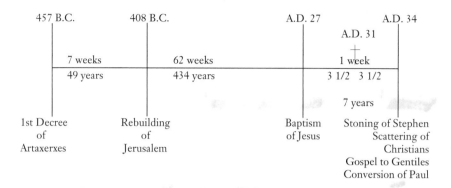

The End of the Seventieth Week

We have established 457 B.C. as the beginning date for Daniel's seventy weeks. We have seen that the sixty-nine weeks, or 483 years, ended in A.D. 27 with Jesus' baptism. The next questions become: When did the seventy weeks end, and what event marked its termination?

Seventy prophetic weeks equal 490 prophetic days or literal years. Simple addition tells us that if we add 490 years to 457 B.C., we reach A.D. 34. What happened in A.D. 34 to mark the conclusion of the seventy weeks? This date is too late for the crucifixion and resurrection of Jesus which took place three or four years earlier. Some other event must be considered.

The stoning of Stephen, described in Acts 7, is an event that has attracted considerable attention as marking the end of the seventy weeks—both for its theological significance as well as its timing. The narrative records no specific date for Stephen's death, but indirect evidence places it in A.D. 34 How do we arrive at this conclusion?

The estimated date for Stephen's martyrdom is based on the career of the apostle Paul. He was still unconverted at Stephen's death, since he stood by and held the coats of those who stoned him (Acts 7:58). A short time later, Saul left for Damascus to persecute Christians there. On the way to Damascus he was converted from Saul the Pharisee to Paul the Christian apostle (9:1-9). If Paul's conversion can be dated, the stoning of Stephen can also be placed within narrow limits.

In Galatians 1, Paul gives some biographical details about his career as an apostle, referring especially to his visits to Jerusalem. He made only brief and infrequent visits to Jerusalem, and he gives us some chronological information about them. He says the first visit came three years after his conversion (vs. 18); the second occurred fourteen years after the first (2:1). Then shortly after his second visit to Jerusalem, Paul left on his second missionary journey, which took him to Corinth (Acts 18). While at Corinth, Paul appeared before the proconsul Gallio (vs. 12). So Paul would have stood before Gallio seventeen years following his conversion (fourteen years between his second and first visit to Jerusalem added to the three years between his first Jerusalem visit and his conversion). From an inscription found in Corinth, we know that Gallio's one-year proconsulship in Corinth occurred in A.D. 51. If the seventeen years for Paul's two visits to Jerusalem are subtracted from the date of Paul's appearance before Gallio, then his conversion and Stephen's stoning should be dated to A.D. 34. This date, A.D. 34, is the one New Testament scholars commonly favor for Stephen's death and Paul's conversion. We can't be so precise as to determine the month or day, but it is a close estimate for the year itself.

Thus this book takes the position that Daniel's seventy weeks came to an end in A.D. 34, with the stoning of Stephen and the conversion of Paul. We have already discussed the theological significance of Stephen's death in the context of the last phrase of Daniel 9:24 (see above). There, we said there were four areas of theological significance related to Stephen's martyrdom: (1) the group to whom Stephen gave his final speech—the Sanhedrin, the highest religious body in the land; (2) the form of his speech—a covenant lawsuit speech like those given by Old Testament prophets; (3) the prophetic nature of his experience at the time of his death when he looked up in vision into heaven itself; and (4) the fact that Paul's conversion has its roots in Stephen's death, so that Paul, the apostle to the Gentiles, takes the place of Stephen, the powerful preacher to Israel. For these reasons, Stephen's death at the end of the seventy weeks can be seen as a highly significant point of transition from the era of Israel as the elect nation of God to the era of the church.

The Seven Weeks

Daniel 9:25 goes on to say, "It [Jerusalem] will be rebuilt with streets and a trench, but in times of trouble." We cannot date specifically from history the completion of this phase of Jerusalem's rebuilding, but it is clear from the books of Ezra and Nehemiah that this construction took place in a troubled time. When Ezra returned, he started rebuilding the city, but the western Persian governors soon intervened and got the work stopped (Ezra 4:7-12). When Nehemiah took up the project anew, his opponents wanted to assassinate him. He resisted their efforts and refused to interrupt his work on the city (Nehemiah 4). Thus the rebuilding of Jerusalem certainly took place in a troubled time.

The prophecy seems to point to some event marking a completion of this first phase of construction in 408 B.C. at the end of the first seven weeks, or forty-nine years (vs. 25). We are not able to determine specifically what event would correspond to this part of the prophecy. The reason we cannot date this event specifically is that we do not possess any historical documents which deal with that matter. The historical records of the Old Testament end about 420 B.C., so they don't reach to 408 B.C. Neither do Josephus, 1 and 2 Maccabees, inscriptions, nor papyri deal directly with the events of that time. Here we need to be careful not to abuse an argument from silence as either supporting or opposing the prophecy. The lack of documentation for a particular period is not negative evidence against a certain event happening. Neither is it positive evidence that some other event happened. It is simply neutral and presents us with a historical vacuum on that point. The prophecy should be judged and interpreted according to the points for which we do possess historical documentation—not upon those points where it is lacking. We have an abundance of evidence dealing with 457 B.C. and A.D. 27, and we have good indirect evidence dealing with

A.D. 34. Our lack of direct evidence dealing with 408 B.C. does not negate these other points, and certainly this period was a troubled time— as the prophecy predicted. Future discoveries may fill in this vacuum, but for the present we must rest content with the evidence currently available.

■ Getting Into the Word

Daniel 9:26

Read 9:24-27 several times. Then work through the following items related to verse 26.

1. The three sentences of verse 26 list three things that will take place after the end of the sixty-two weeks (i.e., after the end of the sixty-ninth week). List those three things in your Daniel notebook.
2. Who is "the Anointed One"? What does it mean for the Anointed One to be "cut off"? Your marginal references will help here. So will the references to "cut off" in your concordance.
3. Who will come and destroy the city and the sanctuary? What historical event might the prophecy be describing?
4. What is the significance of the wording in the last phrase of verse 26 referring to a "flood"? Read the section in your Bible dictionary about the destruction of Jerusalem in A.D. 70. What insights does this give you regarding verse 26? List these in your Daniel notebook.

■ Exploring the Word

The Cutting Off of the Anointed One

Daniel 9:26 begins by saying, "After the sixty-two 'sevens,' the Anointed One will be cut off." These sixty-two weeks, first mentioned in verse 25, follow the first seven weeks and comprise the second interval of prophetic time within the seventy weeks. Thus the sixty-two weeks conclude with the end of the sixty-ninth week of the seventy-week prophecy.

But verse 26 says "*after* the sixty-two 'sevens' " (emphasis supplied), thus taking us slightly *beyond* the end of the sixty-nine week. In other words, the Anointed One is not cut off right at the point at which the sixty-two weeks end, but slightly beyond that point. The specific use of the Hebrew word for "after" emphasizes this.

Where are we if we are just beyond the end of the sixty-ninth week? The answer is quite evident: We are in the seventieth week. Verse 26 does not specify exactly where in that week the Anointed One is to be cut off. That detail comes up in verse 27.

As we saw earlier, the sixty-nine weeks come to an end in A.D. 27 when the Messiah appeared to officially begin His public ministry. Sometime after the commencement of that ministry He was to be "cut off." The verb translated "cut off" is used here as a Hebrew idiom which means "to be killed." To be cut off is to be cut off from the land of the living, to die (Genesis 9:11). But the verb here is in the passive form, meaning that the Anointed One is not going to die of His own volition; somebody is going to do this to Him. He is going to *be* cut off, *be* killed. This stipulation of the prophecy was fulfilled when the religious leaders of Judea conspired with the Roman governmental authorities to have Jesus of Nazareth crucified like a common criminal (Matt. 27:1, 2).

In the Old Testament, we have two strands of messianic prophecies delineating Messiah's fate. One kind tells of His glorious reign (Zechariah 9:9). The other describes a Messiah who will suffer and even die (see Isaiah 53:7-9). How are we to understand the relative sequence of these two types of prophecies?

Many Jews of Jesus' time expected the prophecy of a victorious, ruling Messiah to be fulfilled first and in their day. He would cast off the hated Roman yoke from Jewish shoulders. In the experience of Jesus of Nazareth, however, these prophecies developed in a different sequence. First the cross, then the crown. First His suffering, death, and resurrection; then the establishment of the glorious future kingdom at His second advent. One we look back to, one we still anticipate. Daniel 9, with its precise chronological sequence, is a major link that helps establish the true biblical order of the Messiah's works.

The Messiah Rejected

The next phrase of this prophecy in verse 26 is a short—but difficult—one. The NIV translates it: "The Anointed One . . . will have nothing." This is a good translation because the phrase in the original language has to do with possession. Literally, the Hebrew words mean "There shall not be [X] to/for him." Notice that the direct object is missing from this phrase, as has been indicated by the X in the translation above. The indirect object, *him*, is present and refers clearly to the Messiah, the Anointed One. But what is it that will not be to or for Him? The NIV, the RSV, and other versions supply the word, *thing*, making the phrase mean, "There shall be no*thing* for him." That would be a prophetic picture of the Messiah's poverty. Certainly Jesus of Nazareth had few, if any, material possessions beyond the clothes He wore. He Himself said, "Foxes have holes and birds of the air have nests, but the Son of Man has no place to lay his head" (Matthew 8:20).

It may be suggested, however, that there is something more important to God, and His Messiah, than mere material possessions. People are of greater importance to God than their possessions. In fact, the next phrase of the prophecy in Daniel 9:26 places its stress on people: "The people of the ruler who will come. . . ." Thus it seems that the missing word is better supplied by the word *people* than the word *thing*. Thus we can translate this phrase: "There shall not be people for him," or more freely, "No one shall be for him."

This is a picture of rejection, not poverty. And this rejection takes place at a particular time, at the time when He was to be cut off. This is not a general rejection floating freely in time; it is a specific rejection occurring at the time of His death. This rejection was fulfilled in the experience of Jesus of Nazareth. When He went to the cross, He did so because the religious leaders and the tide of public opinion had turned against Him. The fickle crowd turned away from the popular enthusiasm they had displayed in favor of Jesus earlier during the final week of His ministry (Matt. 21:1-11). Now, with equal enthusiasm, they shouted in favor of the death sentence against Him (Matt. 27:20-26). His own disciples who stood about the foot of the cross did not understand what this was all about. Even after the cross they murmured, "We had hoped that he was the one who was going to redeem Israel" (Luke 24:21). At the time of Jesus' death, "no one was for him."

More Destruction

The next phrase of the prophecy in Daniel 9:26 shifts the focus from the Messiah to the Jewish people and what will happen to them. "The people of the ruler who will come will destroy the city and the sanctuary." Verse 26 begins with a prophecy of Jerusalem's reconstruction and ends with a prophecy of its re-destruction! Enclosed within these two historical poles and their extension in prophetic time lies the career of the Messiah. After that career was over, at some later point not specified, the city was to revert to ruins like those which Nebuchadnezzar had left behind when he conquered Jerusalem in 586 B.C.

The Romans accomplished this re-destruction of the city when they conquered and destroyed Jerusalem in A.D. 70. Visitors to the city today can still see the results of the Babylonian destruction of 586 B.C. in the archaeological garden on the eastern slope of Mount Ophel. Those same tourists can see the effects of the Roman destruction in A.D. 70 in the archaeological excavations around the southern retaining wall of the temple complex and in the archaeological museum nearby known as the Burnt House. These remains give vivid evidence of the destruction prophesied by Daniel. It can also be seen on the Arch of Titus in Rome where the booty taken from Judea, including the lampstand, or Menorah, from the sanctuary is depicted in sculpted stone relief.

Who are the "people of the ruler [or 'prince,' Hebrew: *nagid*]" who carried out this destruction? The Romans clearly destroyed

Jerusalem in A.D. 70, so it has been suggested that this verse refers to the Roman people, or army, and that the "ruler" must refer either to the Roman general who led the army against Jerusalem or to the Caesar who ordered the attack. This generalization, however, fails to take into account some of the specific language used here.

The word used in verse 26 for "prince" or "ruler" is *nagid*, the same word used in verse 25 for "the Anointed One, the ruler," also known as Messiah, the Prince. Note the following pattern of word use in this prophecy:

verse 25	Messiah *nagid*	
verse 26a	Messiah	—
verse 26b	—	*nagid*

In verse 25, the designation, "Messiah *nagid*," forms a word pair—"the Anointed One, the ruler"—so that the two words are linked in a technical way in verse 25. Verse 26a breaks the word pair apart and uses the first word of the pair. Then verse 26b uses the second word of the pair. This pattern suggests that all three references are to the same Messiah Prince designated by the first occurrence of this word pair in verse 25. If so, then "the people of the ruler who will come" refers to the people of the Messiah. It is they who are going to destroy Jerusalem and the sanctuary. The Messiah was a Jewish figure, and thus His people must be the Jewish people of that time. This same point is emphasized here by the use of the word *people* instead of the more correct military term *host* or *army*.

If this interpretation is correct, in what sense did the people of the Jewish Messiah Prince destroy the city and the sanctuary in A.D. 70?

The Roman army was indeed the physical agent which brought about the literal destruction of Jerusalem. But why did they destroy it? They did so because Judea had rebelled against Rome. If Judea had not rebelled, the Roman army would never have come there, and Jerusalem would have been spared. We are dealing here with causes and resulting events. The cause of Jerusalem's destruction was the Jewish rebellion; the event which resulted from that rebellion was the destruction of the city and its temple. In that sense, it can be said that the people of the Jewish Messiah Prince caused or brought about the destruction of Jerusalem in A.D. 70.

The final phrase of verse 26 amplifies the picture of that war and its consequences. "The end will come like a flood: War will continue until the end, and desolations have been decreed." The figurative language of a flood is a very apt description for the way the Roman army finally flowed into Jerusalem to conquer it. Isaiah described the assault of the Assyrian army in similar language: "Therefore the Lord is about to bring against them the mighty flood waters of the River—the king of Assyria with all his pomp. It will overflow all its channels, run over all its banks and sweep on into Judah, swirling over it, passing through it and reaching up to the neck. Its outspread wings will cover the breadth of your land, O Immanuel!" (Isaiah 8:7, 8). In the same way, Daniel prophesied, the Roman army will overflow Jerusalem and its temple like a flood. Jerusalem's northern wall was always the weakest of its defenses because there were valleys on the other three sides of the city. It was at this northern wall that the Roman troops finally penetrated the defenses, bringing desolation that is still well revealed today by the archaeologist's spade.

■ Getting Into the Word

Daniel 9:27

Once more, read Daniel 9:24-27 through several times before dealing with the following items:

1. What three things does verse 27 set forth that bring the prophecy of verses 24 to 27 to a close? List these three sentences in your Daniel notebook.
2. What do you think verse 27 means when it says that the covenant will be confirmed for one week? Who is it being confirmed with? Who is doing the confirming? How does the fact that this occurs during the last week (or seven-year period) of the seventy-week prophecy affect your answers?

3. When verse 27 says "He will put an end to sacrifice and offering" in the midst of the week, who do you think is referred to as "he"? How did he put an end to sacrifice and offering?
4. List all the aspects of the life and work of the Messiah that you can discover from Daniel 9:24-27. Summarize the data from all the statements about the Messiah in this passage into a single word picture or phrase.

■ Exploring the Word

In some ways, the last verse of Daniel 9 is the most difficult of the chapter. It begins with two more statements about the work of the Messiah and then shifts back again to the work of Rome, the desolater.

Confirming the Covenant

Verse 27 makes two predictions concerning the Messiah. The first states, "He will confirm a covenant with many for one 'seven.' " This does not refer to the inception of a new covenant; it refers instead to an attempt to strengthen or renew a covenant already in existence. When Hebrew writers wanted to refer to the inception of a new covenant, they used the verb "to cut" to express that action. "To cut" a covenant was to make a new covenant. But that is not the verb used here in verse 27. It says, instead, that the covenant would be "confirmed," meaning "made strong," or "strengthened." The verb used here is related to the Hebrew word for "a strong man," a "warrior."

This strengthening or reconfirming of an already-existing covenant refers to the covenant that was currently in force between God and Israel. It is not the offer of the new covenant to the church. This strengthening, or confirming, of the covenant was God's final offer and call to the people of Israel as His elect people. This offer was made to them through Jesus, the Messiah. Jesus described to them what they could have had. His Sermon on the

Mount at the beginning of His ministry was based upon an amplification of the old covenant. Taking several of the commandments of the old covenant and amplifying them, Jesus showed that they penetrate to the motives of the heart (Matt. 5:17-48). Jesus was the true messenger of the covenant. Unfortunately, His hearers did not fully accept this great view of what Israel might have been under the Messiah's covenant leadership. It was this failure to grasp all that God was holding out to them that caused Jesus to weep bitterly over Jerusalem during the last week of His earthly ministry (Matthew 23:37-39).

The End of the Sacrificial System

The second prediction of Daniel 9:27 foretold the end of the sacrificial system. Physically, the temple and its offerings came to an end when the Romans destroyed Jerusalem in A.D. 70. But that is not what this phrase of the prophecy is talking about, because it gives a time frame for the end of the sacrifices and offerings that does not extend to A.D. 70.

Verse 27 begins by saying that Messiah would confirm the offer of the old covenant for one week. As we have seen from the dates worked out above, that week extended from the beginning of Jesus' public ministry in A.D. 27 to the stoning of Stephen in A.D. 34. The interesting thing about the duration of this seventieth week is that it extends beyond the cross, thus showing the gracious mercy of God whose voice of invitation went out to His elect people even after His Son was crucified. Not until the deacon-prophet Stephen brought God's covenant lawsuit before the Sanhedrin did Israel's day as God's elect people pass. Individual Jews are still accepted by God on the basis of the life, death, and work of Jesus the Messiah, but national Israel is no longer God's elect nation. That time has passed. The church, spiritual Israel, gathered from all nations of the earth, now occupies that position (Gal. 3:28, 29; Rom. 9:6-8).

The second phrase of verse 27 says "in the middle of the 'seven' he will put an end to sacrifice and offering." The week referred to here is the seventieth week mentioned earlier in the same verse. We have seen that the seventieth week extended from A.D. 27 to A.D. 34. Thus the ending of the sacrifice and offering in the middle of that week should be located in A.D. 31.

Who is the one putting an end to these sacrifices and offerings? The antecedent to "He" is the Messiah Prince, not a Roman ruler. True, the Romans caused the direct physical cessation of the temple and its sacrifices by their destruction of the temple in A.D. 70. But even more important was the spiritual end of the sacrifices in the theological sense that they were no longer necessary after the death of Jesus. He Himself was the Passover lamb (1 Corinthians 5:7). With His death, the type of all of the Old Testament sacrifices met their antitype. They were no longer necessary. God signified this by rending the veil in the temple at the time that Jesus died (Matt. 27:51). Thus, in the sense of Daniel 9:27, the sacrifices came to an end in A.D. 31 when Jesus died on the cross.

One question that arises here is: When did Jesus die? He died in the midst of the final week which we have dated A.D. 27–34. Thus the midpoint of that week is A.D. 31. Can we prove beyond a shadow of doubt that Jesus died in A.D. 31?

Not yet. The problem is the precision that is required to establish such a date. At first glance, it appears to be a simple problem: just find a year within the range of A.D. 25-35 on which the Passover date of Nisan 14 fell on a Friday, which is the day on which the Gospels place the crucifixion and death of Jesus (Luke 23:54-56). To work on this problem, two sets of tables are necessary: (1) a table of new moon dates, and (2) a table with the Julian day number equivalent of these new moon dates. In other words, one must first work out the date for the Passover according to the Jewish lunar calendar in effect in Jesus' time, and then one must consult the appropriate tables to determine what day of the week that was.

The problem lies in attaining the precision necessary to pin down this date to a single year to the exclusion of all others. This requires astronomical, observational, and historical accuracy to within less than one twenty-four-hour period. Historically, the Gospels themselves still leave questions. The Synoptic Gospels appear to date the Passover meal Jesus ate with His disciples to Thursday night of the Passion Week (Matt. 26:2-19; Mark 14:1-16; Luke 22:1-15). John, on the other hand, appears to imply that on that year Passover fell on Friday (John 18:28; 19:14). How do we reconcile these accounts?

One suggestion is that John was calculating his date using the Roman reckoning in which the new day began at midnight, while the Synoptic writers were calculating the date using the Jewish method of beginning the day at sunset. But there may be more to it than that.

To determine the day of Passover, it is astronomically necessary to determine when the first crescent of the new moon could have been seen in Judea. Computer programs designed to make these types of calculations have been getting better and better. With these new programs, it is now possible to determine that Nisan 14 could easily have fallen on a Thursday night in A.D. 31. It is more doubtful that the date could be stretched to a Friday night that year.

Observationally, we also need to know what atmospheric conditions were like to observe the sky on those nights. Just because a new moon mathematically *should* have been visible does not mean that conditions were optimal to observe it visually. If they were not, the official beginning of the lunar month was delayed by a day. In Jesus' time, the lunar calendar of the Jews was also complicated by the fact that it was necessary to insert an extra, or thirteenth, month every third year or so to keep the lunar year in line with the solar year.

The variability of all these factors demonstrate why it is difficult to date the Passover of Jesus' death with precision. Without going into further detail, we can fairly say that all these factors narrow the historical choice down to either A.D. 30 or 31. Since the latter choice correlates best with the dates for the other historical points for the prophecy of Daniel 9, we have utilized A.D. 31 as the year in the spring of which Jesus was crucified. Those readers especially interested in this problem will find a listing of technical works on this subject in the suggested readings at the end of this chapter.

share with others in need. Isn't it time to clean out your closets?
Community Services needs coffee cans with lids that they can fill with beans. If you have any or know of anyone who does, bring to church and give to James.

YOUR DAILY PRAYER for the Holy Spirit's intervention in the lives of the names in the Net98 Prayer box could be the last prayer that is needed to create a desire to attend Net98. PLEASE DON'T FAIL TO PRAY FOR THE NAMES IN THE PRAYER BOX DAILY! You and I might not be here if it had not been for another saint's prayer. It will cost you nothing to be the catalyst that might save someone's life. Do it for the Honor and Glory of God!

Prayer partners are needed for the students at BMA. If you'd like to be a part of the prayer patch program, contact Sue Shobe, 610-562-4533, or pick up a postcard from the bulletin board. There's a huge need!! Don't let the students go it alone.

Join the pastor and elders for forty days of prayer and fasting for Net 98! Prayer will make a difference. People who are interested in participating are encouraged to find a partner and get a copy of the prayer and fast schedule from Pastor Peter. To find out more, check out the bulletin board.

The Mothers Group and Women's Ministries are sponsoring a Baby Shower in a Basket for Christine Walsh. Christine is expecting a boy in September. She has a real need for baby items. If you'd like to donate good used baby clothes, or if you'd like to give a gift-- especially newborn and up to 6 months size clothes, give the items to Tanya or Tami by September 12. This is an opportunity to show Christine and her family that we still care and love her. Please help!

<u>Change in Membership list:</u>
Bennett's phone number is 560-0668

<u>Funds in the red</u>:
Church expense: $2438.78	Personal Ministries 157.87
Satellite equip: 2515.16	Local Evangelism 28.25
Church School: 10918.00	Net 98 5308.47

to *Church Life*

Today--If you're visiting with us today, welcome and please join us for a fellowship meal after the service with Care Group #1.

September 8--Mothers Group at 10:00 am. This week will be a sharing time with Tina Bennett. Bring a favorite magazine article, CD, or book to share. Childcare provided.

September 8--School board meeting, 7:00 pm. Note date change due to holiday.

September 9--Our next Ladies Night Out. Meet us at Lanvina on Columbia Av at 6:30 pm for a fun evening of fellowship and great food. Need details or directions? See one of our Women's Ministries Committee members--Cecelia Hershey, Crystal Woodruff, Kathy Smaela, Lisa Musser, Minda Angelo, Tami Horst, or Tina Bennett.

September 12--Care Group #2 fellowship meal

September 13--Men's Ministry! 8:00 am at the church. An introduction to the gospel in Revelation will be presented by Dan Musser.

September 14--Church board meeting, 7:00 pm

September 18 and 19--Western Campmeeting at Laurel Lake Camp with Randy Maxwell, author of "If My People Pray". Come see the new and improved Laurel Lake and grow in your walk with Jesus as Randy shares from God's Word!! For more info, see Pastor Peter or Bryan.

September 19--Care Group #3 fellowship meal

September 20--Lay Advisory meeting at Laurel Lake, 8:00 am.

September 22--Mothers Group Bible Study, unit 8, at 10:00 am. Childcare provided.

September 26--Care Group #4 fellowship meal

September 27 - 29--The Allegheny East and Pennsylvania Conferences are presenting a Vegetarian Cuisine Instructors Course at BMA. The course is designed to teach the necessary skills for teaching a cooking class in your community. To register, call 745-3370

Community Services still is in need of clothes in good condition to

The Fall of Rome

The final statement of this entire prophecy of Daniel 9:24-27 comes in the last half of verse 27. Following the literal word order, the original Hebrew of this prediction states: "Upon the wing of abomination [shall come] the desolater, until the end that is decreed is poured out on him." The first part of this translation is my own; the last part comes directly from the NIV. In the NIV, the first part of the sentence contains some additional words which the translators have added in an attempt to make sense out of the verse. But by doing so, they have obscured the meaning further.

"Upon the wing of" should be seen as an idiom which means to follow closely. In other words, the abominations come first, followed quickly by the desolation. The desolation was caused by the Roman army after its conquest of Jerusalem. The abominations were those things going on in Jerusalem preceding its destruction and desolation. As the Roman troops broke through the northern defenses of the city, one contingent of Judean troops retreated into the very temple building itself. It was a strong, substantial structure and therefore made a good final fortress. This required the Roman soldiers to attack the temple building, even though their general wished to spare it. In the ensuing fight, the temple caught fire and burned. It was never God's purpose that His temple would be turned into a fortress for fighting in war, and to do so introduced the ultimate in secular abominations into that holy space. After that abominable course of action came the destruction and desolation, exactly as the prophecy described.

But the Romans themselves were not to go unpunished either. God permitted these events to occur because the people of Judea forsook His divine protection by their rejection of the Messiah. The Roman troops were, therefore, instruments of God's judgment at the time. The same type of thing occurred in the Old Testament when Assyria was permitted to conquer Samaria but then received its own just judgment (Nahum). In the same way, Babylon was permitted to conquer Jerusalem but was later to receive its own just judgment (Jer. 50, 51). Now the Romans were permitted to carry out the same kind of judgment upon Jerusalem, but Rome, too, was to be judged. That was also the message of some of the other prophecies of Daniel—that Rome would have its day upon the stage of history, but like the other powers that preceded it, Rome would also fall (Dan. 2:40-44; 7:7, 8, 23, 24; 8:25). Thus the title of Gibbon's famous work of history, *The Decline and Fall of the Roman Empire*, actually illustrates the fulfillment of the final prophetic statement in Daniel 9.

Summary

In summarizing the contents of this prophecy, we should focus our attention on the various aspects of the work of the Messiah that it outlines. These may be seen as follows:

1. Dan. 9:24c—He would make the great atonement.
2. Dan. 9:24d—That atonement would bring in everlasting righteousness.
3. Dan. 9:24f—The heavenly sanctuary would be anointed for the commencement of His high priestly work.
4. Dan. 9:25—The date for the coming of the Messiah.
5. Dan. 6:26a—The Messiah killed.
6. Dan. 9:26b—The Messiah rejected at His death.
7. Dan. 9:27a—The Messiah makes the final great offer of the old covenant to Israel.
8. Dan. 9:27b—The Messiah brings the sacrificial system to an end.

If we take all eight of these points and boil them down into one image, a central picture results. That picture is one of the Messiah as *sacrifice*. His death, His rejection at His death, the date for His death, and the manifold results of His death are featured prominently in this prophecy. Those results include atonement and righteousness, an end of the sacrificial system, and a beginning of a new priesthood in the heavenly sanctuary. This picture of the Messiah as sacrifice is a prelude and vital introduction to the prophecies of Daniel 8 and 7 that flow in reverse order from chapter 9. Daniel 9 forms a presupposition for the later events contained in those prophecies.

■ Applying the Word

Daniel 9

1. What can I learn about prayer from Daniel 9:4-19? What specific items do I need to put into practice in my prayer life?
2. What can I learn from Daniel 9 about God's care for His people? In what ways can that knowledge strengthen my daily Christian walk?
3. What meaning do the time prophecies of Daniel 9:24-27 have for my life today? What do they say about God?
4. What can I learn about the plan of salvation from Daniel 9:24-27? What is my present relationship to God's great covenant of salvation? In what specific ways could it improve?
5. What can I learn about history from Daniel 9 and specifically from verses 24-27? In what ways does that knowledge affect me in daily living?

■ Researching the Word

1. Using the *NIV Exhaustive Concordance*, look up the word *ruler* (Hebrew: *nagid*) used in Daniel 9:25, 26. (You can do the same word study with *Strong's Exhaustive Concordance of the Bible* using the word *prince*.) Where is this same word used elsewhere in Daniel and to whom does it apply? Does the usage of this word elsewhere in Daniel tell you anything about whom it refers to in Daniel 9:25-27? Where is the word used elsewhere in the Old Testament, and to whom is it applied?
2. Study the literary structure of the prophecy in Daniel 9:25-27 by outlining the successive thoughts in these verses. Does your outline indicate that the thoughts of this prophecy appear in an orderly fashion, or do they seem to be given in random order? Do the successive thoughts build on those that have gone before? Do they help to explain each other?

3. Using the *NIV Exhaustive Concordance*, study the word *seven* (Hebrew: *sheba*). (You can do the same word study with *Strong's Exhaustive Concordance of the Bible* using the word *week*.) How is this word translated in other passages in Daniel? In other passages of the Old Testament outside of Daniel? Do you think that this word has been translated correctly? Could all of the events of this prophecy occur in seventy weeks of literal time? Why, or why not?

■ Further Study of the Word

1. For a better understanding of the different ways in which this prophecy has been interpreted from different points of view, see the survey of this subject by G. F. Hasel, "Interpretations of the Chronology of the Seventy Weeks."
2. For a better understanding of ancient calendars, and in particular the historical materials supporting 457 B.C. as the starting date for the prophecy of the seventy weeks, see S. H. Horn and L. H. Wood, *The Chronology of Ezra 7*.
3. For the best and most detailed Seventh-day Adventist study of the question of the year in which Christ died, see the discussion in F. D. Nichol, ed., *The SDA Bible Commentary*, 5:247-265.
4. For further study of the year-day principle, see W. H. Shea, *Selected Studies on Prophetic Interpretation*, 67-110.

CHAPTER EIGHT

Christe
As Priest

Daniel 8

Daniel 8 presents the prophetic preview, from Daniel's point in time, of two great conflicts to come. The first of these pitted Persia against Greece. In the vision, the prophet saw each of these two powers represented by an animal. A ram symbolized Persia (8:3, 20) and a goat symbolized Greece (vss. 5, 21). The clash between these two powers was represented by head-to-head combat between the two animals. Greece won, and the Persian ram was cast down to the ground and trampled upon by the goat (vss. 6, 7).

The second great conflict present in Daniel 8 pitted Rome against the forces of heaven. Rome was represented by the symbol of a little horn (vs. 9). Historically speaking, Rome existed in two major phases. There was the classical, or Imperial, phase—the Rome of the Caesars. Later came the religious or spiritual phase—the Rome of the popes. While the prophecy symbolizes both phases of Rome, the emphasis is upon the second phase.

According to the vision, a special target of contention between these two powers was to be the sanctuary or temple in heaven (vs. 11). Obviously, there is no physical way for an earthly power to attack a heavenly structure. The attack is spiritual, or theological, and that is what the symbols in the second half of this vision point toward. The challenge to the heavenly sanctuary is created by turning the attention of men and women to an earthly substitute, by turning their attention to religious rites in an earthly context which take the place of the true heavenly rites.

This struggle over the sanctuary was to go on for a prolonged period of time according to the time element connected with this prophecy—2300 evening-mornings, or days (vs. 14), which equal 2300 historical years (see chapter 6 above). We are not shown the complete end of this phase of the conflict; that awaits the fuller picture of these events in Daniel 7. Chapter 8, however, does give us assurance that this conflict will be resolved in God's own prophetic time and in God's way.

■ Getting Into the Word

Daniel 8:1-8, 15-22

Read Daniel 8 through once. Then reread verses 1-8 and 15-22 before answering the following questions:

1. The first prophetic symbol in this chapter is the ram (vs. 3). In your Daniel notebook, list all the identifying characteristics of the ram found in verses 3 and 4.
2. The goat is the second prophetic symbol in chapter 8. List all the identifying characteristics of the goat given in verses 5-8. Describe the relationship between the ram and the goat.
3. In verses 15-22, Gabriel is sent to Daniel to identify the ram and the goat. What further facts can you discover for each of those symbols from these verses? What do these verses tell you about the identity of both the goat's large horn and the four horns that replace it?

■ Exploring the Word

The Persian Ram, Daniel 8:1-4

In his introduction to this vision, Daniel says God gave it to him in the "third year of King Belshazzar" (8:1). In terms of our calendar, Belshazzar's third year equals approximately 548 B.C. Major changes were developing in the Near East at that time. Babylon was on the decline, and Persia was on the rise (see map of the Persian Empire on page 87). In this vision, God showed Daniel just how far Persia would go. But even more, He also showed him the powers

THE PERSIAN EMPIRE

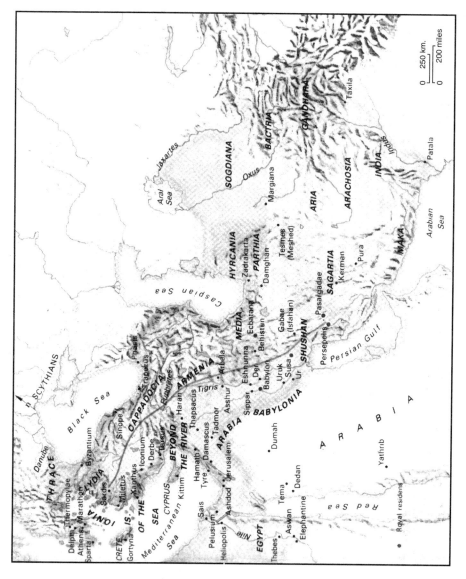

MEDIA Satrapy under Darius I
=== Canal built between the Gulf of Suez and the Nile
—— Royal Way

that would follow Persia.

The visions recorded earlier in Daniel came as dreams in the night. This was true of Nebuchadnezzar (2:1; 4:5), and it was true of Daniel (7:1). But the vision of chapter 8 comes to Daniel during the daytime. He seems to be in Susa, or Shushan, in the eastern province of Elam (vs. 2). This was the same place where the action of the book of Esther took place (Esther 1:2).

Elam was a border state between Babylonia and Persia. Sometimes it was under the control of Babylon; sometimes it was under the control of Persia. And at other times it was able to stand free and independent of both those powers.

In vision, Daniel seemed transported eastward from Babylon until he came to stand on the west bank of the Ulai river near Susa. He looked eastward across that river and saw a ram coming toward him from the east. It had two horns on its head, but they were uneven. The higher one came up later (vs. 3). Later, Gabriel, who was sent to Daniel to interpret the vision to him, explained this feature. "The two-horned ram that you saw represents the kings of Media and Persia" (vs. 20).

The Medes and the Persians were related peoples who occupied the Iranian plateau—the Medes in the north and the Persians in the south. The Medes were the more powerful of the two, and they gave the Assyrians considerable difficulty on their eastern border from the ninth to the seventh centuries B.C. The royal houses of the Medes and Persians intermarried, and eventually, under Cyrus, the Persians became the stronger of the two. Cyrus conquered Media and incorporated it into his kingdom, hence the combined name of the Medo-Persian Empire (vss. 3, 20). This dual power is represented by the ram in this vision.

As Daniel watched, the ram charged off into three different directions. The accompanying statement makes it obvious that this represented conquests by this power: "No animal could stand against him, and none could rescue from his power" (vs. 4). The three directions of conquest were toward the north, the west, and the south. The major conquest of the Persians toward the north was the kingdom of Lydia in Anatolia, or ancient Turkey. Cyrus conquered this area in 547 B.C. To the west, Persia, under Cyrus, conquered Babylon in 539 B.C. Daniel 5 and 6 refer to this event and its immediate consequences. To the south, Cyrus' son Cambyses conquered Egypt in 525 B.C. In this way, the Medo-Persian Empire was extended in these three directions.

The Greek Goat, Daniel 8:5-8

Flushed with success, the Persian emperors tried to extend their conquests one step further in the north. They invaded Greece. Two different Persian kings, Darius I in 490 B.C. and Xerxes in 480 B.C., tried to subdue Greece. But after some initial successes, both were eventually turned back and had to return home. Thus ended the Persian attempts to conquer Greece (see map of the Greek Empire on page 91).

But the Greek goat (vss. 5, 21) did not forget this national humiliation of a Persian invasion and the destruction they had wrought. Thus when the prophecy speaks about the eventual clash between these two powers, it says that the goat ran at the ram "furiously" (vs. 6). Greece was out to even the score, and it did so—and then some. Alexander the Great defeated the Persians, and his victorious army marched all the way to the valley of the Indus River in northwestern India before returning.

All of this was symbolized by the actions of the goat in Daniel 8. In verse 21, Gabriel identifies the goat as Greece, adding, "The large horn between his eyes is the first king"—an obvious reference to Alexander. The rapidity of the Greek conquest is referred to by the symbolism of the goat flying across the earth (vs. 5). The defeat of the Persians and their last king, Darius III, is indicated by the way in which the goat treated the ram, "striking the ram and shattering his two horns. The ram was powerless to stand against him; the goat knocked him to the ground and trampled on him; and none could rescue the ram from his power" (vs. 7).

But Alexander did not live to enjoy the fruits of his conquests. At the young age of thirty-three, he died in Babylon after his return

THE EMPIRE OF
ALEXANDER THE GREAT

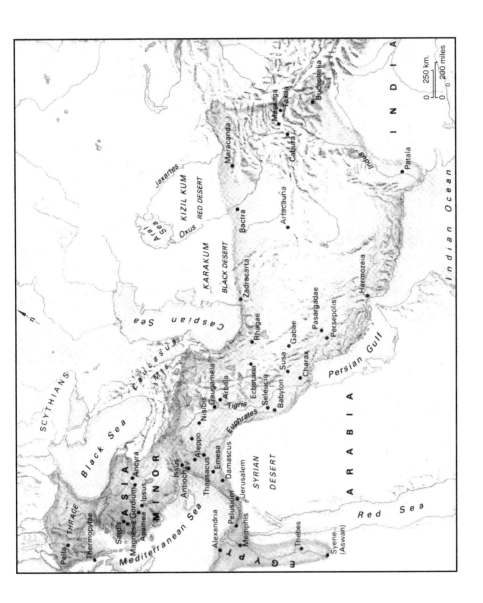

from India. His fate has been immortalized in a poem which contrasts his achievements with those of Jesus:

> Jesus and Alexander died at thirty-three.
> One lived and died for self,
> The other died for you and me.

The prophecy of Daniel 8 predicted Alexander's death. "The goat became very great, but at the height of his power his large horn was broken off" (v. 8). At the height of his powers and conquest, Alexander died in 323 B.C. He had a son, but this son did not inherit the kingdom (Dan. 11:4). Instead, Alexander's kingdom was divided among his generals. There was fighting among them for a period of about twenty years. But by 301 B.C., four kingdoms had emerged from the political chaos that ensued after the death of Alexander (8:8, 22). These were: (1) Macedonia under Cassander; (2) Thrace and northwestern Asia Minor under Lysimachus; (3) Syria and Babylonia under Seleucus; and (4) Egypt under Ptolemy. (These developments are depicted in a series of maps found in F. D. Nichol, ed., *The Seventh-day Adventist Bible Commentary*, 4:824, 825. See also the map of the divisions of the Greek Empire on page 95). These factions continued to battle back and forth, but the later prophecies of Daniel (chapter 11) came to concentrate on the struggles between the king of the north (Syria) and the king of the south (Egypt).

■ Getting Into the Word

Daniel 8:9-12, 23-25

Read Daniel 8 straight through once; then focus on verses 9-12 and 23-25, reading them again carefully before answering the following questions:

1. Where did the small horn of verse 9 come from? In what directions did it expand its power? What is the "beautiful" land? To help you answer this question, use a con-

cordance, and look for all the other uses in Daniel of the word "beautiful" in the NIV (or "pleasant" and "glorious" in the KJV). What light do verses 23-25 throw on the identity of the "beautiful" land?

2. List the small horn's activities against God and His kingdom as given in verses 10-12. In a parallel column in your Daniel notebook, list the activities of the small horn as explained by Gabriel in verses 23-25. To the best of your ability, describe each of those activities.

3. Who is the "Prince of the host" (vs. 11) or the "Prince of princes" (vs. 25)? Using a concordance, look up all the references in Daniel to the word "prince." How do these other uses help you identify the "Prince of the host"? In Daniel 8, what is the relationship of the small horn to this Prince?

■ Exploring the Word

The Little Horn of Rome: Phase I, Daniel 8:9

The four Hellenistic (Greek) kingdoms of the eastern Mediterranean region were represented in this prophecy by the four horns that came up in the place of Alexander's horn which was broken off (8:8, 22). After they had been established, a new power came on the scene of action (see the map of the Roman Empire on page 99. This power was represented by a "small horn" (vs. 9). Up to this point in the prophecy, the commentators have been relatively uniform in their interpretations of the symbols. For the most part, they follow the historical outline presented above. At this point in the vision, however, they diverge in a marked way.

One school of interpreters holds that the little horn represents an individual king, Antiochus IV Epiphanes, a Greek king of the Syrian kingdom. A second school of thought holds that this new horn represents Rome. The position taken in this volume follows the latter view. I have elaborated upon that view in chapter two of my book, *Selected Studies in Prophetic Interpretation*. Those who would like more details on this point can consult that work. (See also chapter 6 of the

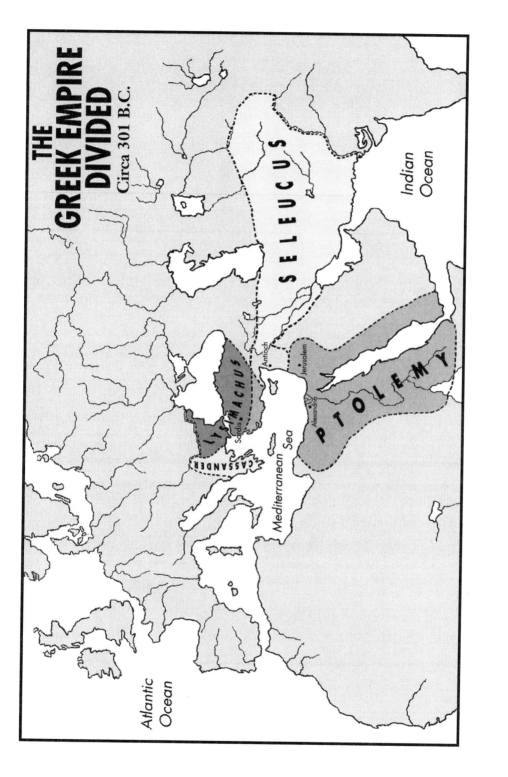

THE
GREEK EMPIRE
DIVIDED
Circa 301 B.C.

Indian
Ocean

S E L E U C U S

L Y S I M A C H U S

CASSANDER

Antioch

Sardis

Jerusalem

Alexandria

P T O L E M Y

Mediterranean Sea

Atlantic
Ocean

present volume.) Here, we can only note a few points in passing. There are seven reasons why Antiochus cannot be the small horn of Daniel 8. We will note three of the major ones.

First, the vision presents a progression in terms of the power utilized by the kingdoms involved. The Persian ram "magnified himself" (vs. 4, RSV). The Greek goat "magnified himself exceedingly" (vs. 8, RSV). The little horn then "magnified itself, even to the host of heaven . . . , even up to the prince of the host" (vss. 10, 11, RSV). This progression from the comparative to the superlative would be true in terms of the Roman Empire, but it would not be true in terms of an individual ruler such as Antiochus Epiphanes.

Second, Antiochus Epiphanes (175-163 B.C.) ruled in Syria about the *middle* of the Seleucid dynasty, which lasted from 301 B.C.until 64 B.C. He was the seventh king out of twenty-seven in the Seleucid dynasty. The little-horn power, however, appears on the scene of action "in the latter part of their reign" (vs. 23), that is, at the *latter* end of the rule of the four Greek kingdoms. In contrast, Rome did appear on the scene at the latter part of the rule of these four kingdoms, conquering each in turn—Greece in 168 B.C., Asia Minor in 133 B.C. (by inheritance), Syria in 64 B.C., and Egypt in 31 B.C. Thus Rome fulfills this characteristic of the vision, but Antiochus Epiphanes does not.

Third, we should note the direction of conquest specified by the vision. The little horn was to conquer to the east, the south, and the beautiful land (vs. 9). Antiochus IV had some success toward the south. In 169 B.C. he conquered the eastern half of the Egyptian delta. In 168 B.C. he came back to finish the job, but he was not able to do so. Instead, he was turned back by a Roman ambassador and never returned to Egypt again. On his eastern campaign, Antiochus had some initial success, but he later died on this campaign. His record was even worse with regard to the "beautiful land," or Judea. When he came to the throne, this province belonged to his kingdom. But because of his persecution of the Jews, they rose up in revolt and threw off the Syrian yoke. In contrast to the vision, Antiochus Epiphanes did not conquer the "beautiful land," rather, he was the one responsible for losing it. Rome, on the other hand, made major conquests in all three of the directions specified by the vision. Here again, Rome fits the characteristics of the vision, but Antiochus does not.

Based on these reasons, we will take the position in this volume that the small horn in the vision of Daniel 8 represents Rome.

The first thing the small horn did after its appearance was to make conquests toward the east, the south, and the "beautiful land." These, as we have seen, correspond to the territorial conquests of Imperial Rome. In terms of conquering the four Greek horns, Rome conquered to the east in 168 and 133 B.C.; it conquered the "beautiful land" of Judea at the same time it conquered Syria in 63 B.C.; and it conquered Egypt to the south in 31 B.C.

The Little Horn of Rome: Phase II, Daniel 8:10-12

The territorial conquests to the east, south, and the beautiful land in Daniel 8:9 represent territorial conquests by *Imperial* Rome. With verse 10, however, a transition takes place. The small horn of Rome has a new target, but it is not on earth. It is in heaven. The next three verses identify the targets of the small horn as the "starry host" of heaven (vs. 10), the "Prince" who leads that host (vs. 11), and the sanctuary in heaven along with the service carried on there (vss. 11, 12). This transition from horizontal earthly conquests to a vertical assault on heaven is referred to as the vertical dimension of apocalyptic.

This vertical dimension of apocalyptic also heralds a new phase of the work of the little horn. Conquest of territory in the east, south, and beautiful land is a military-political type of activity. An attack upon heaven, even if it is described in symbolic terms, is a distinctively religious activity. Thus with this phase of the work of the little horn, the prophecy has entered upon its religious phase.

The vertical dimension of apocalyptic is demonstrated in this passage both by the verbs of motion used and also by the targets of the little horn's activity. "It grew until it reached the host of the heavens, and it threw some of the starry host down to the earth and trampled on them" (vs. 10). The symbolic actions depicted here operate in

THE ROMAN EMPIRE,
1ST CENTURY B.C. TO A.D. 150

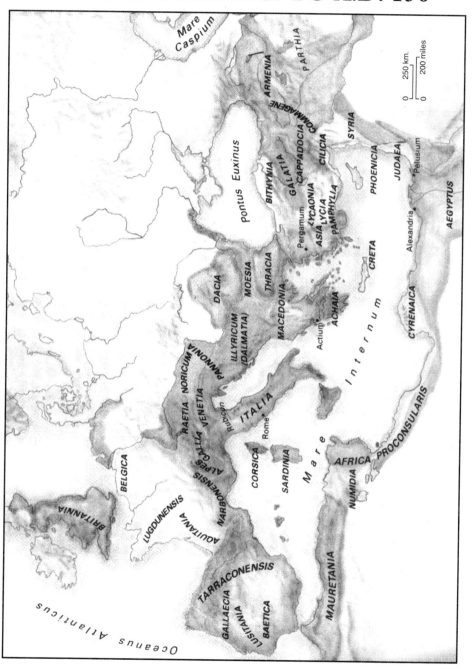

two opposite directions. The little horn reaches *up* to heaven, which is the vertical dimension, and then he throws *down* the stars to the earth in the other direction. But he is not content with merely throwing the stars down to the earth; he goes on to trample upon them, crushing them.

In this vision, the stars are not symbols for angels as they are in some other Bible symbolism. This does not refer to the casting down of Satan and a third of the angels at the time of his original rebellion. That occurred long before the historical action portrayed here was carried out by this religious power. Revelation 12:7-9 places the casting down of Satan and his angels back at the beginning of his great controversy with God. Nor did Satan trample on his angels, for he needed them to carry out his purposes. The casting down of the stars, spoken of here in Daniel 8:10, is explained in verse 24, "He will destroy the mighty men and the holy people." The saints of the Most High are the targets of the little horn, and that tells us that the little horn was to be a persecuting power. The saints are compared to stars elsewhere in Daniel; when they finally emerge victorious, "they will shine like the brightness of the heavens" (Daniel 12:3).

Of course, Imperial Rome *did* persecute Christians from time to time—first on a local basis and later on an empire-wide basis. But persecution was carried out for a longer time and to a greater extent by religious Rome under the papacy. The list of these persecutions is extensive.

The Crusades of the eleventh through the thirteenth centuries against "infidels" in the Middle East were holy wars directed by the papacy. From these, the idea of crusades against Christian "heretics" was developed, leading to attacks on the Albigenses in southern France and the Waldenses in northern Italy in the thirteenth century.

A later form of the inquisition was developed in Spain. And since Spain controlled a considerable portion of the New World, the inquisition was exported to Latin America, where it was carried on until the early nineteenth century. Testimony to this fact is the Museum of the Inquisition in Lima, Peru, housed in the actual building in which this type of persecution was carried out. From Spain, this type of activity was also exported to Holland, where the Duke of Alva led the Spanish troops in suppressing and killing Dutch Protestants in 1568.

France also saw aggressive action against Protestants. Thousands of Huguenots fell on St. Bartholomew's Day in 1572. Again, when the French king revoked the Edict of Toleration in 1685, many of the Huguenots had to flee to other countries. All this activity correlates well with the type of persecution the little horn is said to carry out by casting down to the ground the stars, or the saints of the Most High, and trampling upon them (vs. 10).

The vision next brings to view a chief opponent of the little horn; he is known as the "Prince of the host" (vs. 11). The little horn "set itself up to be as great as the Prince of the host" (vs 11) but was not able to do any harm to Him personally, although it was able to harm His followers. The word translated *Prince* is a political title, but in this chapter it is used in a priestly way. To Him belongs the sanctuary and the *tamid*, or daily service that went on there. This is indicated by the personal pronouns used with those objects. "The place of *his* [the Prince's] sanctuary was brought low" (vs. 11, emphasis supplied). The Hebrew verb used here means "to throw or cast down."

The word used for "Prince" is also a messianic term. We found the Messiah Prince mentioned in Daniel 9:25, 26 in the prophecy about the Messiah in relation to His people in the Promised Land. The word used here for "Prince" (*sar*) is a different Hebrew word than that used in Daniel 9 (*nagid*). This usage in Daniel 8 reflects the Prince's heavenly position. The name or title for God is not used in this chapter. In this chapter, the Prince is the chief protagonist on God's side. Thus this Prince can be compared to the heavenly Michael who elsewhere in Daniel (10:13, 21; 12:1) is mentioned as a prince (*sar*).

As the religious phase of Rome, the little horn has attacked the saints and has been able to harm some of them. He has challenged the Messiah Prince, Jesus Christ, in His heavenly setting, but he has not been able to do any harm to Him. He does, however, attack His sanctuary. It is cast down to the earth and is trampled upon (vs. 13). The Hebrew verb used for this casting down is *shalak*. The NIV translation, "brought low," does not capture the strength of this verb. It is commonly used for throwing a stone or a similar action. In this case, the translation, "cast down" (KJV and the NKJV), is to be preferred.

What does it mean for the heavenly sanctuary to be cast down to earth and trampled upon? Clearly, this is not a literal, physical casting down. There is no elevator between heaven and earth upon which the sanctuary building can go up and down. This is symbolic action. What would it mean to bring a heavenly sanctuary down to earth? It means that what was correctly represented as being located in heaven has now, in the eyes of human beings, been brought down here where we are by the activities of the little horn. The small horn now represents the heavenly ministry of Jesus Christ as requiring human or priestly activities on earth to mediate its grace to humanity. Human intermediaries have been interjected between God and the people. One of the central issues of the Reformation was a rejection of this very point. Martin Luther claimed that every Christian has immediate access to Christ's ministry in heaven. Each individual may have personal access to Jesus Christ and God; human, priestly intermediaries are not necessary for such access. "For there is one God and one mediator between God and men, the man Christ Jesus" (1 Tim. 2:5). This leaves no room for the mediation of priests, saints, angels, or Mary—as in the Roman system.

The final act carried out by the little horn against the sanctuary was to attempt to control the "daily" or "continual" ministry that goes on there. The NIV says the little horn "took away the daily sacrifice from him [the Prince]" (vs. 11). In actuality, the verb is in the passive: it "was taken away from him" (RSV). The clear implication, of course, is that it was the little horn that did this. More importantly, many versions, including the NIV, have supplied the word *sacrifice* here in connection with the word *daily*. Elsewhere in the Old Testament, this Hebrew word *tamid* (daily) is used as a modifier, referring to something that goes on daily, continually, or constantly. Here, however, the word is used as a noun; no word follows it for it to modify. Many Bible versions have supplied the word *sacrifice* because *tamid*, "daily," is sometimes used to modify the offering or sacrifice that was burnt daily on the altar in the courtyard of the earthly sanctuary (Exod. 29:38, 42). But *tamid* was also used to modify a number of other activities carried on in the sanctuary. It was used for the burning of the lamps of the seven-branched lampstand (Exod. 27:20, 21), for the burning of incense on the altar of incense (Exod. 30:8), and for the bread of the Presence on the table of shewbread (Exod. 25:30). It was also used for other activities connected with the sanctuary (Exod. 28:29, 38; 1 Chron. 16:6).

It is necessary then to translate *tamid* with a word that comprehends all of these activities connected with the sanctuary, not just the one idea of sacrifice. A word that is more broad and inclusive, encompassing all of these activities, is *ministry*. All these activities which *tamid* is used to describe are activities carried out by the priest in the courtyard and the holy place of the sanctuary. They were part of his daily ministry there. It is this type of ministry that Jesus carries out in the heavenly sanctuary (Heb. 8:1) and which the little-horn power attempted to counterfeit. It attempted to turn the eyes of mankind from Jesus' true, original ministry in heaven to an earthly, human substitute. That is the *tamid* which the little-horn power attempted to take over and control.

It ultimately failed in this attempt, however, for the true heavenly ministry of Jesus continued. Eventually, by means of the Reformation and subsequent events, the eyes of people were again directed to Jesus' ministry in the heavenly sanctuary as the source of salvation.

The struggle and conflict envisioned here in Daniel 8:10-12 was of a distinctly religious nature. It involved persecution. It involved an attack upon the person of Christ. It attempted to point the attention of people away from His heavenly sanctuary to an earthly substitute. And it attempted to point the attention of people away from His heavenly ministry to an earthly human priesthood and their actions. All this was the work of the medieval papacy, the religious phase of Rome.

Why was this conflict so important? Because it dealt with the

source of the plan of salvation. It was a struggle between two different plans of salvation—the original heavenly one and a later earthly
substitute. Why do Seventh-day Adventists make so much out of
the eighth chapter of Daniel? Because it involves the very plan of
salvation. What could be more important?

It is also important to note that Daniel 8 does not paint a picture
of the final resolution of this problem. When the vision faded from
the prophet's eyes, the little horn still "prospered in everything it
did" (vs. 12). However, verses 13 and 14 provide an assurance that
this problem would eventually be resolved, but chapter 8 does not
explain that resolution in detail. The full significance of what was
involved in resolving this problem is depicted in Daniel 7, which we
will study in the next chapter.

■ Getting Into the Word

Daniel 8:13-27

**Read all of Daniel 8 once again. Then focus your attention
on verses 13-27 as you answer these questions:**

1. **What is the relationship of the question asked in verse 13 to
   verses 11 and 12? What answer is provided in verse 14?**
2. **What is an "evening and a morning?" See Genesis 1:5, 8, 13
   to help you formulate your answer.**
3. **Verse 14 falls in the symbolic half (as opposed to the explanatory half) of Daniel 8. How do Ezekiel 4:6 and Numbers 14:34 help us unlock the symbolism of the time period
   given in Daniel 8:14?**
4. **According to verse 14, what is to happen to the sanctuary at
   the end of the 2300 evenings and mornings? Compare verse
   14 in a number of other Bible translations for a broader
   understanding of this event. What words do they use in place
   of "reconsecrated"?**
5. **Verse 14 provides us with the last prophetic symbols to be
   found in Daniel 8. In verse 15, Gabriel is sent to explain**

each of the symbols. List those symbols that are explained in verses 15-27. Which symbol does Gabriel leave unexplained? In what ways does that unexplained portion relate to the time explanations of Daniel 9 (especially verses 20-27)? How do 9:21-23 relate to 8:26, 27?
6. What indications can you find in Daniel 8:15-27 that the vision of Daniel 8 will extend until the end of time? List these in your Daniel notebook.

■ Exploring the Word

The Two Angels Speak: Daniel 8:13, 14

The visual portion of the prophecy of Daniel 8 ends with verse 12. As the screen of the prophet's view went blank, a new phenomenon occurred. Two angels came within range of his hearing, and he listened in on their conversation. In verse 13, the first angel asked a question. The second angel gave the answer in verse 14.

The NIV correctly translates the first part of the first angel's question as: "*How long* will it take for the vision to be fulfilled?" (vs. 13, emphasis supplied). The rest of the question goes on to identify the vision in question—"the vision concerning the daily sacrifice, the rebellion that causes desolation, and the surrender of the sanctuary and of the host that will be trampled underfoot?" The second angel's answer is found in verse 14: "It will take 2,300 evenings and mornings; then the sanctuary will be reconsecrated." Each element in this important verse needs to be examined in detail.

Establishing Dates for the 2300 Days

It is important to note that the question is about the length of *the vision*, not about the length of the activities of the little horn. The activities of the little horn are included within this vision, indeed they mark its climax, but they are not all there is to the vision. The vision also includes the Persian ram, the Greek goat, and the four horns that precede the little horn of Rome's two phases. So when the angel asks, "How long is the vision?" the word *vision*, includes the whole of what Daniel saw in chapter 8—from the Persian ram to the little horn. This fact gives us an approximate starting point for the 2300-day time-period mentioned in verse 14.

The vision starts with the Persian ram. Therefore, the 2300 evening-mornings should begin with the Persian period. The prophecy does not give us a precise starting point within that period; we must obtain that point from Daniel 9. In the preceding chapter on the prophecy of Daniel 9, we paid considerable attention to the starting point for the prophecy of the seventy weeks (see pp. 61-66). From a study of the decrees of Ezra and Nehemiah and the chronology related to them, we established the date of 457 B.C. as the starting point of the seventy weeks. It remains now to connect these prophecies—that of chapter 9 and the vision of chapter 8—on a more specific basis. There are several lines of evidence for this linkage.

The first point is that Daniel 9:24 says the seventy weeks were "cut off" for Daniel's people and the holy city of Jerusalem. The NIV, along with a number of modern versions, prefers to translate this verb as "decreed." Unfortunately, this verb, *hatak*, occurs only this one time in the Old Testament, so in terms of the Bible itself, there is no comparative material with which we can evaluate it for possible alternate meanings. In such a case, we must go to the next most helpful source of such information—post-biblical Hebrew. This word, *hatak*, is used about a dozen times in post-biblical Jewish sources. In all but one instance it means "to cut." In only one case does it have the meaning "to decree" or "to determine." Clearly, its dominant meaning in post-biblical Hebrew sources is "to cut," and thus that is the most likely meaning here in Daniel 9.

Another argument pointing to the same conclusion is the fact that the meaning of the roots of Hebrew words generally developed from the concrete to the abstract. In this case, the idea of "cutting" is the concrete, and the idea of "decreeing" is the more abstract idea. It isn't clear whether by Daniel's time the word *hatak* had developed from the concrete meaning "to cut" to the more abstract idea of "to decree" or "to determine." But certainly the earlier concrete idea of "to cut" was present in the word in Daniel's time. Thus the linguistic evidence—both the root meaning and the dominant usage—favor the meaning of "to cut" here in Daniel 9:24. Daniel 9:24 says that seventy weeks are to be "cut off" for the Jewish people. If a time period is "cut off," it must be cut off from another time period. From what longer time period could the seventy weeks be cut off? The most readily available time period is the 2300 days of the preceding chapter, Daniel 8.

The second point linking chapters 9 and 8 of Daniel is the fact that Daniel obviously doesn't understand the second angel's climactic answer (8:14) to the question of the first angel (vs. 13). Verse 16 specifically commissions Gabriel to explain the vision to Daniel, including this exchange between the two angels. However, when we examine Gabriel's explanation as given in the remainder of chapter 8, we see that he explains virtually all the elements of the symbolic vision except the angel's statement about time in verse 14. In verse 26, Gabriel simply assures Daniel that the time element is "true." It was that particular element over which Daniel was especially confused (vs. 27). Thus when the same angel comes much later (in Daniel 9) to further explain matters to Daniel, we would certainly expect his explanation to be related especially to what Daniel did not understand about the preceding vision of chapter 8.

The specific words used by the angel, as recorded in the Hebrew text, make that connection even more direct. This constitutes the third argument for connecting these two time periods in chapters 8 and 9. When Gabriel came to give Daniel the prophecy of chapter 9, he pointed Daniel back to the preceding prophecy in a specific way: "Therefore, consider the message [which I Gabriel bring to you] and understand the vision [*mareh*]" (Dan. 9:23). There are two Hebrew words used for "vision" in the book of Daniel. One is *mareh*, and it refers to the appearance of a personal being in vision. An example is found in Daniel 10:5-7 where Daniel encounters the person of God. Of this he says, "I, Daniel, was the only one who saw the vision [*mareh*]" (vs. 7). The other word for "vision" in Daniel is *hazon*. This refers to a symbolic vision such as those containing beasts and their actions. An example of this is found in Daniel 8:1, 2 where this word is used three times to refer to the symbolic vision of the ram, goat, and horns.

In Daniel 8, both types of vision are present. From verse 1 to verse 12 there was a *hazon*, a symbolic vision. By verses 13 and 14, however, the *hazon* vision was over, and two angels, two personal beings, appeared. This appearance was a *mareh*. The Hebrew wording of Daniel 8:26 makes it clear that chapter 8 contains both types of visions: "The vision [*mareh*] of the evenings and mornings that has been given you is true, but seal up the vision [*hazon*], for it concerns the distant future."

When Gabriel came to Daniel in 9:23 and told Daniel that he had come to help him understand the "vision," he used the word *mareh*. What *mareh* is Gabriel referring to? Obviously this had to be a vision that Daniel had already received. Thus when Gabriel pointed Daniel back to a preceding *mareh* vision, he was pointing him right back to Daniel 8:26, which, in turn, refers to Daniel 8:14. Thus there is a direct link between Daniel 9:23 and Daniel 8:14 through Daniel 8:26. Gabriel did not give Daniel the prophecy of chapter 9 in order to explain the whole vision of Daniel 8; he gave it to him in order to explain the first part of the time element of that vision. The seventy weeks of Daniel 9 were to be cut off of the 2300 days of Daniel 8 as the Hebrew wording of Gabriel's statement makes plain.

The language of Daniel 9, and its connection with Daniel 8, thus give a more specific date to the time period of Daniel 8. Daniel 8 indicates that it was to begin, in general, during the Persian period, and Daniel 9 pins down the beginning date as 457 B.C. (see the discussion of this date in the preceding chapter dealing with Daniel 9). If one adds 2300 evening-mornings, or days, to 457 B.C. on the basis of the year-for-a-day principle (Eze. 4:6; Num. 14:34), those 2300 years extend to the year A.D. 1844. In this way we have established dates for both the beginning and the end of the time period in Daniel 8:14.

What Happened at the End of the 2300 Days?

With the dates established for this time period, we may ask: What was to happen at the end of this time period? What was to happen in 1844?

Daniel 8:14 says, "Then the sanctuary will be reconsecrated." The sanctuary referred to in this verse is the sanctuary referred to previously in verses 11 and 12—the heavenly sanctuary. It was the same heavenly sanctuary that the little-horn power figuratively attempted to cast down to earth in the eyes of humanity. In so doing, it attempted to take over the prerogatives of that heavenly sanctuary, to usurp them for itself. Thus there have been two rival plans of sanctuary ministry and salvation—the heavenly original and the earthly substitute. There have been two rival sanctuaries and two rival priesthoods. There have been two rival high priests who have officiated over these plans. At some point in the history of this struggle, there must come a time for a decision between these two plans and their results. There has to come a time of judgment that will decide between them. This judgment is what is brought to view in the time period of Daniel 8:14, the 2300 days. The "cleansing" (KJV) or "reconsecration" (NIV) of the sanctuary thus has to do with righting the wrongs that the little horn has created in its attempt to establish an earthly substitute for the work of the heavenly sanctuary. Through this judgment it will become evident that all during this struggle the true sanctuary was the one in heaven (compare Heb. 8:2). It will become evident that the true priesthood was the priesthood in which Jesus is involved in heaven (compare Heb. 8:1). It will become evident that the true services of the true sanctuary were those located in heaven with Christ, the priestly Prince.

The verb the Hebrew text uses to express this manifold restoration is *sadaq*, meaning "to be right or righteous." In Hebrew this is a very rich, broad word with various shades of meaning. In its broader aspects it takes in the various words—"cleansed," "reconsecrated," "vindicated," "restored," "victorious"—with which it has been translated. It is an umbrella word which includes all these other shades of meaning. The sanctuary has been defiled symbolically by the little horn; it will be cleansed by this judgment. It has been cast down in terms of symbolic action; it will be restored to heaven again, figuratively. The earthly judgments against the saints have been going against the judgments of the heavenly sanctuary; now it will be seen that the heavenly decisions were right and that those of earthly courts were wrong. Now the wrong decisions of earthly courts will be overturned, and the clear judgments of heaven will be made manifest. In all these ways, the sanctuary will be set right. It will be right; it will emerge victorious; it will be vindicated; it will be cleansed of the earthly contamination from which it has suffered. Thus "to be right" or "righteous" is the broad, rich theological meaning which encompasses all of these other shades of meaning. That whole rich and variegated picture will be brought about by a heavenly judgment in which all these aspects will be made manifest.

That heavenly judgment occurs at the end of the 2300 days as is affirmed by various lines of evidence.

First, the situation or problem of Daniel 8:11-13 requires such a judgment to resolve it. Second, the heavenly judgment was shown Daniel in vision in chapter 7:9-14, which is in a parallel position in that vision with what is found here in Daniel 8:13, 14. An angel announces the coming of the judgment in Daniel 8:14, but it is not shown to the prophet at that point; it is shown to him in vision in Daniel 7:9-14. That is one reason these prophecies need to be studied in reverse order—because the announcement of the judgment in Daniel 8 leads logically to the picture of that judgment in Daniel 7. The other line of evidence for this judgment comes from typology found in the book of Leviticus.

Links and Parallels Between Daniel 8 and Leviticus

It may seem strange, at first, to call attention to the book of Leviticus in the middle of discussing a prophetic book such as Daniel. Leviticus is a book of law, not prophecy. But when one considers the nature of the content of this prophecy, it can be seen more clearly how these two sources connect. They connect through the sanctuary. Daniel 8 is ultimately a prophecy about the sanctuary. Leviticus is a book of laws and regulations about what happened in the earthly sanctuary. Thus there is a natural, logical connection between these two books, and that link is reinforced by the nature of the symbols used in Daniel 8. A careful consideration of those symbols shows just how much Daniel 8 is a sanctuary prophecy.

First, there is the very word *sanctuary* itself that is used three times in Daniel 8 (vss. 11, 13, and 14).

Second, there is the word *tamid*, meaning "daily" or "continual." Although this word could be used as an ordinary adverb to modify other actions outside the sanctuary, it was commonly used for various priestly activities that took place within the temple.

Third, there is the symbol of a ram that was used to represent Persia. The ram was a domesticated animal, in contrast to the wild beasts of the field that are found as symbols in Daniel 7. The ram was also an animal that was used for sacrifice in the sanctuary service.

Fourth, there is the symbol of a goat used to represent Greece. It, too, was a domesticated animal that was used for sacrifice.

Fifth, there is the "evening-morning" time unit that is employed in Daniel 8. The prophecy does not simply say "days"; it uses a compound unit of "evening-mornings." What is an evening-morning? Genesis 1 indicates that the days of Creation week consisted of an evening and a morning, so chronologically an evening-morning is equivalent to one whole twenty-four-hour day.

Beyond that, however, there may be a theological reason for selecting this time unit for the prophecy. Numbers 9:14-23 tells the story of the Israelites setting out on their travels in the Sinai peninsula. With them went the very presence of God, represented by the cloud over the sanctuary. When that cloud turned into a pillar of fire in the evening, the high priest knew that it was time to offer the evening sacrifice. When it turned back into a pillar of cloud in the morning, he knew that it was time to offer the morning sacrifice. Thus an evening-morning was also a sanctuary day, delineated by God Himself to indicate the times in that day when He wanted the various aspects of His service conducted.

From these five reasons we can see that Daniel 8 is a prophecy that draws heavily from the sanctuary services for its symbolism. So to understand that symbolism, we should turn to the book in the Bible that tells us the most about the sanctuary. The last portion of Exodus (chapters 25–40) tells us about how the sanctuary was built; the book of Leviticus tells about how the sanctuary was put into use and about the services that went on there.

There were basically two types of services in the sanctuary—the daily and the yearly. The daily services were those that were carried out every day. They are known by the word that we encounter in Daniel—*tamid*. The other kind of services were those that came around only once a year. These were generally festivals of celebration and thanksgiving such as the Passover and the Feast of Tabernacles (Lev. 23).

There was one of these annual festivals, however, which more than any of the others, brought an end to the yearly round of daily sacrifices and services. That was the Day of Atonement, *yom kippur*. All of the daily services met their final conclusion in that yearly service. With the blood of the Lord's goat, the sanctuary was cleansed of its record of sin for the past year and was made new and fresh all over again to begin another round of sacrifices for the next calendar year (Lev. 16). Thus in Leviticus we meet these two great aspects of the sanctuary service—the daily and the yearly.

We meet them also in Daniel 8. The daily is referred to as the *tamid*, and we see it as an object of contention between the small horn and the Prince (vs. 11). This daily ministry in the heavenly sanctuary actually belonged to the Prince, but the little horn contended with him for it. In attempting to take over control of the services of the sanctuary in the eyes of men, this small-horn power introduced false elements into that service (vs. 12). A false priesthood ministered for the people in a way that was not prescribed by God. When that happened in the earthly sanctuary in Old Testament times, the sanctuary was defiled. Defilement took place, for example, when its holiness was corrupted by idols (Lev. 20:1-3; Jer. 7:30, 31) or by a priesthood that was not fit to serve there (Lev. 21:6-8; Eze. 22:26). This type of defilement had to be cared for in a certain way, and that was through the services of the Day of Atonement.

But there was another element—the record of forgiven sins—that was introduced into the sanctuary. In Leviticus 4, we find instructions for the sin offering. In chapters 5 and 6, we find instructions for the guilt offering. When these types of sins were treated by these sacrifices, the blood or the flesh of the sacrifices was handled in a certain way. Either the blood was taken into the sanctuary or the priest was to eat a portion of the sacrifice in a holy place. Both procedures transferred the forgiven sin from the sinner to the sanctuary. This is made clear in the conclusions to these actions as described in Leviticus 4:20, 26, 31, 35. When the priest had completed his manipulation of the blood from the slain sacrifice, he had made atonement for the sinner, and he was forgiven. An Israelite did not have to wait until the Day of Atonement to find out if he was forgiven; he was forgiven from the moment the sacrifice was made and the priest handled the elements from the sacrifice in the appropriate way.

There is a very instructive case in relation to this point in Leviticus 10:16-20. The services of the sanctuary had just begun, and the priests were not yet very familiar with them. When Moses found out that the priests had taken neither the blood nor the flesh of the sacrifice into the sanctuary, he was very upset. He sternly reprimanded them. The importance of taking the blood or the flesh into the sanctuary lay in the fact that the sacrifice for sin was thus registered or transferred in one way or another. All this was also part of the daily service.

When the daily service of the sanctuary shifted to the yearly service on the Day of Atonement, all the sacrifices of the year were incorporated into the blood of the Lord's goat that was taken into the Most Holy Place only this once and applied to the mercy seat of the Ark of the Covenant. Thus the entire year's accumulation of sins that had been transferred from the sinner to the sanctuary through the daily sacrifices were "gathered up" as it were in the single sacrifice of the yearly service. That is why there was no confessing of sin over the head of the Lord's goat on the Day of Atonement (Lev. 16:8, 9). The sins had already been confessed over the heads of the individual sin offerings throughout the year (4:29). With the blood of the Lord's goat on the Day of Atonement, the priest made atonement for the Most Holy Place, the holy place, and the altar in the courtyard of the sanctuary (16:16-18).

Now the sanctuary was cleansed. It was restored to its former state of purity and was ready to begin another round of sacrificial services for the next year (vss. 22-25). A final disposition of sin was made when all the sins, which had been forgiven and recorded in the sanctuary throughout the year, were brought out of the sanctuary, placed upon the head of the goat for Azazel, and sent into the wilderness, never to be seen by the people of Israel again (vss. 20-22).

Daniel 8 contains these same two elements—the daily and the yearly—now set in a prophetic relationship of type and antitype. Leviticus is the type, and Daniel is the antitype. The comparison can be seen as follows:

Daily Service
a. Leviticus 1–15
b. During the 2300 days

Yearly Service
a. Leviticus 16
b. At the end of the 2300 days

Just as there was a cleansing and restoration of the sanctuary on the Day of Atonement, just so would there also be a full restoration of the heavenly sanctuary when the judgment—the antitypical Day of Atonement—began at the end of the 2300 days in A.D. 1844 (Dan. 8:14).

But the question comes up: What is it from which the heavenly sanctuary has to be cleansed or restored?

First, there is the matter of what the little horn has attempted to do to it. In symbol, the little horn has reached into heaven itself and defiled the purity of that sanctuary with its machinations. In Old Testament times, this was done *literally* by conquerors (Eze. 4:6-8; 7:20-24; 24:21), false priests (Lev. 22:15; 2 Chron. 36:13; Zeph. 3:1-4), and idolaters. This reached its final culmination under the last king of Judah, Zedekiah. Of his times we read: "Furthermore, all the leaders of the priests and the people became more and more unfaithful, following all the detestable practices of the nations and defiling the temple of the Lord, which he had consecrated in Jerusalem" (2 Chron. 36:14).

What befell the temple in literal terms can be projected into the realm of the heavenly sanctuary in symbolic terms. When the judgment convenes in the heavenly sanctuary, however, all the long-standing questions about the plan of salvation will be made clear. That which has been impugned, or made obscure, will now stand pure and clear in the mercy and justice of God that shines forth from the heavenly sanctuary. The truth from that heavenly sanctuary about what has really been going on there will be made clear. Thus the sanctuary is said to be "cleansed" (Daniel 8:14, KJV), "reconsecrated" (NIV), or "returned to its rightful state" (RSV).

But the judgment of the Day of Atonement in the Old Testament took care of more than just the impurities that had been introduced by foreigners or false priests. It also took care of, in a final way, the record of the forgiven sins of the saints, the righteous Israelites (Lev. 16:16, 22). Thus the Day of Atonement accomplished two major events: (1) the cleansing or restoration of the sanctuary from the record of the sins of the righteous, and (2) its cleansing from any impurity that had been introduced by false conduct in relation to the sanctuary itself. Leviticus 16:16 says, "In this way he will make atonement for the Most Holy Place because of the uncleanness and rebellion [sins] of the Israelites, whatever their sins have been."

The uncleanness referred to is the state of uncleanness that defiles the sanctuary (chapters 11–15). The rebellion is the personal and corporate sins of Israel (1–7). In terms of the typological parallels in the book of Daniel, the sins of the righteous that are dealt with in the final heavenly judgment correspond to the forgiven sins of the Israelites that were recorded daily in the sanctuary; the uncleanness that the little horn has symbolically introduced into the sanctuary by defiling the knowledge of the work of the true sanctuary for humanity corresponds to the state of impurity or uncleanness from which the Old Testament sanctuary was cleansed. The pattern is this:

Leviticus 1–7	**Leviticus 11–15**	**Leviticus 16**
Sins of the righteous forgiven and recorded in the sanctuary	States of impurity and uncleanness that defile the sanctuary	Cleansing and restoration of the sanctuary by final judgment upon both

Daniel 8:14a	**Daniel 8:10-12**	**Daniel 8:14b**
Activities of the Prince, as the heavenly high priest. True application of the "daily" service during the 2300 days	Activities of the little horn. False application of the "daily" service	Judgment at the end of the 2300 evening-mornings, at the climax of the "daily" services

Thus a fuller knowledge of the function of the sanctuary in the book of Leviticus can indeed illuminate the references to the sanctuary in the prophecy of Daniel 8. But the book of Daniel has more to say on this subject with the vision of Daniel 7. That will be the focus of our attention in the next chapter.

Summary

The amount of discussion that has been devoted to this prophecy might imply that this is a complicated topic. In actuality, it is not. The prophecy begins with the story of the Persian ram—its origin, its successes, and its final demise. Then it goes on to the Greek goat and its initial successes and final dissolution. That dissolution led to the division of the Greek Empire into four smaller kingdoms distributed around the eastern Mediterranean basin. Into this region came a new power represented by a little horn that grew greater and greater. Its greatness was first revealed by its conquest in the regions of the former Greek kingdoms. It successfully conquered and absorbed all four of those kingdoms.

In its later phase of existence, this power in Rome took on a more religious character. In this phase, it represents the church that has its seat in Rome, the church that had such a powerful influence in Europe throughout the Middle Ages. During those centuries, it exercised its power as a persecuting force, and this is clearly revealed by the Roman church's history. Its theology reveals something else: an approach to the plan of salvation that has been carried out through channels that are not approved of by the Bible. In this way, it has actually come to be something of a rival to the plan of salvation that it claimed to minister. This organization, which started out so well, actually came to find itself in opposition to the purposes of God through its desire to exercise control.

In this way a rivalry developed. On the one hand was the true heavenly sanctuary from which the true plan of salvation was ministered by the true High Priest, Jesus Christ. On the other hand was an earthly power attempting to divert attention away from that heavenly sanctuary and its Priest and its services and focus, instead, on an earthly substitute.

How long would this rivalry last? How would it be brought to an end? What are the results of the two alternate plans of salvation? The answers to these questions will all be made manifest in the judgment. This judgment at the end of time is what the prophecy is talking about when it refers to the (heavenly) sanctuary being cleansed, restored, and justified at the end of the 2300 evening-mornings. We can learn more about this "yearly" service, coming at the end of the "daily" services, by considering parallels from the book of Leviticus. Leviticus, chapters 1–15 represent the daily, and chapter 16 describes the yearly. That yearly service, or Day of Atonement, was a day of judgment for ancient Israel. Likewise, the antitypical Day of Atonement brings to view a judgment in the heavenly sanctuary that will determine all who truly belong to the camp of the saints of the Most High.

It is not our part to judge who those saints will be; that is God's part in His judgment. Only He knows how much light and truth any individual has received. Our task is to apply ourselves to His Word so we may truly come to know Him as our Lord and Saviour. Our task is to receive His Spirit so that we may live for Him. All other aspects of judgment we may safely leave with Him, our God of mercy and justice.

■ Applying the Word

Daniel 8

1. How does the fact that these ancient kingdoms actually came on the scene of action just as prophesied in Daniel 8 contribute to my confidence in the accuracy of this prophecy, including its final aspects of judgment and restoration?

2. Daniel 8 raises the issue of human intermediaries mediating between myself and God. When I compare the problem of human mediation raised in Daniel 8 with the priesthood of Jesus on my behalf described in Hebrews 7:23–8:13; 1 John 1:8–2:2; and Romans 8:31-39, what superior blessings can I claim as mine through the ministry of

Christ in the heavenly sanctuary?

3. Daniel 8:14 teaches that the sanctuary will be "reconsecrated" (NIV), "restored" (RSV), or "cleansed" (KJV). What does that process mean for my life?

4. What grounds for hope and joy do I have in the heavenly judgment? In what ways can this hope and joy improve the quality of my daily life?

■ Researching the Word

1. Using an exhaustive concordance, study the word "sanctuary." List all the meanings for sanctuary you can find. Study also the use of the words "tabernacle" and "temple." How many different sanctuaries for worship has God authorized throughout history? Compare your findings with the discussion of these words in a good Bible dictionary or Bible encyclopedia.

2. The ministry of the angel Gabriel features largely in Daniel 8 and 9. Use a concordance to discover what you can about Gabriel's ministry in the rest of the Bible. Do the same for the angel Michael who shows up in Daniel 12:1. Next, discover all the other references to the ministry of angels in the book of Daniel. Then use your concordance to study the words *angel*, *angels*, and *archangel* in the rest of the Bible. In your Daniel notebook, write summaries of your conclusions regarding the role of Gabriel, Michael, and the ministry of angels in both Daniel and the rest of the Bible.

■ Further Study of the Word

1. For the approach other commentaries take to the study of Daniel 8, see F. D. Nichol, ed., *The SDA Bible Commentary*, 4:839-847, and M. Maxwell, *God Cares*, 1:145-188.

2. For a general overview of the judgment at the end of the 2300 days, see E. G. White, *The Great Controversy*, chapters 23-25.

3. For a survey of judgment scenes in the Old Testament prophets, see W. H. Shea, *Selected Studies in Prophetic Interpretation*, chapter 1. For a rejection of Antiochus Epiphanes as figuring in the prophecy of Daniel 8, see chapter 2 of the same work. Chapter 3 of that book treats the year-day principle in more detail.

4. For five special studies on Daniel 8, see F. Holbrook, ed., *Symposium on Daniel*, chapters 6–10.

5. For three special studies on Leviticus, see F. Holbrook, ed., *The Seventy Weeks, Leviticus, and the Nature of Prophecy*, chapters 5–7.

6. For a special study on the subject of the relationship between justification, sanctification, and faith to the judgment in heaven, see F. Holbrook, ed., *Symposium on Daniel*, 339-388.

CHAPTER NINE

Christ
As King

Daniel 7

Daniel 7 is the most detailed and complete of the symbolic visions in the book of Daniel. It begins with the contemporary kingdom of Babylon under which Daniel lived at the time the vision was given. It continues all the way down through human history and ends with the kingdom of God that will ultimately be set up. Thus it covers the whole time from Daniel's day to ours—and beyond into eternity. Chapter 2 covers a similar time span, but it does so in less detail. There we simply find the kingdoms involved represented by different metals, whereas in Daniel 7 they are symbolized by different beasts that can convey more detailed characteristics. Those characteristics represent the activities of the kingdoms. The other main prophecies in the book of Daniel cover shorter time periods in their prophetic content than does chapter 7. Daniel 8 starts with Persia, not Babylon, and it does not extend to the final kingdom of God. Chapter 9 is even shorter, covering only the period from Persian to Roman times. Chapter 11 does extend to the final kingdom of God, but it starts with Persia, not Babylon. Thus it can be said that Daniel 7 is the most complete and detailed symbolic vision in the book.

Chapter 7 spells out the fourfold kingdoms of this earth that would dominate the Mediterranean world for many centuries. However, unlike the prophecy in chapter 8, the angel's explanation of the vision to Daniel does not name any of these kingdoms. How, then, are we to identify these beast-kingdoms? The answer is that they must be identified by cross-correlating them with other prophecies in Daniel that do name these successive kingdoms or identify them in some other way. Basically, there are four of these great "outline" prophecies in Daniel—chapters 2, 7, 8, and 11. (Daniel 9, the other major prophecy in the book, is of a different nature. It does not outline the nations that were to rise and fall. As a matter of fact, it does not even mention them, except indirectly. Rather, chapter 9 concentrates upon the prophetic history of the Jewish people and thus lies outside the realm of the outline prophecies that describe the fourfold rise and fall of kingdoms.) In terms of symbols, Daniel 7 gives the most complete representation of the sequence of world kingdoms.

But the climax of the vision in chapter 7 does not come with the final beast. The climax comes, rather, in what happens after the final beast, when God takes charge of human history and brings it to an end (vss. 13, 14, 26-28). How does God do that? Daniel 7 provides an interesting answer. When God takes over, one final phase to world history remains before He sets up His eternal kingdom. Chapter 7 assures us that God's kingdom will be set up, but just how does He go about it? The answer comes in verses 9-14. We will study that passage in detail.

As we study Daniel 7, we will concentrate on key words. How do we identify key words? One way is to see what words occur most frequently in a given passage. If a biblical author uses a word over and over again, that word and the thought it represents must have been very much uppermost in his mind. Daniel 7 contains several words that are used with considerable frequency. One of those is "dominion," used seven times in chapter 7. (Note that the NIV is not consistent in translating the word as "dominion." Synonyms are used.)

As we consider this key word, we should ask: Who has dominion? We will see that chapter 7 indicates that the first beast was to have dominion for a time, but then it was to lose it to the second beast. Then the second beast was to lose dominion to the third beast, and so on, until the sequence is finished. A practical question comes up at this point: Are human beings always to suffer under these constantly changing kingdoms and their governments? Many of these governments were oppressive and unjust—especially to God's righteous people. Is this to be the common lot of humanity forever? The prophecy assures us that it will not ever be so. God will step in and put an end to these earthly kingdoms and their injustice. He will set up a kingdom of His own making, "wherein dwelleth righteousness" (2 Peter 3:13, KJV). In God's eter-

nal kingdom, we will enjoy peace, prosperity, and the eternal vigor of youth and immortality (Rev. 21:1-4). God's dominion will be radically different from any kind of dominion that human beings have enjoyed previously. That is what Daniel 7 assures us.

From that conclusion, we need to go back and look at the details to see how we will arrive at that point in the course of history.

■ Getting Into the Word

Daniel 7:1-6, 15-18

Read Daniel 7 through one time carefully. Then reread verses 1-6 and 15-18 before doing the following exercises:

1. Daniel 2, 8, and 7 each deal with the same kingdoms in parallel fashion. To see this parallelism clearly, copy the following chart into your Daniel notebook, and fill in the blanks.

Kingdoms	Daniel 2	Daniel 8	Daniel 7	Interpretation
1st kingdom	Head of gold	——	Lion	
2nd kingdom		Ram		
3rd kingdom				
4th kingdom				

a. The key to the interpretation of the first kingdom can be unlocked by examining the explanation of the first metal in Daniel 2.

b. The key to the interpretation of the second and third kingdoms is found in the explanation of the ram and the he-goat at the end of chapter 8. (By the time of Daniel 8, the first kingdom was moving off the scene of action. Thus Daniel 8 begins with the second kingdom.)

c. The fourth kingdom of chapters 2, 8, and 7 is the same in each case. It is the world power that follows the third kingdom.

2. **Compare the bear in 7:5 with the ram in 8:3, 4. Compare the leopard in 7:6 with the goat in 8:5-8. What similarities do you find for each pair?**

■ Exploring the Word

The Setting

Daniel 7:1 tells us that Daniel received the vision of this chapter as a dream or night vision while he was asleep. In that sense, it was similar to the two night dreams Nebuchadnezzar received as recorded in chapters 2 and 4. In these previous cases, Daniel had functioned as an inspired wise man who could go in to the king and explain his dreams to him. In this case, however, the dream was given directly to God's servant without the intermediary of the pagan king.

All of this happened in the first year of Belshazzar, or about 550 B.C. We have already referred several times previously to the unusual circumstances under which Belshazzar came to the throne (see the Bible Amplifier volume treating Daniel 1–7 as history). His father, Nabonidus, left Babylon to live in Tema, in Arabia, for a period of ten years, from about 550 B.C. to about 540 B.C. He returned just in time to try to defend Babylon from the Persians. But he came back too late, and that defense was unsuccessful. The vision of Daniel 7 was given at the beginning of that unusual ten-year period, at a time when Nabonidus had just left for the desert of Arabia and Belshazzar had just been put in charge of affairs in Babylon as co-king with his father. Why would God have given this particular vision at that special time? There may have been at least one good reason.

By 550 B.C. it was already evident that the kingdom of Babylon was weakening and on its way to being overthrown by some other power. Thus one function of this vision was to spell out the events that would take place when this happened. These developments were not to take the people of God by surprise. Ten years later when the Persian bear took over from the Babylonian lion, the people of God would find assurance that they were indeed being led by God—that

He had given evidence through His prophet that He was still in charge of human affairs and that He knew what would happen. Thus one explanation for the giving of this vision at this particular time was to strengthen the faith of the people of Judah during their captivity.

The First Three Beasts

Daniel saw a series of beasts coming up out of the water of the great sea (7:3). Revelation 17:15 tells us that in apocalyptic prophecies such as those of Daniel and Revelation, waters represent multitudes of people. So we can see these kingdoms arising out of great populations. But those multitudes of people were located in and around what is known as the great sea (7:2). Thus this symbol of water was not just a general representation of all kinds of people everywhere. It specifically referred to the peoples in one particular place. For biblical people, the great sea meant the Mediterranean Sea. This means, then, that these powers were Mediterranean kingdoms. As their identifications are developed below, we will see that this sequence begins with Babylon and continues on through Medo-Persia, Greece, and Rome.

Where were these four powers located? They were all situated around, or even *in*, the Mediterranean Sea. That is self-evident for Greece and Rome, but what about Babylon and Medo-Persia? How could they be classified as Mediterranean powers? One needs to look at their conquests.

Nebuchadnezzar led the Babylonian army into Syria and Palestine on many occasions. We have the records of these campaigns preserved on Babylonian tablets in the annals for the first thirteen years of his reign. Thus Babylon was a Mediterranean power by virtue of conquest. This was even more true of Persia, which inherited Syria and Palestine when it conquered Babylon. It went beyond the Babylonian limits, however, and conquered Egypt and twice invaded Greece, although it did not hold it as a part of its kingdom. Thus we have four Mediterranean powers represented here: Rome and Greece by right of geographical location, and Babylon and Persia, which became Mediterranean powers by conquest.

It is significant to point out the Mediterranean focus of this prophecy, since the question sometimes arises why India and China are not represented in this prophecy of world empires. It was not the purpose of the prophecy to cover all the history of all the world. It focused upon one major and very influential segment of that history—that which took place around the Mediterranean basin, the location of God's special covenant people, Israel.

It is also of interest to note here that although the prophecy does depict certain details regarding these beasts, they are basically inactive. After they popped up out of the sea, they didn't go anywhere. They did not charge off in one direction or another to complete their conquests. They were animate, but inactive. In contrast, the ram in Daniel 8 charges westward, and the goat charges east. We do not have such directional elements here in chapter 7. The vision is more pictorial in nature. It shows us the beasts and their characteristics and lets us decode them with the interpreting angel's help (see vss. 15-27). Conquests are indicated—for example, by means of the ribs in the bear's mouth—but they are shown statically as events having already taken place, rather than being represented by actions depicted as taking place in the prophecy itself.

The First Beast

The first beast is a lion (vs. 4). The interpreting angel does not tell us what kingdom the lion represents. We must make that identification by connecting this prophecy with Daniel 2. There, in the metallic image, we see the head of gold in first place (vs. 32). In that prophecy, the prophet himself identifies the head of gold for us. He said to Nebuchadnezzar, "You are that head of gold" (vs. 38). As if to clarify that he was talking about kingdoms and not just Nebuchadnezzar, Daniel went on to say, "After you, another kingdom will rise, inferior to yours" (vs. 39).

This connection is clarified by the use of numbers. The prophecies in both chapters (2 and 7) use some elements from the sequence of first, second, third, and fourth. It isn't just that we can count four metals in the image of Daniel 2 and four beasts in the vision of chapter 7; the prophet himself has counted them for us before. Clearly, therefore, the sequence is the same in both chapters. Since Daniel 2 begins with the golden head and identifies it for us as Babylon, that cross-connection points directly to the lion, the first beast in Daniel 7, as also representing Babylon (see the map of the Babylonian Empire on page 129).

The lion was a particularly appropriate representation of Babylon. In the city of Babylon, lions were depicted in detail by means of colored bricks on the great processional way and the Ishtar gate to which it led. This was the main entrance to Babylon from the north. Lions made of colored bricks appeared also on the outer wall of the throne room in the palace. In addition, the great lion of Babylon, a huge statue carved from black basalt stone, stood in the courtyard of the palace. Lions were also kept in the royal zoo, as the story of Daniel 6 tells us. Daniel undoubtedly walked many, many times past these representations of lions. The lion is, therefore, a singularly appropriate representation of the kingdom of Babylon.

What detailed characteristics of this lion does the vision provide? This lion started out with the wings of an eagle, but then those wings were torn off, and the lion was given the heart of a man. Elsewhere in Daniel, wings represent speed of conquest, as is seen by comparing the leopard representing Greece in 7:6 with the goat representing Greece in 8:5. So tearing off the eagle's wings from the lion would represent the decline of its voracious and conquering nature. When did this happen?

The history of the Neo-Babylonian kingdom can be divided into two main segments: the reign of Nebuchadnezzar (605-562 B.C.) and those kings who followed after him (562-539 B.C.). Nebuchadnezzar ruled Babylon about twice as long as did the five kings who followed him (including Belshazzar) combined. In addition, these five kings were much more ineffective than Nebuchadnezzar was. He built up the kingdom of Babylon, and they frittered it away, as shown, for example, by the prolonged absence of Nabonidus from Babylon. So this succession of weak-hearted rulers could well be represented by the "the heart of a man" that was given, symbolically, to the now wingless lion (7:4).

The other possibility is that this is a representation of Nebuchadnezzar's own experience as described especially in Daniel 4. When the sentence of God's judgment fell upon him, he went out and lived among the animals of the field. He was in this mental state for a period of seven years. During this time he was, of course, incapacitated from carrying out any affairs of state such as leading military campaigns that would be represented by the wings of an eagle. At the end of this period of insanity, Nebuchadnezzar's mental faculties returned, and he was restored to his kingdom. His mind—or heart—came back to him as he joined mankind again. The vision could be referring to either of these scenarios; however, the former seems slightly more in keeping with the viewpoint of the prophecy.

The Second Beast

The second beast in the vision of chapter 7 was a bear (vs. 5). The bear is a mountain dweller, making it an apt symbol for a mountainous country such as Media, which was later joined to the country of Persia on the elevated plateau of Iran. To reach Medo-Persia, the forces of Assyria or Babylon had to march up through the Zagros mountains. Nebuchadnezzar built the famous hanging gardens of Babylon for his Median wife because she was lonesome for her native mountains and bored by the flat plain of Mesopotamia.

This bear had an unusual feature—he was lopsided. One side was raised up higher than the other side. The ram in 8:3 has the same characteristic in that one horn was raised up over the other horn. The interpretation given in verse 20 is that the two horns represent the dual kingdoms of Media and Persia. Combined, they make up the Medo-Persian Empire (see map on page 87). The lopsided bear in Daniel 7 should logically represent the same combination. The Median power was stronger at first, but then the Persian part arose and eventually became more prominent than the Medes (8:3). Thus the bear in chapter 7 and the ram in chapter 8 represent the same power—Medo-Persia.

The other feature of the bear in Daniel 7 is that he had three ribs in his mouth. In the natural world, this would represent animals he had eaten. In the prophetic symbol, therefore, this should represent

THE RISE OF THE
NEO-BABYLONIAN EMPIRE

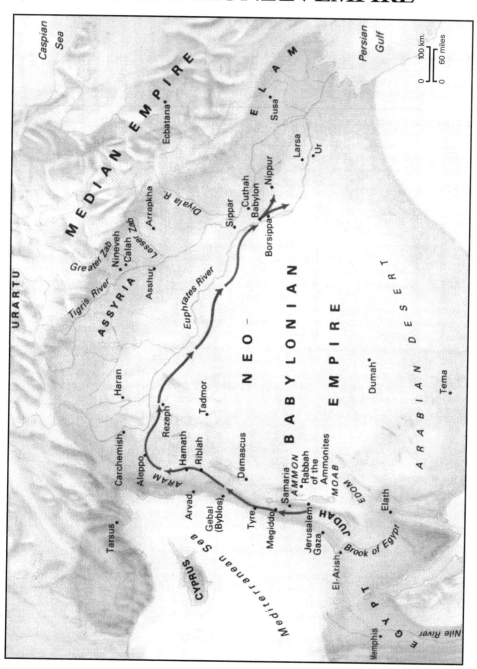

the kingdoms the bear power had absorbed or conquered. Daniel 8:4 depicts the same characteristic when it notes that the ram charged off in three directions—to the north, the west, and the south. Thus the three directions of conquest in chapter 8 and the three ribs of conquest in chapter 7 both represent the same thing—three major conquests of the Medo-Persians. In the commentary on Daniel 8, we identified these conquests as Lydia in Asia Minor to the north of Persia, Babylon to the west, and Egypt to the south. Cyrus conquered Lydia and Babylon, and Cambyses, his son, conquered Egypt.

The Third Beast

The third beast of Daniel 7 is the leopard (vs. 6). This is clearly not a natural leopard, but a symbolic figure. This leopard has a four-fold nature; he has four heads and four wings. This fourfold nature matches well with the four horns that came out of the head of the Greek goat in 8:8. The angel identifies that goat by name as Greece in verse 21. So we can apply that same identification to the leopard in chapter 7. In Daniel 8, the goat flew over the ground without touching it; in chapter 7, the leopard is given wings to accomplish the same purpose. Once again, the common characteristics between the beasts in these two chapters establish a correlation that allows us to identify the leopard in chapter 7 and the goat in chapter 8 as one and the same—the kingdom of Greece (see map on page 91). The fourfold nature of these two beasts refers to the divisions into which the Greek kingdom split after the death of Alexander (see map on page 95).

Thus far we have been able to identify the first three beasts of Daniel 7 by cross correlations with the symbols in other chapters in the book where they are specifically named. The cross-correlation with Daniel 2 identifies the lion in chapter 7 as Babylon. Cross-correlations with chapter 8 identify the next two beasts in Daniel 7, the bear and the leopard, as Medo-Persia and Greece. This is also the order in which these powers appeared historically. Persia conquered Babylon under Cyrus, and that conquest is recorded for us right in the book of Daniel itself (chapter 5). Alexander the Great then led the armies of Macedonian Greece to defeat and conquer Persia. Thus the identifications made in the book of Daniel have proved to be correct by historical comparisons from outside that book.

■ Getting Into the Word

Daniel 7:7, 8, 19-26

Read Daniel 7 through yet again. Focus on verses 7, 8, and 19-26. Then do the following exercises:

1. In your Daniel notebook, list all the characteristics of the fourth beast that are given in both the first and second sections of chapter 7. As far as possible, provide an explanation for the meaning of each characteristic.
2. List all the characteristics of the little horn found in verse 8 and in the explanation of the vision in verses 19-26. Try to determine an explanation for the meaning of each characteristic.
3. Compare the little horn of Daniel 7 with the little or small horn of Daniel 8. (Remember that both chapters are divided into sections, the first describing the vision, and the second explaining it.) Is the little horn of chapter 7 the same power as that of the small horn of chapter 8? Are they different powers? What evidence can you provide for your answer?

■ Exploring the Word

The Fourth Beast

The fourth beast of 7:7 is not identified for us by name anywhere in the book of Daniel—not in chapter 2 nor in chapter 8 nor in chapter 11. That leaves us with a historical question: What power succeeded Greece?

Historically, the answer is quite simple. It was Rome. This was seen in our discussion of the four horns of the goat in 8:8. These four horns represented the four main divisions of Alexander's empire—mainland Greece, Asia Minor, Syria (including Babylon), and Egypt. Who was eventually responsible for the overthrow of all four of these kingdoms? The answer is Rome (see map on page 99). Rome first conquered Greece. Then it had Asia Minor willed to it by the king of Pergamum who had no male offspring. Next, Syria, along with Judea, fell to Pompey and his legions. Finally, Egypt, the last of the four, fell to Rome. In this way, Rome made its conquest of the eastern Mediterranean basin complete. The fourth beast that followed the four heads of the leopard can readily be identified as Rome.

Daniel does not describe the appearance of the fourth beast as completely as he does the third; for that reason it is sometimes called the "nondescript" beast. Whatever it may have looked like, the fourth beast shocked Daniel by its appearance. It was, he said, "terrifying and frightening and very powerful" (7:7). This power went on and "crushed and devoured its victims and trampled underfoot whatever was left" (vs. 7). The picture is one of very, very thorough conquests. Archaeology has shown how thorough Roman engineers were in destroying previously existent cities in order to make way for the new Roman occupation. Jerusalem itself was an example. When Rome conquered and destroyed Jerusalem in A.D. 70, the debris from that destruction was scraped into a valley on the west side of the city. Today, that valley, the Tyropoean, no longer even exists because it has been completely filled with the Roman debris from the destruction of the city. Roman destruction of the Herodian, or Second Temple, was so thorough that even today archaeologists still do not know for sure where it stood on the temple platform. Jesus prophesied of this when He predicted that not "one stone" of the temple would "be left on another; every one will be thrown down" (Matt. 24:2).

The prophecy gives an interesting detail about this fourth beast; it says it had teeth of iron (Dan. 7:7). These iron teeth further represent the conquering and destructive nature of this kingdom, but it also forms a direct link with the fourth kingdom in Daniel 2, where the fourth kingdom was represented by the iron legs of the image (2:33, 40). Iron was connected with the fourth kingdom in each prophecy, indicating that the powers represented were one and the same. In both cases, Rome is the kingdom brought to view.

The other major characteristic of this fourth beast given in Daniel 7 is that it had ten horns. In the second half of the chapter, the angel interpreter gives us the explanation: "The ten horns are ten kings who will come from this kingdom" (vs. 24). One might at first take this literally and look for ten caesars to come out of Rome. However, it should be noted that there is a precedent in Daniel for using the word *king* to mean "kingdom." As we have already noted in Daniel 2, the prophet told Nebuchadnezzar, "You, O king, . . . are that head of gold" (vss. 36, 38). He immediately went on to say, "After you, another kingdom will arise" (vs. 39). This same parallel usage is found in Daniel 7. In his first and more simple explanation, the angel said to Daniel, "the four great beasts are four kingdoms [literally, 'kings'] that will rise from the earth" (vs. 17). Then later in the chapter, the angel tells Daniel, "The fourth beast is a fourth kingdom that will appear on earth" (vs. 23). Thus in the original Aramaic text of Daniel 7, there is an example of "king" and "kingdom" being used with parallel meanings, just as in chapter 2.

With this usage in mind, we can see that the ten horns represent not individual kings, but kingdoms that arose out of the political and military turmoil occurring when Imperial Rome broke up under the assaults of the barbarian tribes from the east and the north. This historical process took a couple of centuries to accomplish, beginning in the fifth century A.D. or even before. Gradually the barbarian tribes that had filled the vacuum left by the fall of Imperial Rome settled down to occupy their respective territories, and eventually they evolved into what we now view as the modern nations of Europe. The list of these as commonly given includes the Ostrogoths, Visigoths, Franks, Vandals, Suevi, Alamanni, Anglo-Saxons, Heruli, Lombards, and Burgundians (see the map of the divisions of the Roman Empire on page 135).

It is not necessary to be adamant about precisely what tribes were involved. There was a flux in the number of tribes migrating through Europe, and so likewise, there has also been a flux in the number of modern nations derived from them. We can take the number ten as

Atlantic
Ocean

ANGLES
SAXONS

F R A N K S

ALEMANNI

BURGUNDIANS

LOMBARDS

O S T R O G O T H S

SUEVI

VISIGOTHS

HERULI

VANDALS

Mediterranean
Sea

**THE
ROMAN EMPIRE
DIVIDED**

Although boundaries were rather fluid, this map represents the
general positions of the ten divisions of the Roman Empire as
they were circa 476 A.D.

a representative number for the corporate whole of such tribes and nations. A historic debate over this point occurred during the presession for the 1888 Seventh-day Adventist General Conference session. The particular point at issue was whether the Alamanni or the Huns belonged in the list. The debate was sharp and pointed and became very partisan—so much so that participants went around asking, "Are you a Hun or an Alamanni?" There is no need to try to split hairs that fine. It is clear historically that when Imperial Rome crumbled, the tribes that took over its territories evolved into approximately ten kingdoms. No other single empire succeeded Imperial Rome after its fall and division. Daniel 2:43 suggests that after Rome's fall, its former territory—represented by the toes and feet (2:43, 42)—would remain divided until the setting up of God's eternal kingdom (vss. 44, 45).

The Little Horn

The division of Imperial Rome made way for the rise of yet another power. This power is represented by another horn, an eleventh one (7:8). There is something about this power, however, that set it apart from the other ten. It was distinctly a religious power, while the others were political in nature. Just as there was a distinctly religious phase to the work of the little horn in Daniel 8 (see vss. 9, 10), so the little horn here in chapter 7 also swings into operation as a distinctly religious power. That religious character is demonstrated by the great words that it speaks against the Most High God and by its persecution of God's saints (vss. 8, 25). This religious characteristic stands in contrast to the purely political actions of the four powers that have appeared previously in the prophecy. In the discussion of the little horn in Daniel 8, we concluded that this religious phase of its work represented the Roman Church headed up by the papacy, since this was the religious phase of Rome that succeeded the imperial phase. The same identification fits well here in chapter 7 for a number of reasons.

First, we should note where this little horn comes from. It originated from the fourth or Roman beast (vs. 8), not any of the previous three. Thus this power must be Roman in character. But it is not Imperial Rome itself, for that power was represented by the beast from which this horn grew.

Second, the time this horn arose should be noted. It came up *after* the other ten horns were already in place. That means it arose on the ruins of the broken empire of Imperial Rome. That is exactly when the papacy really came to the fore. The capital of the Roman Empire had been moved to Constantinople by Justinian in the sixth century A.D. That left a power vacuum in the city of Rome itself, when it was not under the control of the barbarian tribes. With the aid of Justinian, that vacuum was soon filled by the bishop of Rome. Justinian decreed that the bishop of Rome was the head of all the churches (A.D. 533). He also sent his army to liberate Rome from the Gothic siege (A.D. 537-538). He even gave the Roman bishop certain civil powers. In the words of Revelation 13:2, "the dragon gave the beast his power and his throne and great authority."

Third, three horns were plucked up before the little horn. An interesting phenomenon occurred in the sixth century A.D. During that century, there were a series of wars that were both political and religious in nature. They were political because some of the barbarian tribes suffered defeats during the course of these wars. But those defeated tribes were Christian! Here we have the spectacle of one Christian power—the Roman Empire led by the emperor and the bishop of Rome—opposing other Christian powers such as the Ostrogoths, the Vandals, and perhaps the Visigoths. These tribes were Christians, but they embraced a particular kind of Christianity. They were Arians. The Arians believed that Christ was a created being and thus of lesser stature than God the Father. This doctrine was not acceptable to the bishop in Rome, and he fought it with the arm of the state. From the point of view of the state, the defeat of these powers accomplished certain desirable political ends. From the point of view of the church, the defeat of these Arian powers accomplished the plucking up of heresy. The military arm of the state was employed for the theological aims of the church. Thus were these three tribal horns, or powers, plucked up before this new horn of papal Rome.

Fourth, this power was a persecuting power. This is explicitly stated in 7:15, 21. We discussed this feature of the little horn's work in chapter 5 (see the volume on Daniel 1–7 in the Bible Amplifier series) and also in the preceding chapter in our treatment of 8:10. The same recital of persecution listed there can be applied here also.

Fifth, this power attempted to do something with God's law. The prediction was that he will "try to change the set times and the laws" (vs. 25). There are two words for time in this verse. One is *iddan*, used to describe the duration of the little horn's persecution of the saints; it would last three and a half times ("a time, [two] times and half a time"). The word *iddan* means a span of time. The other word for time used in this verse is *zeman* (plural, *zimmin*). "He will . . . try to change the set times and the laws." This Aramaic word has more of a function of a point in time, but it is in the plural form indicating repeated points of time. These are connected with God's law (the word for "law" is singular in the original language). The feature of God's law that best fits this description is the fourth commandment where the recurring seventh day is featured as a point of time, or as regularly occurring points of time.

The New Testament indicates that the early Christian church observed the Sabbath (see Acts 13:14, 44, 16:13; 17:2; 18:4), but gradually the practice of worshiping on the first day of the week was introduced. The process was a gradual, complex one, and anti-semitism played a considerable part in the church's desire to distance itself from the biblical Sabbath. According to some early church historians, this movement to abandon the seventh-day Sabbath developed most rapidly in Rome and Alexandria, but eventually it became widespread. The Church of Rome considers its sponsorship of this shift in worship practice from the seventh day of the week to the first to be a result of its *magisterium*, or teaching authority from God. (For more on this change, see chapter 5 in the volume on Daniel 1–7.)

Sixth, this power was to speak great words against the Most High, or commit blasphemy. A number of the claims made for this power fall into this category, including some of its titles and its functions such as forgiveness of sins by a priest, excommunication, and the interdict (the exclusion of individuals and whole populations from participation in spiritual things). The sixth century A.D., in which the bishop of Rome rose to special prominence, was also a time for the production of what have come to be called pseudodecretals, or false documents, making wide-ranging claims for the powers of the papacy. (See chapter 5 in *Daniel 1–7* for a more detailed examination of these claims.)

Seventh, there is the link between the little horn of 7:8 and the little horn of 8:9. Both horns are modified with the same adjective— "little" (or "small") when starting out, but both grew to be great. This word *little* or *small* is of interest in itself. The Hebrew word translated "little" in Daniel 8 is not the usual Hebrew word for "little." Daniel had a much more common word readily available to him, but he chose this relatively rare word in order to match it with the Aramaic word for "little" used in chapter 7 to describe the horn depicted there. The distinct linguistic connection between these two prophetic symbols shows that they are the same entity. All the characteristics we have examined earlier in connection with the little horn in Daniel 8—persecution, rivalry with Christ's heavenly ministry, and directing mankind to an earthly substitute for the heavenly sanctuary—can also be applied to those given to the little horn described here in chapter 7.

Eighth, there are the dates for the duration of the persecution and dominion carried out by this power. This time period is identified as three and a half "times" in 7:25. These "times" (vs. 25) can be identified as years on the basis of parallels with 4:16, 23, and 25 where seven "times," or years, were to pass over Nebuchadnezzar until he regained his sanity. The Greek Old Testament even translates "times" as "years" in Daniel 4. The "times" of Daniel 4 were literal Babylonian calendar years, but here in chapter 7 we are dealing with symbolic years in an apocalyptic prophecy. Revelation 12 makes this same equation of "times" with "years." Verse 6 allots 1260 days for this same persecuting of the church, and verse 14 restates that same time period as three and a half "times," a phrase quoted from Daniel 7:25. Each of the 1260 symbolic days in these three and a half years needs to be interpreted according to the rule of a day-for-a-year (see chapter 6 of this book for further discussion of this principle of prophetic interpretation). In Revelation 11:2 and 13:5 this same time period is identified as forty-two months. Thus the mathematics of this equation can be worked out to show that 1260 days equals forty-two months equals three and a half years or "times." A prophetic month thus equals 30 days uniformly. It has been rounded off from other calendars for ease of calculation.

All these prophecies indicate that the period of domination by the little horn power was to last 1260 years. The beginning of this period can be dated to A.D. 538. Justinian's decree making the bishop of Rome the head of all the churches took place in A.D. 533. That decree could not go into effect, however, until the city of Rome itself was liberated from the control of the Ostrogoths. That took place in A.D. 538 when the Ostrogoths' siege of Rome was broken by the general Belisarius, who led the emperor's troops in pursuit of the Goths all the way to their capital of Ravenna. The Ostrogoths were not completely eliminated until A.D. 555, but in 538 the bishop of Rome stood free and clear to exercise the authority with which he had been invested by the emperor. This was the first time in sixty years (A.D. 476-538) that the bishop of Rome had been out from under the influence of barbarian tribes.

The end of this 1260 year prophetic period is even easier to document. It came with the fall of papacy and the exile of the pope in 1798 by the troops of France. Napoleon crossed the Alps into northern Italy in 1796. At Campo Formio he defeated the Austrians in 1797. The French Directory, which was atheistic in its orientation, ordered Napoleon to conquer Rome and abolish the papacy. Napoleon, however, was called away to other duties, leaving the Italian campaign of the French army under the direction of General Berthier. Berthier seized the city of Rome on February 10, 1798, and deposed Pope Pius VI on February 15. The pope was taken captive and died the next year. In addition to the church's massive losses of land and priests in France during the French Revolution, the head of the church was now dethroned.

But it was not ever to remain so. Beginning with the Concordat in 1801 between Napoleon and the papacy, the restoration of the Roman Church started with the new pope, Pius VII. Since then, the influence of the papacy has continued to expand up through the present. In the terms of Revelation 13:3, "One of the heads of the beast seemed to have had a fatal wound [in 1798], but the fatal wound had been healed [beginning in 1801]." Thus the year 1798 marks a fitting end to the great prophetic period outlined in Daniel 7:25.

From these eight points about the activities of the little horn, we can draw up a summary that will help us in identifying it. The fourth beast of this prophecy represented Imperial Rome. That empire was to be broken up, and as predicted, it happened with the barbarian invasions of the mid-first millennium A.D. After the rise of those divisions, a new power came to prominence, represented by the little horn in this prophecy. It had its origin from the Roman beast and was therefore Roman in character. In contrast to the previous political powers depicted in this prophecy, however, the little horn was distinctly religious in character. This religious nature was demonstrated by its persecution of the saints, its blasphemy, and its attack—through the forces of the state— upon those Christian powers which disagreed with its theology. These Arian wars of the sixth century added to the prestige of the bishop of Rome and his church. The power of the little horn was not to last forever; the prophecy limited it to a prophetic time period of 1260 day-years. These began with the liberation of Rome in A.D. 538 and came to an end with the conquest of Rome and the deposing of the pope in A.D. 1798. Thus the Roman Church and its leadership fit the characteristics of this power as outlined above.

It should be recalled, however, that God alone can read the conscience. When we identify the work of this religious power by means of the characteristics present in this prophecy, we are not speaking about the individual consciences of believers. Rather, we are dealing here with a political and theological system which went astray from its spiritual origins. That drift has led to unbiblical beliefs and practices, but individuals may have participated in that communion with a complete sincerity which God recognizes and will honor.

■ Getting Into the Word

Daniel 7:9-14, 21, 22, 26, 27

Read Daniel 7 once again in its entirety. Then focus on verses 9-14 and verses 21, 22, 26, 27. Remember that the second half of the chapter is an explanation of the first half.

1. In your own words, briefly describe what is happening in these verses.
2. Who is the "Ancient of Days"? Who is the son of man? A concordance will help you as you examine the second title.
3. List all the judgmentlike language in these verses.
4. Where do the saints, or people of the Most High, fit into this prophecy?

■ Exploring the Word

The Heavenly Court Scene

One would naturally think that the way to solve the problems introduced by the different nations outlined in this prophecy would be for God to set up His kingdom, a kingdom of a radically different nature. And that *is* the ultimate answer this prophecy provides to the problems under which human beings suffer (7:14, 27). The prophecy describes an intermediate stage which leads to that final result. The prophecy presents that intermediate stage in terms of a judgment. In other words, when human history concludes, God will sit in judgment upon it and upon the people involved in it (7:9, 10, 26). This judgment is distinct from the executive phase of judgment, which takes place when Christ comes the second time and passes out His rewards (see, for example, Revelation 22:12). The judgment described here takes place in heaven before Christ comes to earth. For that reason, it is sometimes referred to as the preadvent judgment, which also locates it in terms of time.

The Setting of the Judgment

A large number of prophecies in the Old Testament speak about God's judgment from His sanctuary—either the earthly temple or the heavenly temple. Examples can be found in Isaiah 6, Ezekiel 1, Micah 1, Amos 1, and 1 Kings 22. These were limited, local judgments, either upon the people of Israel or upon their enemies. These judgments were a microcosm of what Daniel 7:9-14 indicates will happen at the end of time on cosmic scale. This great final cosmic judgment will conclude the plan of salvation. When this judgment in heaven is finished, Christ can come for His people—those who have been clearly identified by that judgment as the saints of the Most High. Then those saints will be taken home to their eternal reward.

As evidence for the fact that a new work of judgment takes place at this time, the scene set in heaven begins with the preparations for that work. This involves bringing the fiery, glorious throne of God into the heavenly courtroom, His audience chamber. Archaeology provides some interesting examples of this very type of thing. The kings of the ancient world commonly had a large, separate chamber in which to hold court and audiences. There citizens or ambassadors appeared before the king to present their cases or describe their negotiations. Audience chambers commonly had a raised dias or platform at one end of the room. The king's throne was portable, and his servants would bring it out of the palace to place it upon that platform. Then when the royal audience was over, the throne would be taken back into the palace until the next time the king was to hold court.

The heavenly throne scene of Daniel 7 portrays a similar setting. Daniel saw the flaming, fiery chariot of God, His portable throne, coming into the heavenly audience chamber. "Thrones were set in place" (vs. 9). The fire is Daniel's description of the glory that surrounds the personal being of God; it is not literal fire. Three times in verses 9 and 10 God's glory is described as "fire." Fire is not only descriptive of the glory Daniel saw, but it is appropriate as one of the results of the judgment. God's enemies are to be destroyed by fire—a fire that comes from Him who conducts this judgment (vss.

11, 26). The movement involved here shows action, and it reveals that action to be a new activity. Our God is not a static God; He is dynamically active. There is movement to judgment. This judgment takes place when that movement brings God into this scene. In other words, this is a judgment that takes place at a certain point in time.

The outline of the prophecy can give us an idea of when that judgment was to begin. First, the prophecy describes four beast-kingdoms that were to rise and fall—Babylon, Medo-Persia, Greece, and Rome. But the judgment still has not convened. Then Rome was to be divided, and the little horn was to arise after those divisions. Following that, the little horn was to have its prolonged period of religio-political dominion, lasting, as we have described above, from A.D. 538 to 1798. After that, the judgment comes. So even before we turn to Daniel 8 for more precise dating, we have an implied date for this judgment here in chapter 7. It must begin sometime after 1798. The prophecy of chapter 7 does not say exactly how long after 1798 the judgment was to begin, but chapter 8 gives us the answer in the 2300-day prophecy. That prophecy brought us, as we have seen in the previous chapter, to A.D. 1844. Daniel 8:14 refers to the event that was to occur in 1844 as the cleansing, or restoration, of the (heavenly) sanctuary. This cleansing of the sanctuary was a time of judgment, as we discovered by comparing Daniel 8 with Leviticus. Daniel 7:9-14, 26 talks about the same judgment scene—with one difference. In Daniel 8, the prophet was only *told* about the judgment; he listened in on the conversation of two angels who assured him that the judgment would come at the end of the 2300-day period. Here in chapter 7, however, the prophet was *shown* the heavenly court session as a scene of his vision. What he was told about in 8:14 he was shown in 7:9-14, 26. Daniel 7 gives an approximate date for the judgment (sometime after 1798), while chapter 8 gives its exact date as beginning in 1844 at the end of the 2300 days. These two points occur in parallel positions in their respective visions, and they explain each other in various ways.

The prophecy of Daniel 7 next goes on to describe the person of God, who comes in to begin this judgment (vs. 9). He is surrounded by the glorious appearance of fire. The hair of His head is described as white like wool, giving, in human appearance, the look of great age. The same thing is emphasized by the title He is given here—"the Ancient of Days" (vs. 9). This title is used for God nowhere else in the entire Bible. What is its significance here?

When God takes up the work of judgment, He judges human beings who have lived in every age of earth's history. But none of them have outlived God or lived at a time before Him. God could say to all the people judged in the judgment, "I knew you; I was contemporary with you. You did nothing that lay outside the realm of my knowledge." He is also a pure and righteous judge. Human courts may, or may not, give just judgments, but God's judgment is always just and righteous (Rev. 15:3, 4; 16:4-7; 19:2). This is represented by the white color of His garments.

Daniel next sees the angels come into this heavenly court (vs. 10). The judgment cannot start without the angels being there as well as God. What function do the angels serve in the judgment?

Chapter 7 poetically describes the angels in the judgment scene in these words: "Thousands upon thousands attended him; ten thousand times ten thousand stood before him" (vs. 10). This poetic progression is not given to express a literal number of angels; it is given to express totality. All of God's faithful angels will be there. Every human being who has ever lived has had a guardian angel, and all those guardian angels will be there in the judgment to testify for their charges. Believers will not be unrepresented in that judgment. With Christ, our High Priest and Advocate, and our guardian angel present, we will be well represented.

The concluding statement of this opening passage from the judgment section states, "The court was seated, and the books were opened" (vss. 10, 26). The scene here is typical of what we know of human courts. The judge comes in and takes his seat. Those in attendance in the court sit down, and then they get to work. They have to examine the materials of the case. The records are opened. So it is in the heavenly judgment. There are record "books" of some sort that are examined (vs. 10). For that reason, this judgment has been called an "investigative judgment." The records obviously are the records of the lives of those being judged. Did they accept Christ as their Saviour and receive forgiveness for their repentance? Or did they turn away from the great salvation offered in Christ? Did they accept God as Lord of their lives and live for Him, or not? All of this is recorded in these books. The ultimate question in the judgment is this: What was your relationship to Christ? The decision is ours; God does not change it. He merely reviews the decisions that have been made to see who will enter the eternal kingdom with the saints of the Most High and who will not. This naturally leads to the consequence that when Christ comes, He comes ready to distribute His rewards (Matt. 16:27). These rewards have been decided upon in this preadvent, investigative judgment. This judgment is the necessary intermediate stage between the last phase of human history and the beginning of heaven's history.

An Interlude

At this point in the prophecy, there is an interlude, or parenthesis. It is found in verses 11 and 12. In verses 9 and 10, the prophet saw events from the viewpoint of heaven; he was shown the beginning of the preadvent judgment taking place in heaven. But in verses 11 and 12, Daniel's viewpoint is brought back down to earth temporarily, and he is shown earthly events. These deal mainly with the destruction of the fourth beast and the little horn. It is true that Imperial Rome came to an end in the latter part of the fifth century A.D. How, then, does Daniel view its destruction along with the little horn at the close of world history?

Imperial Rome does not live on in exactly the same way it did during the early centuries of this era, but the ten horns which represent its divisions do live on in the modern nations of Europe that are descendants of the tribal divisions of that empire. To carry these horns through to the end, the fourth beast continues in the prophecy, although in modified form. The same point is made in Revelation 13:1-3; 17:3, 9-12. The fourth beast carrying its various horns, along with what started out as the little horn, will remain until the end and be destroyed by fire (Dan. 7:11). The NIV has done well to put verse 12 in parentheses, for that is where it belongs. Verse 12 reflects back upon the fate of the first three beast-kingdoms: "The other beasts had been stripped of their authority, but were allowed to live for a period of time." Babylon was conquered by Persia in 539 B.C., but it lasted as a city until A.D. 75. Greece still exists today, but not with the power of Alexander's empire. Until recent years, Iran (Persia) was ruled by Shahs who considered themselves direct descendants of the Persian kings (the Achaemenids) of the sixth through the fourth centuries B.C. In this way, each of these powers lived on after its dominion was taken away.

The Son of Man and the Conclusion of the Judgment

With Daniel 7:13, the prophet's view returns to the heavenly court scene. Verses 13 and 14 depict the conclusion of the judgment, when Christ receives full authority from the Father just prior to returning to earth at the second advent. Some have seen verses 13 and 14 as referring to the second advent itself. But that interpretation does not correlate well with the explanation of verses 13 and 14 given in verses 26 and 27. The Millerites made the mistake of identifying verses 13 and 14 with the second advent. Only after their disappointment on October 22, 1844, did they come to understand that what was predicted here was an event that was to transpire in heaven. It is not the coming of Christ to earth, but the coming of Christ to God the Father in heaven—an event that takes place in heaven before Jesus comes to earth.

Christ is described here in Daniel 7 as the "son of man" (vs. 13). Jesus used this title for Himself many times according to the Gospels (for just a few instances, see Matt. 9:6; 11:19; 12:8; 13:41; 16:13; 16:28, etc.). This was a well-understood messianic title in His time. Some scholars think that Jesus' use of this title goes directly back to Daniel 7:13. In any event, He surely was identifying Himself with that figure. In Daniel, however, the title serves a slightly different purpose. It is descriptive. It is preceded by the comparative preposition, "like." Daniel saw someone in heaven who looked "like a son of man," that is, He looked like a human being. From the point of view of Daniel's time, such a title is quite remarkable. Daniel saw God and the angels in heaven (vss. 9, 10). There is nothing remarkable about that; that is their normal dwelling place. But then Daniel sees someone who looks like a human being up in heaven!

Even more remarkable, this human being is receiving universal rulership. "He was given authority, glory and sovereign power; all peoples, nations and men of every language worshiped him. His dominion is an everlasting dominion that will not pass away, and his kingdom is one that will never be destroyed" (vs. 14). There are two dimensions here. The first is time. In contrast to the temporary kingdoms of earth, the kingdom and dominion that this "son of man" receives will go on forever; it will never be interrupted or given to another. The other dimension includes the earth, the horizontal dimension. Everybody who lives on the surface of the earth in those days will worship and serve Him. The whole earth will be full of His glory.

Who is this Son of man? Jesus has identified this figure for us by His use of it in the Gospels to apply to Himself. But what about the time perspective of Daniel? What identity would this figure have in terms of this vision in the sixth century B.C.?

We have already referred to the fact that the Son of man looked like a human being. But there was another aspect to His appearance—He is accompanied by clouds (vs. 13). A word study of "clouds" in a concordance yields references (after those to atmospheric clouds are excluded) that suggest clouds are an attribute of divinity. Psalm 97:2 is an example. "Clouds and thick darkness surround him; righteousness and justice are the foundation of his throne." Thus we find an interesting combination here in Daniel 7. The title "son of man" refers to His humanity, while the description of clouds accompanying Him refers to His divinity. Thus the language of the vision gives evidence that the "son of man" is a divine-human being. How can this be? There is only one Being in all the history of the universe who combined those elements in Himself, and that was Jesus Christ. By virtue of the Incarnation, He combined both divinity and humanity in His one person. As Daniel was shown a view of the judgment that was to take place well into the Christian era, long after his own time, he was also shown a view of the resurrected God-man ministering in that judgment, and ultimately receiving the benefit of that judgment by reaffirming his kingship over the saved of the human race.

The combination of the Father and Son here in this vision—the

Ancient of Days and the Son of man—brings together some prophetic time symbols from Daniel 8. The great time prophecy which extended to the beginning of this judgment was measured in the unusual time units of "evening-mornings" (8:14). In the preceding chapter, we identified these "evening-mornings" from Genesis 1 as a twenty-four-hour day; we also identified them as a sanctuary day using Numbers 9:15 and following. The Lord marked off the sanctuary day by a pillar of fire over the sanctuary during the night and a pillar of cloud over it during the day. These same two elements are brought together again in Daniel 8:14 and 7:9,13. The fire that surrounds the Ancient of Days reminds us of the pillar of fire over the sanctuary, and the Son of Man comes with clouds, like those that were seen over the sanctuary during the day. Thus 8:14 gives us sanctuary days marked off by fire in the evening and by a cloud in the day; 7:9, 13 gives us those same two elements coming together at the end of the 2300 sanctuary days. When the judgment was to start, these two heavenly elements came together.

Basically, three events result from this judgment: (1) the wicked are destroyed (7:11, 26); (2) the kingship of the Son of man is reaffirmed (vss. 13, 14); and (3) the saints of the Most High inherit the kingdom (vs. 27). The last verse of the angel's explanation is very important, for it gives the final solution to the problems the saints have suffered on earth. In God's great eternal kingdom, they will "worship and obey him [the Son of Man]" (vs. 27). Verses 14 and 27 are reciprocals. Both describe the people of God who will be in the eternal kingdom. Verse 14 tells who will rule over them—the Son of Man. Verse 27 tells what they will do in relationship to Him—they will serve Him in worship, and they will obey Him. Some of these people will be those who have suffered unjustly from human courts. The divine court in heaven will redress these wrongs. That is what verse 22 means when it refers to the time when "the Ancient of Days came and pronounced judgment in favor of the saints of the Most High, and the time came when they possessed the kingdom." In many cases in human courts, there are two sides to an issue. For example, both sides may claim a piece of property. When the court makes its decision, it will decide in favor of one party and against the other. So it is with the divine court. It will decide *against* the wicked and *in favor* of the righteous. To decide in favor of the righteous, God must know the righteous and know that they are—through Christ—righteous. Then they will be vindicated by God in judgment; "vindicated" is one of the meanings of the verb that is employed in Daniel 8:14 and translated as "cleansed" in the KJV and "reconsecrated" in the NIV.

Summary

In this symbolic vision, God gave Daniel a mighty overview of history from his own day to the end of time. This depiction began with four beast nations—a lion representing Babylon, a bear standing for Medo-Persia, a leopard symbolizing Greece, and a final beast representing Rome. These kingdoms had already covered 1,000 years from Daniel's time. The prophecy does not foresee any further world empires like these. Instead, the fourth kingdom was to break up into divisions represented by ten horns. After those divisions were in place, an eleventh horn came up. It started out little and then became great. It was distinct in nature from the other powers depicted. Its nature was religious, in contrast to the political powers that had gone before. This religious power came to exercise political powers, however, through a union of purpose between church and state.

This was the form of the church that developed during the Middle Ages, when the church reached the zenith of its power. The prophecy identifies eight major characteristics of this medieval Roman Church. These all occurred as predicted by the prophecy. Prominent among these was persecution which was carried out by the Roman Church as amply demonstrated by historical sources (see chapter 5 in the *Daniel 1–7* Bible Amplifier volume). What had started out as a persecuted body under the caesars now turned around under the popes to do the persecuting. The prophecy further states that this power would attempt to change God's law, especially those aspects connected with time. This points to the fourth, or Sabbath, commandment. This power has claimed special authority over the Sabbath, enabling it to transfer that sacred institution to another day, Sunday, the first day of the week. The historical sources quoted toward the end of chapter 5 in *Daniel 1–7* demonstrate just how this course of action has worked out.

The conditions caused by these beast nations and the little horn were not to last forever. Dominion was to pass from one to another, and thus these powers rose and fell on the scene of action. But God had a more final answer ready. That final answer has been introduced by the judgment that is taking place in heaven now, according to the description of Daniel 7:9-14. When that great final judgment in heaven comes to an end, the kingship of God's eternal kingdom will be reaffirmed to the Son of man, Jesus Christ. Then He will return to earth and gather up all His saints, those living and those resurrected, and take them to His kingdom. And so shall we ever be with the Lord. "Even so, Come, Lord Jesus" (Rev. 22:20, KJV). God is ultimately in control of the direction of human history as it moves inexorably toward His goal, and that goal will come about soon.

Summary of Parallel Outline Prophecies			
Identification	Daniel 2	Daniel 7	Daniel 8
Babylon	Gold	Lion	not represented
Persia	Silver	Bear	Ram
Greece	Bronze	Leopard	Goat
divisions	not represented	4 heads and wings	4 horns
Rome, Imperial	Iron	4th beast	little horn, phase 1
divisions	iron and clay	10 horns	not represented
Rome, papal	not represented	little horn	little horn, phase 2
Preadvent judgment	not represented	heavenly court scene, Ancient of Days	cleansing of the sanctuary at the end of 2300 days
Kingdom of God	Stone kingdom	Saints of Most High ruled by Son of man	not represented

■ Applying the Word

Daniel 7

1. In what ways is it helpful to me to know that the Son of man is depicted as being both divine and human?
2. How should I relate to the fact that the heavenly judgment is taking place at the present time? What does (or should) the certainty of judgment do for my daily Christian life?
3. As a Christian, what reasons can I provide for personal confidence in the judgment?

■ Researching the Word

1. Read the book of Daniel through from beginning to end, looking especially for pictures of the Messiah. How many do you find? List them in your Daniel notebook, and describe what each picture says about the work of the Messiah.
2. Using a concordance, look up every reference in the Bible to the use of "books" in the judgment. List the names of the various books that will be used. In your notebook, write a composite description of the purpose and use of these books.

■ Further Study of the Word

1. On the subject of heavenly court scenes depicted elsewhere in the Bible outside of Daniel, see W. H. Shea, *Selected Studies in Prophetic Interpretation*, chapter 1.
2. On the subject of Daniel 7 in general and especially its judgment scene, see W. H. Shea, *Selected Studies in Prophetic Interpretation*, chapter 5.
3. On the subject of the breakup of the Greek kingdom that was divided into the four heads of the leopard in Daniel 7, see F. D. Nichol, ed., *The SDA Bible Commentary*, 4:822-826.

4. For the events surrounding the date of A.D. 538, see L. E. Froom, *Prophetic Faith of Our Fathers*, 1:492-517.
5. For the events surrounding the date of A.D. 1798, see L. E. Froom, *Prophetic Faith of Our Fathers*, 2:723-782.
6. For a parallel and useful recent exposition of Daniel 7, see M. Maxwell, *God Cares*, 1:101-144.

CHAPTER TEN

Summary Chapters 9, 8, and 7

Daniel 9—Christ As Sacrifice
Daniel 8—Christ As Priest
Daniel 7—Christ As King

Some obvious connections exist between the three prophecies listed above. They describe some of the same events and cover some of the same historical periods. But other connections between these prophecies are not as readily apparent. One such connection, which the Adventist pioneers (and the Millerites before them) emphasized, is the connection between the time prophecies of Daniel 8 and 9. As described in detail in the preceding chapters, the seventy weeks of chapter 9 have been cut off from the longer time period in chapter 8—the 2300 days. As a matter of fact, the original language makes that link even more specific.

But there is yet another kind of link between these prophecies which we have not emphasized. That link lies in the fact that as one progresses through these prophecies, successive steps in the ministry of Christ are brought to view. We may have failed to readily recognize this progression due to the fact that these prophecies are presented in Semitic thought order, that is, in an order that reasons from effect back to cause. In modern western European thought processes, we reason from cause to effect. The ancients could do that too, but they commonly thought and wrote in the reverse of this order. This feature explains much about the connections between these prophecies and why they appear in the order that they do. When we understand this feature of these prophecies, the logical progression in the work of Christ the Messiah becomes clear. In this way an even stronger link is forged between these three prophecies. This summary chapter will focus on these connections.

■ Getting Into the Word

Daniel 7–9

Reread Daniel 7–9, looking especially for references regarding Christ and His work.

1. Which one of these three prophecies is the longest or covers the most history? Which is the shortest? Where does each begin and end?
2. What is the nature of Christ's work in Daniel 9, and how does that work relate to His work in Daniel 8?
3. What is the nature of the work of Christ in Daniel 8, and how does that work relate to His work in Daniel 7?
4. If Daniel 7 is the end of this series of prophecies, as suggested by the arrangement in this volume, what is the climax of Christ's ministry in chapter 7? What type of work does it involve?

■ Exploring the Word

Summary of Daniel 9: Christ as Sacrifice

From our study of Daniel 9 (see chapter 7 above), we may summarize as follows the main emphases in that prophecy regarding the work of the Messiah. The prophecy of Daniel 9 foretold:

1. The time for the appearing of the Messiah (vs. 25)
2. That He would be "cut off," that is, killed (vs. 26a)
3. That He would bring the sacrificial system to an end (vs. 27a)
4. That He would make a strong offer of the covenant to many people in His teaching and ministry (vs. 27a)
5. That He would make the great atonement for iniquity (vs. 24c)

6. That by making this atonement He would bring in everlasting righteousness (vs. 24d)

7. That a new sanctuary in heaven would be anointed or dedicated for His work as our high priest (vss. 24-25)

All the specifications of this prophecy with regard to the Messiah were fulfilled in the life, death, resurrection, and ascension of Jesus of Nazareth. He becomes its center and focus; all else in it revolves around Him. The list given above can be condensed into one central teaching about Jesus Christ as the Messiah: He was the great suffering Servant of God who came to give His life as a sacrifice for sin. The picture that lies at the heart of the prophecy of Daniel 9 is the picture of *Jesus as sacrifice*.

Summary of Daniel 8: Christ as Priest

Moving to Daniel 8, we come to a prophecy of a different character. The prophecy in this chapter is a symbolic prophecy involving beast-nations and horns, along with symbolic actions characterizing their future course. The outline of the first half of the prophecy is relatively straightforward, and the details are agreed upon by most commentators. The action begins with the ascendancy of the Medo-Persian ram (vss. 3, 20), followed by the Greek goat (vss. 5, 21). The Greek goat's great horn is Alexander, whose reign is followed by the breakup of his empire into four kingdoms symbolized by the four horns (vss. 8, 21, 22).

Pagan Rome

At this point a new "little" horn comes upon the scene. Historicist commentators see this little horn as Rome, whose conquests to the east, south, and the glorious land of Judea are described in Daniel 8:9. Most interpreters in other prophetic schools identify this little horn with Antiochus IV Epiphanes. This interpretation has been dealt with in detail earlier in this book and need not be discussed further here. This volume takes the position that we are dealing with Rome under this symbol.

Papal Rome

A new phase of Rome begins in verse 10. This new phase is symbolized by actions that introduce the horn's vertical dimension beyond the stellar heaven in contrast with the horizontal conquests it has carried out previously. The symbolic nature of these actions should be stressed. We are not dealing with a literal horn, nor did it literally reach up to heaven. This is a symbol for a human organization that makes a fourfold attack against God: (1) it persecutes the saints of the Most High, or the holy people; (2) it casts down the sanctuary in heaven (thus implying, in contrast, its elevation of an earthly temple in which it dwells and functions; compare 2 Thess. 2:3, 4); (3) it attacks the "daily" or "continual" (not a single sacrifice as some translators would have it, but a "ministration" that covers all types of activity going on in the heavenly sanctuary on a daily basis); and (4) it attacks the Prince to whom the sanctuary belongs (8:11, 12, 24, 25).

In other words, the climax of this prophecy describes a great conflict pitting the heavenly Prince against the little horn, a conflict involving nothing less than the plan of salvation. On one hand is the true plan of salvation, ministered by the true heavenly High Priest. On the other hand is a substitute, an earthly priesthood functioning in earthly temples designed to take the eyes of mankind off the true High Priest in His true sanctuary (compare Heb. 8:1, 2). Who is this great heavenly High Priest, and who is this priestly Prince? None other than Jesus Christ. His priesthood is identified especially in Hebrews 7–9. And the anointing of His sanctuary in heaven is referred to in the prophecies of Daniel (9:24, 25). The prophecy of Daniel 8 presents *Jesus as priest*.

Summary of Daniel 7: Christ as King

In the great prophecy of Daniel 7, we also have a succession of kingdoms symbolized by a series of beasts. These can be readily identified as Babylon, Medo-Persia, Greece, and Rome (7:3-7, 17). The kingdom or empire of Rome was then to be broken up, as symbolized by the ten horns upon the head of the Roman beast. Among these ten horns would sprout another "little" horn. The prophecy gives a number of characteristics by which we can determine that it does the same type of work as does the little horn of Daniel 8. Thus we can identify this little horn as a Roman horn—the religious phase of that power (7:7, 8, 20, 21, 23-25; see also the discussion in the previous chapter).

A particular period of time was allotted to this little horn for it to exercise power and dominion. Verse 25 specifies this time period as three and a half "times," or years. Applying the year-day principle to this time prophecy, we identify its 1260 years with the Middle or Dark Ages, from A.D. 538 to A.D. 1798.

God has an answer to all the beast-kingdoms and horns found in this prophecy. The answer is His judgment. That judgment is described in Daniel 7:9-10, 13-14. Here the prophet looks into the heavenly sanctuary and sees the great heavenly tribunal begin (vss. 9, 10). The Ancient of Days comes to sit upon His throne, placed upon a dais at the commencement of this court session. All the angels gather, the court sits in judgment, and the books of record out of which the judgment is to be conducted are opened.

Three important decisions stem from this judgment: (1)The saints of the Most High will go into the heavenly kingdom (vs. 22); (2)the little horn, the beasts, and those allied with them will be destroyed (vss. 11, 22, 26); and (3)the kingship of the eternal kingdom of God is reaffirmed to the Son of man (vss. 13, 14). The Son of man is brought before the Ancient of Days by a retinue of angels and with the clouds of heaven. He is awarded direct and physical rule over God's eternal kingdom. Emphatically, we are told that His kingdom will include all who will dwell on earth in the future and that this kingdom, in contrast with those that have gone before it, will last forever and ever. It will never be interrupted or brought to an end.

Who, then, is this Son of man who receives the eternal kingdom? Jesus took this very title Himself when He made such statements as, "The Son of man is come to seek and to save that which was lost" (Luke 19:10, KJV). Revelation 14:14 makes this connection explicit using the same title, phrased in the same way, in the same context (the clouds of heaven), in a reference to the second coming of Jesus.

From a New Testament perspective, therefore, there can be no question that this title, Son of man, refers to King Jesus. At the heart of the prophecy of Daniel 7, therefore, is the picture of *Jesus as king*.

Interrelations of Daniel 7, 8, 9

We have identified three pictures of Jesus at the heart of three prophecies in the heart of the book of Daniel. In chapter 9, the picture is one of *Jesus as sacrifice*. In chapter 8, the picture that emerges is that of *Jesus as priest*. And in chapter 7, the picture is of *Jesus as king*.

At this point a question may arise about the order in which these features have been presented. Why are the portrayals not presented in the sequence of their actual occurrence—sacrifice, priest, and king? Why are they presented in the reverse sequence—king (chapter 7); priest (chapter 8); and sacrifice (chapter 9)?

As we noted above, one reason for the literary order has to do with Semitic thought processes. Modern western European thinking reasons from cause to effect; ancient Semitic people commonly reasoned from effect back to cause. Instead of saying, "You are a sinful, wicked, and rebellious people, therefore your land will be destroyed," the biblical prophets could also put the matter the other way around: "Your land will be destroyed." Why? "Because you are a sinful, wicked, and rebellious people." A good biblical example of this kind of thought order can be found in Micah 1:10-15 where the cities that mourn for the exiles are listed first, followed by a list of the cities from which the exiles came. We would put the matter the other way around.

Seventh-day Adventists emphasize that the seventy weeks of Daniel 9 is connected with, or "cut off" from, the 2300 days of chapter 8. This is working backward, if you please. The three pictures of Jesus in these prophecies follow the same kind of pattern, although we are dealing in this case with thematic relations, not time.

We can see the effect of these thematic relations as we read Daniel's book from the beginning. By the time we reach chapter 7 and encounter the picture of the messianic King, the natural questions are:

Who is this Being? Where does He come from? Daniel 8 answers by saying, "The King becomes king, in part, because previously He has been the priest. He is the one who has ministered on behalf of the saints of the Most High; now He can accept them into His kingdom."

But that response simply raises another question: How did He qualify as priest? In order to become a priest, one has to have something to offer, a sacrifice (see Heb. 8:3). Where do we find the answer to that question? In Daniel 9. The sacrifice of chapter 9 enabled the priest of chapter 8 to become priest, and the priesthood of the Prince enabled the Prince of chapter 8 to become the king of chapter 7. There is a logical, consistent, and interrelated sequence here that is quite direct and reasonable when we understand that the sequence begins at the end and works backward as far as the literary order of the book is concerned.

Temporal Relationships

Another way to look at this sequence is to relate the pictures of Jesus to the time elements found in these prophecies. It is evident that Daniel 9 is the shortest of the three prophecies, because its time span extends only for seventy prophetic weeks, or 490 years (9:24). The time period of this prophecy, understood historically, takes us from 457B.C. to first century A.D., Roman times when Jesus walked this earth and was crucified under that power.

The prophecy in chapter 8, on the other hand, is longer in length, simply by virtue of the fact that its time period extends for 2300 "evening-mornings" or days (8:14), which is the symbolic equivalent of 2300 historical years. This takes us from 457B.C. into the Christian Era, through the Middle Ages and beyond, down to relatively recent times—the nineteenth century A.D. This means that the priest of that prophecy has been functioning through a part of that time period (beginning at the ascension in A.D.31).

At the same time, His counterfeit has been active too. But the prophecy of chapter 8 tells about a time when this activity will come to an end. It tells about it verbally; its end is not shown to the prophet in vision. When the visual portion of the prophecy concludes in Daniel 8:12, the little horn is still practicing and prospering.

Likewise, Daniel 8 does not take the saints of the Most High into the final eternal kingdom. It speaks to the fact that there will be a judgment to bring the bad things of that chapter to an end, but it does not refer directly to the reward of the saints at all. That is reserved for the final prophecy in this backward sequence.

In Daniel 7 we see the final culmination when the King receives His kingdom (vss. 13, 14) and the saints are ushered into that eternal realm (vs. 27). This is the longest in length of these three prophecies at the heart of the book of Daniel. Chapter 9 is the short-length prophecy in terms of time; chapter 8 is the intermediate-length prophecy; and chapter 7 is the longest-length prophecy in terms of the events that it describes. These relationships can be summarized by the following diagram:

Three Pictures of Jesus in the Prophecies at the Heart of Daniel

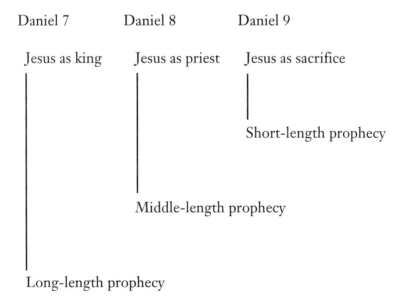

Daniel 7	Daniel 8	Daniel 9
Jesus as king	Jesus as priest	Jesus as sacrifice

Short-length prophecy

Middle-length prophecy

Long-length prophecy

Spiritual Relationships

We are not interested in just the megapicture of what Daniel's prophecies tell us; we are interested also in what they have to say to us personally and how they apply to our own lives. In this case, we can look at these same three prophecies through our own individual spiritual experience with them. They are not just academic or philosophical exercises to prove the foreknowledge of God. They bring to us personal spiritual experiences with the God of these prophecies and with His Son. That Son we have seen in three phases of His work. As we reflect upon these, we see that these three phases of His work take place in our own lives too. As we look back to the cross, through the eyes of Daniel 9, we see Christ as our sacrifice upon the cross. From Him we receive forgiveness in response to our repentance—not through our own merits, but through His atonement that was worked out on the cross as He died for us (Matt. 26:28). The suffering Messiah of chapter 9 is *our* sacrifice for sin (1Peter 2:24). The everlasting righteousness that He thus obtained is for *us*. As we look back in history to the cross and see Him dying there as our Saviour, we claim Him as our Lord. That is the past tense of salvation in these prophecies. We may call that experience justification.

But our salvation does not end there. There is also salvation in the present tense. That is what chapter 8 is talking about in terms of our personal spiritual experience. As we look up to the heavenly sanctuary today, we can know and have confidence that we have a great High Priest there and that it is the same person as the One who died on the cross, Jesus Christ the Righteous (Heb. 8:1-3). He is Himself both the sacrifice and the priest who ministers the sacrifice (Heb. 9:26-28). He is there at the throne of God today interceding for us (1John 2:1, 2; Rom. 8:34). Our prayers go up to Him with the incense of the Holy Spirit (Rev. 8:4). He is our great Mediator, and He is carrying out that role today so that we may receive the Holy Spirit in our lives. He sends forth the promised Comforter to minister to us and live in our hearts, giving us the spiritual strength that we need to live for Christ. This is salvation in the present tense. It is sometimes called sanctification.

But our spiritual experience with these prophecies does not end with justification and sanctification. There is something more awaiting us. That is described for us in the prophecy of chapter 7. There we see the line of history leading into the future where it will culminate in God's kingdom. There King Jesus will lead and govern His people. There the saints of the Most High will find their long-awaited rest. There they will be glorified with their new immortal bodies and eternal life (1Cor. 15:51-53). This eternal life will be lived out as King Jesus leads His people in the kingdom that will occupy the earth made new. The capital of that new world will be the New Jerusalem (Rev. 21, 22). That will be the kingdom of glory. Just as the saints have lived here and now in the kingdom of grace, so one day they will come home to the kingdom of glory. This phase of the plan of salvation is sometimes called glorification.

Thus the three interrelated prophecies of Daniel 9, 8, and 7 bring into view three phases of our spiritual experience. We have a spiritual experience with the Messiah of chapter 9 because He was our sacrifice in the past and from that sacrifice we received atonement and justification. In the present tense, we have a spiritual experience with Him because He has been pictured in chapter 8 as our Great High Priest, the heavenly Prince, our Intercessor, and Mediator. We receive from Him today the sanctification of our lives. Finally one day, according to the promise of the prophecy of chapter 7, those lives will be transformed into the glorified lives of the saints in the new earth. There they will be led by the glorious King Jesus in a kingdom that will be all over glorious. No longer will the dim shadows of sin darken the glory of this earth. In those future days of promise, it will stand forth with all the radiance of God's re-creation.

The prophetic tenses of these prophecies—past, present, and future—may be added into a chart along with the corresponding spiritual experiences—justification, sanctification, and glorification. All of this can be added together to make up the complete picture of how these prophecies are interconnected. The remarkable picture looks something like this when it is fully realized:

Prophecy	Daniel 9	Daniel 8	Daniel 7
Length	Short	Medium	Long
Picture of Christ	Sacrifice	Priest	King
Spiritual point of view	Past	Present	Future
Spiritual experience of salvation	Justification	Sanctification	Glorification

■ Applying the Word

Daniel 7–9

1. How have I personally made sure that Jesus is truly my own sacrifice on the cross and not just the sacrifice for the sins of the world? What does it mean for me to accept Jesus as my Lord and Saviour? In what ways does it add to my confidence in Him as my Saviour to know that His role as sacrifice was prophesied at least six centuries before He came and fulfilled that role?
2. What is my present spiritual experience with my heavenly High Priest? How may I look to Him in faith to receive all the spiritual blessings that He has to bestow upon me? In what specific ways am I living for Him? Am I receiving the daily strength from Him that He offers in the person and presence of the Holy Spirit? What reasons can I give for my answers?
3. How much anticipation do I have for the glorious kingdom of God? Is it something I think about and love to dwell upon—or has it become something I have lost sight of in my busy activities each day? What evidence do I have for my answers?
4. In what ways can I fix my spiritual gaze more firmly upon the final prize and praise God that He has made full salvation available to all who place their faith in Him?

∎ Researching the Word

1. Read through either Romans or Hebrews, and list in three columns those texts that represent the three tenses of salvation that we have found in Daniel 9, 8, and 7.
2. Read through the prophet Jeremiah looking for examples of reasoning from effect to cause (for example, he prophesies of the destruction of the land before he tells the reasons why the land would be destroyed). List the examples you find.

∎ Further Study of the Word

W. H. Shea, *Selected Studies in Prophetic Interpretation*, Revised edition, chapter 6, "Pictures of Jesus in the Heart of the Book of Daniel."

CHAPTER ELEVEN

Daniel's Final Message— Part 1

Daniel 10:1–11:22

Daniel's final prophecy covers three chapters in the book—chapters 10, 11, and 12. Chapter 10 is the introduction, or prologue; chapter 11 is the body of the prophecy; and chapter 12 is the conclusion, or epilogue. All three belong together, as shown by the fact that elements in chapter 10 reappear in chapter 12.

Chapter 11, the body of the prophecy, is the most detailed prophecy in Daniel's book. Previous prophecies have talked about kingdoms; chapter 11 now gets down to the details and talks about individual kings. No symbolic vision precedes this detailed explanation. It is an oral, didactic type of prophecy given directly from the angel Gabriel to the prophet Daniel. The truth of the prophecy is sealed by the appearance of God Himself in chapter 10 and by His oath recorded in chapter 12.

According to the content of chapter 10, a local issue—probably the rebuilding of the temple in Jerusalem—forms part of the situation that is being dealt with. Chapter 11 takes the prophecy from the Persian present (according to Daniel's viewpoint) into the remote future, when God would conclude the plan of salvation and set up His eternal kingdom. That event is described in the first four verses of chapter 12.

Remember that the chapter divisions of the English Bible were not present in the scroll of this book as originally written by Daniel. They were added during the twelfth century A.D. This means that chapter 10 should read consecutively into Daniel 11, and Daniel 11 should read progressively into Daniel 12, unseparated by any major breaks.

■ Getting Into the Word

Daniel 10

Read Daniel 10–12 through once. Then go back and reread chapter 10 before carrying out the following exercises:

1. What indication of a date do we find for the prophecy that begins in Daniel 10? What was Daniel's state of mind in chapter 10? Does the text indicate the nature of the problem that Daniel was praying, mourning, and fasting about? Read Ezra 1–4 (which takes place during this same time period). How might that passage help us understand Daniel's concerns? Especially note Ezra 4:5.

2. What does Daniel's view of the personal presence of God tell us about the divine being? Compare Daniel's vision of God with those found in Ezekiel 1 and Revelation 1. What impressions do you receive from reading such visions?

3. Who came to Daniel's aid in 10:10-12? What indications are there that this might be the same being we find in 8:15, 16 and 9:21-23? List these. What was this being doing just before he came to visit Daniel? According to chapter 10, what did he do after leaving Daniel? What do his activities tell you about divine intervention in human affairs?

4. Who is Michael? Use a concordance to discover other places in the Bible that mention Michael. List each reference and the information it supplies about Michael. What composite picture do you get from these texts?

5. Who is the "prince of Persia"? What does his role appear to be in chapter 10?

■ Exploring the Word

The Date

Daniel 10 begins with a date—the third year of Cyrus (vs. 1). The Persians, under Cyrus, took over Babylon in October of 539 B.C., so Cyrus's first full official year of rulership in Babylon would have begun in the spring of 538 B.C. according to Babylonian and Persian reckoning. Adding three years to 538 B.C. means that this revelation was given to Daniel in the Babylonian-Persian year that began in the spring of 536 B.C. and ended in the spring of 535 B.C. Dates may appear at first to add very little to the story, but they do give us a setting for other events that were happening in the world at the same time.

The Problem

Daniel tells us that a problem was going on at this time, but he does not tell us the nature of the problem. The date, however, gives us a clue. By the third year of Cyrus, the Jews had returned to Judea. In his first year, Cyrus gave the decree permitting them to return, and they had arrived in Jerusalem by the second year. So the problem bothering Daniel was not whether the Jews were going to return to their own land; that had already been accomplished. The problem must have concerned some trouble which the Jewish people had gotten themselves into after arriving in Jerusalem. The book of Ezra tells us that they did indeed find themselves in trouble.

Ezra 1 tells of the decree of Cyrus permitting the Jews to return to their land. Ezra 2 gives the list of those who went back. Ezra 3 tells some of the first things they did when they arrived at the site of the destroyed temple and began to work. They erected the altar and began the sacrifices, but when they came to address building the temple itself, they ran into difficulty. The Samaritans came and wanted to help with the temple construction. They were the mixed descendants of those Israelites who had been left in the land after the Assyrian and Babylonian deportations and non-Jewish people who had been moved in from the east to occupy some of the old Israelite territory. They were polytheists and idolaters. The Jewish returnees, remembering the reason for their captivity, were afraid that the Samaritans would introduce these practices into the new temple, so they refused their offer to help with its reconstruction. That is where the problem arose.

Having been rebuffed, the Samaritans turned to obstructionism. "If you won't let us help you," they said in effect, "we will do everything we can to see that the temple is never rebuilt." And they successfully brought the work to a halt. Ezra 4:5 says, "They [the Samaritans] hired counselors to work against them [the Jews] and frustrate their plans during the entire reign of Cyrus, king of Persia, and down to the reign of Darius, king of Persia." Darius I did not come to the throne until 522 B.C., so this indicates a rather prolonged period of time. From 536 B.C. to 522 B.C. nothing much happened on the temple site in terms of rebuilding.

Ezra says that the Samaritans "hired counselors" to work against the Jews. Where would those counselors carry out their work? Not at Jerusalem, but rather at the centers of political power in the Persian Empire. The most sensitive place for these counselors to try to obstruct the work would be at the court of the king. And since they appear to have had success in getting the work stopped, they must have gotten the ear of the king and his court.

Another person critical to this whole situation was the prince of Persia, and Daniel mentions him later (10:13, 20). Whoever they were talking to, these counselors had success and got the building program in the temple area in Jerusalem stopped. This occurred right about the time that Daniel was fasting about an unspecified problem in chapter 10. Since the major problem for the Jews right at that time was the work stoppage in regard to the rebuilding of the Jerusalem temple, it is logical to put these two pieces of the puzzle together to suggest that this was the problem Daniel was fasting about. The text of Daniel 10 does not say this directly, but this seems the most likely candidate from what we know of the history of that time.

The Appearance of God

Daniel was out by the Tigris River with a few of his friends (10:4). They were concerned about this issue of the temple. Would the temple never be rebuilt? Would God never have His earthly sanctuary to come back to? In Exodus 25:8 God had directed, "Then have them make a sanctuary for me, and I will dwell among them." That directive led to the construction of the tabernacle in the wilderness, followed in turn by Solomon's temple in Jerusalem. But now, that magnificent structure lay in ruins. If there was no temple in which God could dwell and manifest His presence, how could He meet with His people? God soon answered that concern directly by a manifestation of His person.

When God manifested His presence, this is what Daniel saw: "I looked up and there before me was a man dressed in linen, with a belt of finest gold around his waist. His body was like chrysolite, and his face like lightning, his eyes like flaming torches, his arms and legs like the gleam of burnished bronze, and his voice like the sound of a multitude" (Dan. 10:5, 6). This is no ordinary being, not even an angel. The angel Gabriel appears to Daniel later in this chapter, and two other angels appear standing on each side of the river according to chapter 12, but this majestic being outshone them all by far. The prophet tells us of the majesty and glory of the being he saw. He mentions the radiance of His clothes and His body. Then he speaks of His face, His eyes, and His extremities. All over, He was bright and glorious. This is the numinous resplendent effulgence of the personal being of God. We have a hard time finding words to describe this, and so did Daniel. That is why he compared these features to various bright features of nature.

Daniel called this a vision, but he used a particular Hebrew word that refers especially to the appearance of a personal being, in contrast to a symbolic vision such as in Daniel 7 and 8. This could also be called a theophany, a personal appearance of God. At the end of his earthly ministry as a prophet of God, Daniel meets personally the Lord whom he had been serving for all this time. That personal presence of God brought assurance to the prophet. It assured him that his work for God had been accepted and that God was still working on behalf of His people.

Solomon had said at the dedication of the temple that regardless of how great and glorious any earthly temple might be, it was not adequate to contain the great God (2 Chron. 6:18). So it was in Daniel's time. Whether the temple was rebuilt now or later, God was still with His people—and He was still with His prophet. In this vision of God's presence, there was assurance for Daniel personally, and there was assurance for the people of God, that He would help them to overcome the obstacles in their way.

The Day of the Week

There are some clues in these verses that may make it possible for us to estimate rather precisely when this appearance of God came to Daniel. He says that he had been mourning and fasting for three "full" weeks and that then God appeared to him on the twenty-fourth day of the first month—Nisan (10:4). Given the close proximity of these statements, the implication is that the twenty-fourth day of the first month took place immediately at the end of the three weeks of fasting. The original language uses an idiom here to indicate that the weeks were "full." Full weeks come to an end after seven days; they end on Sabbath, the seventh day. Since this vision appeared to Daniel at the end of three full weeks, it must also have come to him on a Sabbath day. That means that this final prophecy of the book of Daniel was most likely given on a Sabbath. This is the only vision in the book that we can date with such precision.

In this regard, there is a rather direct parallel between Daniel and John, who was the recipient of the visions of the book of Revelation. John says he received his vision on the "Lord's day" (Rev. 1:10). As we know from both the Old Testament and the New Testament, the day that the Lord has claimed as His special possession is the Sabbath (Isa. 58:13; Mark 2:28). Thus Daniel received his final prophecy on the Sabbath, and John received the visions of his book on that day too. Both of these men were elderly at the time. Daniel had been in Babylonian captivity for seventy years and was nearing ninety years of age at the time. John received his vision in A.D.96 and had not seen Jesus personally for almost seventy years. We do not know John's precise age, but if he became a disciple of Jesus at about the same age as Daniel when he was carried into exile, then the two men would be approximately the same age at the time they received their visions.

Likewise, both were exiles at the time they received their visions. Daniel was in Babylon, and John was imprisoned on the island of Patmos "because of the word of God and the testimony of Jesus" (Rev. 1:9). Their visions were also of the same character. Both contain a special type of prophecy that is known as apocalyptic. These prophecies narrate history down to its end and the setting up of the kingdom of God.

A comparison can also be made between the form God's appearance took in both Daniel 10 and in Revelation 1. John saw Jesus Christ standing among the lampstands of the sanctuary, dressed like a priest, but also exhibiting the radiance and the glory of the person of God. When one looks elsewhere in the Bible for a further explanation of the appearance of God described in Daniel 10, two texts stand out: Revelation 1 and Ezekiel 1. Ezekiel, like John, saw a similar being with many of the same features. Of this view of God Ezekiel said, "This was the appearance of the likeness of the glory of the Lord" (Eze. 1:28).

To Ezekiel and Daniel, the experience was the same. Ezekiel wrote, "When I saw it [the vision of God], I fell facedown, and I heard the voice of one speaking" (vs. 28). Daniel, too, was overcome in a similar way. He fell into a deep sleep with his face to the ground (Dan. 10:9).

The Angel

The angel Gabriel touched Daniel to restore his strength so that he could receive the prophecy the angel desired to give him. This gave him enough strength to get up on his hands and knees, and then slowly and laboriously he rose to a fully erect stance, even though he was still trembling from the experience (10:10).

This should give us a sense of the might, majesty, and glory of God. There are two contrasting elements in religion that teach us how we should approach God and how we should view Him. These two elements are transcendence and immanence. The transcendence of God says that He is great and mighty and glorious and that He runs the universe from His throne. The immanence of God tells us that He is our friend who has come down to dwell beside us. How can both of these views be true? How can the great majestic God of the universe also stoop low to become our personal friend? That is the great tension of religion, a tension that was ultimately resolved in the Incarnation. Jesus came to live alongside us with His divinity shielded from us by His humanity. Thus the great God of the universe becomes our personal friend in Jesus Christ, and in that capacity He has a tender, loving concern for us. That is part of what the vision of God/Jesus in Ezekiel 1, Daniel 10, and Revelation 1 tells us.

Gabriel we have seen before. He appeared to Daniel to give him the prophecy of 9:24-27. He also appeared to Daniel at the time of the vision of 8:1-12 in order to give to him the interpretation of that symbolic vision. Gabriel is mentioned there as the one whom Daniel had seen "in the earlier vision" (9:21), thus connecting the two prophecies of chapters 8 and 9. Likewise, chapters 10 and 11 are connected to chapters 8 and 9 by Daniel's statement that after receiving the explanation given in chapter 11, he had understanding of the previous vision (10:1). Although Gabriel is not named in chapter 10 or 11, his position next to Michael makes him the logical candidate for the angel that brought this message to the prophet (10:13, 20). Thus these three prophecies are tied together by their common presenter and interpreter, Gabriel. He appeared after the symbolic vision of chapter 8 to explain it to Daniel, and he appeared to present the prophecies of chapters 9 and 11 without any immediately preceding vision. One could almost refer to chapters 8–12 as the book of the Revelations of Gabriel, just as the Apocalypse is referred to as the book of the Revelation of Jesus Christ. We find Gabriel again in the New Testament. He not only gave the prophecy of chapter 9, he also came to announce the completion of one of its major segments when he announced the forthcoming birth of the forerunner of Jesus, John the Baptist (Luke 1:1, 19).

Divine Intervention in Human Affairs

We already know there was a problem over which Daniel was mourning and fasting. It has been suggested that the problem concerning him was the rebuilding of the temple, which had stopped due to the intervention of the Samaritans. Daniel had been fasting and mourning for three weeks. If God's earthly servant was so concerned about this turn of events, why wasn't God Himself doing something about it? He was, and Gabriel tells us so. During the same three-week period during which Daniel had been mourning and fasting, Gabriel and his superior, Michael the archangel, had been wrestling with the prince of Persia (10:12, 13). Thus the prince of Persia must have had something to do with causing the problem.

Most commentaries view the prince of Persia in Daniel 10 as the symbol of an evil angel who works as a national genius or a supervising spirit for Persia. Thus the good angels, Michael and Gabriel, are pitted against him as they battle over the fate of God's people. But neither Satan nor any of his angels were a prince in the kingdom of Persia. Since the chapter names the *king* of Persia, we can readily identify who the *prince* of Persia was at this time. The prince of Persia would be Cambyses, the son of king Cyrus. When Cyrus died, Cambyses succeeded to the throne. Before that, he was the crown prince. Logically, he should be the prince of Persia mentioned in Daniel 10.

Why would Cambyses be mentioned here in Daniel 10? For two main reasons: (1) because of his political influence and power as prince; and (2) because he was very much in opposition to all foreign religious cults. As crown prince, Cambyses was very much involved in the affairs of the province of Babylon. Cyrus even elevated him to the rank of co-king or co-regent for one year, just as Nabonidus had done with Belshazzar for a longer period of time. Cambyses was an ardent Zoroastrian who worshiped the god Ahura Mazda. He had no tolerance for the cults of other gods. Historians have told us that he even destroyed the temples of some of those foreign gods, especially in Egypt. It undoubtedly was no accident that the Jews accomplished nothing toward rebuilding the temple in Jerusalem throughout the reign of Cambyses II (530-522 B.C.). The neglect shown to the temple during that period would certainly be consonant with the policy of Cambyses. Even before his sole reign, Cambyses was of great influence in the province of Babylon, to which Syria and Judah belonged. These provinces were known as Babylon and Beyond the River, meaning the Trans-Euphrates region. Not until the reorganization of the political structure of the empire by Darius I were Syria and Judah split off from the province of Babylon.

Thus if some counselors hired by the Samaritans came to Babylon and encountered Cambyses, he probably would have been happy to oblige them in their request. The Jews were not able to rebuild the temple in Jerusalem through the remainder of Cyrus's reign and during all the reign of Cambyses. Not until a new king, Darius I, came on the scene of action with a new policy were the Jews able to get something done about rebuilding the temple (Ezra 4:5).

Behind the scene of action, however, unseen forces were at work. The powers of heaven were being brought to bear upon the stubborn Persian prince as the angels of God worked to bring about His will. Despite heavenly efforts, however, the choice still resides with man, and as far as we can tell, Cambyses never did yield to these influences. It should also be noted that he came to a sad end, a probable suicide on his way back to Persia from Egypt. He fell upon his sword and died from the wound. Some said it was an accident, while others said it was a suicide. In either event, Cambyses came to a sad end, and part of that sad picture includes his evident opposition to the true God of the Jews.

Michael

Gabriel assures Daniel that the forces of heaven have not yet given up their struggle for the people of God. After leaving Daniel, he would return to continue his struggle with the prince of Persia. He would be supported in this effort by Michael (10:20, 21). Michael is called "one of the chief princes," "your prince," and "the great prince who protects your people" (10:13, 21; 12:1). He is the heavenly prince in contrast to the earthly prince Cambyses. The Old Testament does not tell us everything there is to know about Michael. In order to fill out the picture, we need to go to Jude 9 in the New Testament where Michael is identified as the archangel with the power of the resurrection and to Revelation 12:7 where we find that he was leader of the heavenly host against Satan and his rebel forces in heaven before the creation of man. Clearly, these two New Testament texts can be referring only to Jesus Christ. Therefore, we can safely assume that the Old Testament references to Michael should be understood as referring to Christ also.

Michael is mentioned by name only in Daniel 10 and 12. In Daniel 10, He is involved in a local, limited problem. In Daniel 12, He is involved, as we will see, in a final and universal conflict, the conclusion of the battle between good and evil. Wherever found, all the Michael passages in the Bible have this characteristic: they involve conflict, and Michael is portrayed as the leader in the battle on the side of God. Thus the pictures of Michael in Daniel 10 and 12 make a kind of envelope around the prophecy of chapter 11. Michael is introduced in chapter 10 in connection with the controversy taking place in the prophet's own time (10:13, 21). The final picture of Michael appears at the end of time in the final controversy (12:1). In all of these cases, He protects the people of God. So He did in the sixth century B.C., and so He will do at the end of time.

From the controversy swirling around Michael versus Cambyses, Gabriel goes on to carry Daniel through the prophetic future down to the time when Michael will appear on the scene of action one final time as the plan of salvation draws to its close and Michael takes His people home. That prophetic future narrated by Gabriel is the subject of Daniel 11.

■ Getting Into the Word

Daniel 11:1-22

Read Daniel 11:1-22 through two times. Then work your way through the following exercises:

1. Compare 11:2-4 with 8:3-8, 20-22. In your Daniel note-book, list all the similarities you find between the two passages, including similarities in wording.
2. List each of the symbols in 11:2-4, and attempt to identify them historically based on your previous study of Daniel 8.
3. Daniel 11:5 begins an extensive discussion of the king of the south and the king of the north. According to this chapter, where did these kings come from? What relationship might they sustain to the four winds of 11:4 and the parallel mention of four horns in 8:8, 22? Given the fact that Daniel is thinking of Jerusalem when he mentions the kings of the north and south, what powers or geographic regions might he be referring to?
4. Compare 11:16-22 (especially verses 16 and 22) with 8:9 and 8:23-25. In two columns, list all the similarities you can find between these two passages. What is the "Beautiful Land"? Who is the "prince of the covenant"? Also compare 11:16 with 2:40 and 7:7, 23. What similarities do you find? Next, compare 11:22 with 9:25-27, and list all the similarities you can find. Given your knowledge of Daniel 2, 7, 8, and 9, what is the power being discussed in 11:16-22?

■ Exploring the Word

Daniel 11:1-22

Daniel 11 has been a difficult chapter for interpreters to understand. There is a great amount of detail given, and it can become easy to miss the forest for the trees. In the following section, we will be looking at "the king of the south" and "the king of the north." We will be examining the history of the Persian and Greek kings following the time of Daniel. Chapter 11 brings to view a great many historical details. But all these serve merely to set the stage for the prophecy's overall purpose, which is to carry the action down through the future until the time when Michael will appear on the scene one final time to bring the plan of salvation to a close and take His people home.

Despite its mass of historical detail for the centuries between Daniel's day and the coming of the Messiah, the prophecy of chapter 11, like that of chapters 8 and 9, is concerned with the outworking of the great plan of salvation and the eternal fate of God's people. As such, it is closely linked to the great outline prophecy of chapters 8 and 9 and amplifies that prophecy further as is shown by the following chart:

The Relationship of Daniel 11 to Daniel 8 and 9			
Daniel 11		Daniel 8, 9	
11:2	The kingdom of Persia	8:20	The ram of Persia
11:2	The kingdom of Greece	8:21	The goat of Greece
11:3	A might king appears in Greece	8:21	The large horn as the first king of Greece = Alexander the Great
11:4	The four winds = the scattering of the empire of the great king	8:22	The four kingdoms that rise out of the large horn of Greece
11:16	The Beautiful Land is conquered	8:9	Pagan Rome conquers the the Beautiful Land of Israel
11:22	Prince of the covenant will be destroyed	9:25	Pagan Rome cuts off the Anointed One at Calvary

Persia, Daniel 11:2

Daniel 11:2 refers to three Persian kings who were to "appear," followed by a fourth king. Since Cyrus was on the throne when Gabriel gave Daniel this prophecy, we should begin counting with his son Cambyses as the first of the three. Before leaving for Egypt, Cambyses assassinated his brother Smerdis. But while Cambyses was away, Bardiyya, an imposter, took the throne claiming to be Smerdis. Cambyses was on his way back from Egypt to rectify this situation when he died. After a short time, Darius I Hystaspes took the throne following his military conquest of the rebels against the central government, including the false Smerdis. Darius was not in line for the throne, but he secured that position by means of his military conquests. Thus the three Persian kings who would "appear" (11:2) were Cambyses, the false Smerdis, and Darius I Hystaspes.

The fourth king who followed these three was especially significant; the prophecy says he "will be far richer than all the others. When he has gained power by his wealth, he will stir up everyone against the kingdom of Greece" (11:2). This wealthy king was Xerxes, the Persian king described in the book of Esther. Xerxes was the second of the Persian kings to stir up Greece by invading it; Darius had been the first. Xerxes invaded Greece in 480 B.C. Greece did not retaliate for more than a century, but the Greeks never forgot the humiliation the Persians had visited upon their country. When finally they did come to redress those wrongs, it was in direct response to what the Persians had done to them so many years before. The Greek retaliation took place under Alexander the Great.

Some students of Daniel 11 have said that the author did not know his Persian history well, because he did not go on to enumerate and characterize the Persian kings after Xerxes. This observation misses the point. The purpose of the prophecy was not to give a thorough survey of Persian history, but to trace it to the point at which the next power was introduced on the scene of action. Since Xerxes was the one who eventually brought the Greeks into the realm of Near Eastern politics, there was no need for the prophecy to recite more of Persian history after that point. The prophecy then shifted to the new power on the scene of action in order to trace the rise and fall of these kings and their kingdoms.

Greece, Daniel 11:3, 4

The first king to arise after Greece came on the scene of action is described as a mighty king "who will rule with great power and do as he pleases" (vs. 3). The text does not say so directly, but the clear implication is that this new and powerful king obtained his power and kingdom from his defeat of the Persian kings before him. This king obviously was Alexander the Great. There is a direct linguistic link between Daniel 8:8, 21 and Daniel 11:4 in terms of Alexander's fate; the same Hebrew verb is used in all three verses to express how he was to be "broken." Daniel 11 adds the detail that his kingdom would not go to his direct posterity. This was fulfilled in the life and death of Alexander the Great. He had one young son at the time of his death, but this son did not inherit any part of his father's empire.

Instead, his kingdom was to be divided, "to the four winds of heaven," or to the four directions of the compass. This is the same language used in Daniel 8:8, referring to the breakup of Alexander's empire into the four horns, or kingdoms, that his generals came to control. These divisions have already been discussed in the commentary on chapters 7 and 8, where they were also represented by the four heads and wings on the leopard (7:6) and by the four horns on the head of the goat (8:8, 22). (See the map on page 95.) This is another marker point at which the prophecies of Daniel intersect, and this juncture serves as one of the landmarks as we progress through the complicated political succession of Daniel 11.

Historical Kings of North and South, Daniel 11:5-15

From the standpoint of the Jews living in Judah, the most important divisions of the Greek Empire were Syria, including the province of Babylon, which lay immediately to their north, and Egypt, which lay to their south. These dynasties were known as the Ptolemies in Egypt and the Seleucids in Syria, based on the names of their first rulers, Ptolemy I and Seleucus I respectively (see the map on page 183). During this period, the Jews were first under the control of the Ptolemies and then came under the control of the Seleucids. Finally, as a result of a war of independence, the Jews had their own kings, known as the Maccabean kings of the Hasmonean house. The history of this intertestamental period, as described down to Daniel 11:13, can be followed without great difficulty in history books which cover that period. It can be outlined briefly as follows. (At this point it would be well for the reader to review Daniel 11:5-15 carefully.)

Verse 5 begins with the first prominent king of the south, or Egypt, who may be identified as Ptolemy I Soter. His commander, who came into a kingdom greater than his, may be identified as Seleucus I Nicator. This commander had had to flee from Syria to Egypt, but eventually he was able to win these Syrian lands back from Antigonus, the ruler of Syria. "After some years" (vs. 6), by 250 B.C., the king of the south, Ptolemy II Philadelphus and the king of the north at that time, Antiochus II Theos, formed an alliance, cemented by the diplomatic marriage of Bernice to Antiochus. When Ptolemy died, however, this arrangement fell apart, and Laodice, the former wife of Antiochus, was able to engineer the deaths of Antiochus, Bernice, and Bernice's son (vs. 6).

To avenge the death of Bernice and her son, "one from her family line" (vs. 7), Ptolemy III Euergetes, came against the north and even captured its capital (vs. 7). For a time he controlled much of the territory of the king of the north in Syria, but he later relinquished it and returned to Egypt, carrying away from there much booty and even some of the gods of the Syrians. This is simply an extension of human politics into the realm of the gods, for this indicated that the gods of Egypt had prevailed over the gods of Syria (vs. 8). Ptolemy III returned to Egypt and did not attack the king of the north again for some time (vs. 8b). Then Seleucus II attacked him in retaliation but was not successful (vs. 9).

The sons of the king of the north referred to at the beginning of verse 10 were Seleucus III Ceraunus and Antiochus III Magnus. The former was a short-reigned king (226 B.C. to 223 B.C.), but the latter was a ruler of great importance, hence the significance of his name, Magnus, or "Great." He reigned from 223 B.C. to 187 B.C. The reign of Antiochus III may be divided into unequal thirds. The first third was demarcated by the disastrous battle of Raphia on the border between Egypt and Palestine where he was defeated by Ptolemy IV Philopater of Egypt (vs. 11). From that defeat Antiochus III turned his attention to the east where he attempted to win back possessions of the Seleucid kingdom that had been lost. In this he was largely successful. Following that success, he turned again to the problem of Egypt, and this time he had more success than he did

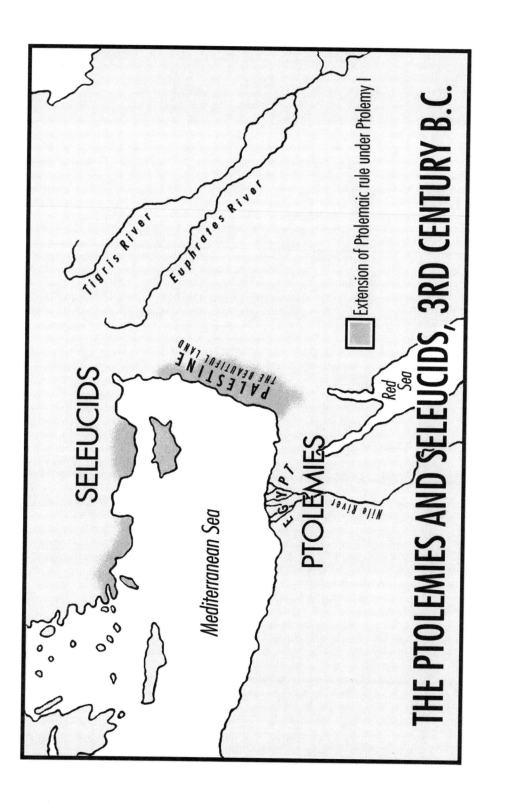

THE PTOLEMIES AND SELEUCIDS, 3RD CENTURY B.C.

SELEUCIDS

PTOLEMIES

Mediterranean Sea

Tigris River

Euphrates River

PALESTINE
THE BEAUTIFUL LAND

EGYPT

Nile River

Red Sea

Extension of Ptolemaic rule under Ptolemy I

in his first encounter (vs. 13). At the battle of Panaeus, in 198 B.C., and as a result of the follow-up from it, the province of Judea came into his hands. Thus the territory of the Jews changed hands, and they were transferred from being vassals of the king of the south to being vassals of the king of the north.

Up to this point, the time of Antiochus III (verse 13), almost all commentators agree upon the identifications of the various kings of the north and the south. The question is: What happened after the time of Antiochus III?

Futurist interpreters take everything from verse 13 to verse 35 as referring to Antiochus IV Epiphanes, whereas preterist interpreters apply everything from this point to the end of the chapter to Antiochus IV. The position of this volume is that only verses 14b and 15 refer to Antiochus IV Epiphanes. Since he was responsible for introducing Rome onto the scene of action in the Middle East, he makes an appropriate transition point to Rome, just as Xerxes made an appropriate transition point to Greece.

By applying only verses 14b and 15 to Antiochus IV Epiphanes, we whittle him down to his proper historical size. He was, after all, only a minor king who ruled a minor kingdom only a short time (175 B.C. to 163 B.C.). He did behave badly toward the Jews in Judea, but the major turning point in his reign was when he had to cave in to diplomatic pressure from Rome. Rome was already the major power on the horizon in the Middle East in the time of Antiochus Epiphanes, and he knew better than to try to thwart its designs. It required only a single Roman ambassador, not an army, to turn back Antiochus Epiphanes from his second invasion of Egypt in 168 B.C.

The first part of verse 14 refers to those who rise up against the king of the south. This could include quite a number of players. First, there was Antiochus III and his Syrian troops. Then there were his confederates. Antiochus III entered into a secret alliance with Philip V of Macedonia to divide up the Ptolemaic possessions outside Egypt. Philip, unfortunately, fell afoul of the Romans and suffered a defeat at their hands in the Second Macedonian War (200 B.C. to 196 B.C.). In spite of his alliance with Philip, Antiochus III declined to oppose the Romans on this occasion. One can also see verse 14a as referring to those Egyptians who rebelled against Ptolomy V in Egypt. These events are recorded in Polybius's work (*The Histories*, 5.107). Last, but not necessarily least, the "many" of verse 14a could include the Jews, previously under Ptolemaic control until delivered from it by Antiochus III. At the time, after having been under Ptolemaic control for more than a century, it must have seemed like a great deliverance. As a token of this promise of a new day, Antiochus III granted special rights to the Jewish religious state of Judea. But this promise soon failed, and the Jews became confirmed antagonists of Antiochus III. So there were indeed many who rose up against the king of the south at this time as Daniel 11:14a records.

What does the rest of this verse mean? This has been a difficult problem in interpretation for a long time. Literally the text reads, "and the sons of the breakers of your people shall be lifted up, bear, be carried. . . ." The first of these two verbs means "to break in" or "to break out" as in breaching a wall. The second verb normally means "to lift up," "to bear," or "carry away." Combining these meanings should result in the sentence saying something like, "the sons of the breakers of your people were taken away." This meaning would be parallel to verse 12 which says, "the army is carried off," and uses the same verb. But who is verse 14 referring to as being taken away? Who are "the sons of the breakers of your people"? It was the Egyptians. As a result of their defeat at the battle of Paneas (198 B.C.), the Egyptians were removed and taken out of the picture as far as Judea or southern Syria were concerned. Thus the phrase in verse 14 should be translated, rather literally, as "the sons of the breakers of your people were taken away [or, will be taken away, in the future prophetic sense]." It means that the Syrians took the Egyptians away by defeating them and thus the oppressors of God's people in Judea were removed.

The final phrase of verse 14 is an interesting one, for it refers to the fulfilling of a vision. Commentators have had considerable difficulty understanding what this phrase means, but if one considers the historical and political changes that took place in Judea at this time, a more direct answer can be determined. When the Syrians defeated the Egyptians at Paneas, the Egyptian horn of the four Greek horns (Dan. 8:7) had been taken out of the way, as far as Judea was concerned. It was replaced by the Syrian horn. Unfortunately for the Jews, that Syrian horn power, soon to be led by Antiochus IV Epiphanes, made life difficult for them by persecuting them.

The persecution by Antiochus IV against the Jews has been seen by many interpreters as constituting the fulfillment of a major portion of the rest of Daniel 11. However, the prophetic statement in verse 14 should caution us against this interpretation; it implies these people—the Syrians under Antiochus IV—will be "without success." No, Antiochus is not the fulfillment of this prophecy. We will have to look for another fulfillment by a greater power on the horizon at that time. We will have to look to Rome.

Daniel 11:15 tells of a campaign against the king of the south conducted by the king of the north. The focus of this campaign centered around a well-fortified city. Various cities and various campaigns of the Seleucid kings have been suggested as the interpretation of these elements, but given the succession of events at this point in the prophecy, the campaign that fits best is Antiochus IV's campaign of 169 B.C. against Egypt. The focus of that campaign centered around the target city of Pelusium, the major city guarding the entrance into the eastern delta of Egypt. Pelusium fell to the troops of Antiochus IV during the campaign, and thus he conquered the eastern half of the delta. Then he returned to Syria for the winter of 169/168 B.C. That was a major error in strategy, and it led to the introduction of the next power in the prophecy.

Imperial Rome, Daniel 11:16-22

Daniel 11:16 introduces a new actor to the scene of action. He is not referred to either as the king of the south or the king of the north, but as "he who comes" (or "the invader" in the NIV). Since Antiochus IV was victorious at the end of verse 15, it seems logical that he should be the one against whom this new power fights. At this point we find the king of the north does not appear again in chapter 11 until verse 40. He disappears from the narrative when this new power is introduced. The king of the north, the Syrian Seleucid king, recedes, and this new power (Rome) takes over.

Emphasizing the fact that this is a new power appearing upon the scene of action, the text says that he "will do as he pleases" (vs. 16). This is a technical phrase used in introducing new powers to the attention of the prophecy. It was used for Greece in verse 3, and now it is used in verse 16 for Rome, the power which came to Antiochus IV Epiphanes and deterred him from his Egyptian conquests. The third important phrase in verse 16 in connection with this new power is the reference to the "Beautiful Land." This power will stand in it, and all of it will be in his hand. This has no conceivable application to Antiochus IV, because Judea was already part of his kingdom when he inherited it from his father. It was not necessary for him to conquer it. Rome, on the other hand, took Judea over by conquest. When Rome conquered Syria in 64 B.C., it included Judea in its conquests. As has already been pointed out, this is a cross-link with the prophecy in Daniel 8, where, in verse 9, the "Beautiful Land" (*sebi*) crops up in terms of the conquests of the little horn.

The other interesting linguistic aspect of verse 16 is the way in which the verse refers to the confrontation between Antiochus IV and Rome. When battles and war are referred to in Daniel 11, the preposition '*al*, "against," is commonly used. But not in this case. Thus the NIV translation, "no one will be able to stand against him," is not entirely accurate. The preposition used in the original Hebrew of this verse is '*el*, "to," or "unto." In other words, when the Roman diplomat came to confront Antiochus IV upon his return to Egypt, he did not come with all of the forces of Rome to back him up. It was a diplomatic mission, one that was successful because of the implied threat of bringing down upon Antiochus IV all the power of Rome. But in terms of the meeting, Rome only came "unto" him, not "against" him.

It is open to question whether verse 16 refers to Rome in general or to a specific Roman general who accomplished these actions. Certainly Pompey and his forces were the ones who stood up with strength in the "Beautiful Land," subjugating it in 63 B.C. On the other hand, in Daniel 8, the little horn is not so much indicative of a specific ruler as it is of a political power including all its rulers. If verse 16 is taken as an introduction of the new power as a whole, then the following verses can be understood as elaborating the fates of individual rulers. That seems to be the course the text follows.

Dealing now with an individual ruler, Daniel 11:17 says "he will determine to come with the might of his entire kingdom." Here is a description of further movement beyond Judea, a campaign to another country. The coming of Rome in verse 17 is not to Judea; that is already described in verse 16. Rome had already conquered the northland; now it continued on to the south, to Egypt. Egypt was not formally incorporated into the Roman Empire until Octavian's success there in 30 B.C., but Julius Caesar entered Egypt and influenced its affairs earlier, in 48 B.C. It is interesting to note that he entered Egypt in pursuit of Pompey, who was killed there by an officer of Ptolemy. If verse 16 is referring to Pompey, who had caused Rome to establish itself in the "Beautiful Land" (11:16) and who had led the action against Egypt, then the next figure on the scene of action is Julius Caesar.

Julius Caesar, then, appears to fit best with verses 17-19. If the first phrase of verse 17 really has to do with bringing terms of peace or arranging an alliance, then Julius was certainly responsible for that. It was through his political and military maneuvers that he propped up the rulership of Cleopatra and Ptolemy XIV. Literally, the next phrase of verse 17 reads, "and he shall give the daughter of women to him to spoil [ruin, corrupt] her, but she shall not stand and she shall not be[long] to him." This fits well with the notorious dalliance between Caesar and Cleopatra. She apparently bore him a child, Caesarian, and followed him to Rome as his consort. Since Caesar was assassinated shortly after that, however, Cleopatra had to flee back to Egypt to protect her throne. For a time she was partly successful, but when Octavian arrived on the scene of action in Egypt, she is supposed to have died by the bite of a poisonous asp. In this sense she did not stand, that is, continue to rule, nor did she belong to Caesar except for a brief time.

Just as "he" (the invader of verse 16) turned his face toward Egypt at the beginning of verse 17, so now at the beginning of verse 18 he turned his face to the *'iyyim*. This word can be translated as "islands" or "coastlands." Coastlands makes better sense here. Julius Caesar conducted three campaigns after he left Egypt—to the Bosporus, to North Africa, and to Spain. The first two, definitely, and the third, probably, can be considered as coastlands to which he turned his face; that is, his military attention. Then came his final denouement, at the hands of his trusted friends and aides. The text appears to refer to this as turning "his insolence back on him" (vs. 18). Caesar's downfall in his last year of rule came about through his increasingly monarchical and dictatorial style of government. He set himself up for his final fall, however, by pardoning, reinstating, and installing in office the very supposed friends who eventually assassinated him on the ides of March 44 B.C. A word play is present here. The word for "abuse," "scorn," "insolence," *herpa*, parallels the word for "dagger" or "sword," *hereb*, the instrument which Caeser's friends turned upon him so viciously. His literal and figurative fall and death are described at the end of verse 19.

Verse 20 gives two characteristics of the person who was to arise in Caesar's place. First, he would send tax collectors throughout the kingdom, and second, he would die in a time of peace, not in battle, even though he had fought many battles earlier in his career. Both of these facets of the career of this figure were fulfilled in the life of Caesar Augustus. He is noted for his census taking in Egypt and elsewhere throughout the kingdom, and these census rolls served as a tax base. The taxation system installed under his administration is well represented by the publicans in the New Testament. Jesus came to be born in Bethlehem as the result of an enrollment by Augustus (Luke 2:1). Augustus died of an illness on August 19, A.D.14, thus fulfilling the latter specification of this portion of the prophecy.

The person who succeeded Augustus was Tiberius, and verse 21 of the prophecy pays attention to the way he gained access to rulership, placing a low evaluation upon him. Tiberius was not the natural born child of Augustus. The son of Livia by a priest also named Tiberius, he came into Augustus' household when Augustus took his mother as his wife by force. According to Roman historians, Tiberius became quite sadistic. Although we cannot completely trust the historians of Rome in his case, there obviously is considerable merit to the evaluation given of Tiberius here in this prophecy. Augustus did not like him or even want him as his successor, but lacking any other logical choice, he had to put up with the idea.

In terms of war, mentioned at the beginning of verse 22, Tiberius was charged especially with taking revenge upon Arminius in Germany, who had wiped out three legions of Roman soldiers. Tiberius was wholly successful in defeating him. He engaged in other occasional wars and acts of savage repression. Included in the latter was his putting down of a provincial rebellion with considerable bloodshed. The prophecy speaks of armies being swept away before him (vs. 22), and this fits Tiberius, but there were many other rulers of ancient times to whom this statement could apply with equal force. The next statement in verse 22, however, is specifically an act of Tiberius.

Daniel 11:22b says "a prince of the covenant" would also be broken before the ruler referred to in this verse. This phrase, "prince of the covenant," is quite specific in its links with Daniel 9:24-27. In other places in the book of Daniel, the word employed for "prince" is *sar*. Here in Daniel 11:22, however, the word used is *nagid*. This word is used only one other place in the book of Daniel—9:24-27. On a linguistic basis, therefore, these two prophecies should be tied together at this point. In 9:24-27 it is also the Messiah Prince (*nagid*, "ruler" in NIV) who makes a strong covenant with many for one week. Hence the "prince" and the "covenant" are linked in both of these prophecies.

Both the historicist and futurist approaches to 9:24-27 see the Messiah Prince mentioned in verse 25 as none other than Jesus Christ. Identifying Jesus as the Messiah Prince of 9:24-27 means that when we come to this time in the prophecy, we have come to the time of Jesus of Nazareth as the fulfillment of those aspects of that prophecy. This gives us a chronological linchpin upon which to hang verse 22 in the narrative of Daniel 11. By the time we reach this point in 11, we have reached the first century A.D., and the events described here should surround that point.

■ Applying the Word

Daniel 10:1–11:22

1. **In 10:2, 3 we find Daniel mourning and fasting, apparently in a state of prayer as he seeks the meaning of God's message to him. How do I relate to times of trouble or need?**

How should I relate to them?

2. What can I learn about God's care for Daniel in chapter 10 that I can apply to my own life?

3. Daniel 11:2-22 displays God's intricate knowledge of history that was still future when the prophecy was given to Daniel. In what ways can a knowledge of God's understanding of the future strengthen my personal faith?

■ Researching the Word

1. Compare Daniel's reaction to his encounter with God in 10:4-9 with the encounters of such men as Isaiah (chapter 6), Ezekiel (chapters 1, 2), and Jeremiah (chapter 1). How was Daniel's reaction like theirs? How did it differ?

2. Daniel 10:1 mentions the third year of Cyrus. This is the last indication in Daniel of a specific time in which a vision was given. Go back to Daniel 1, and list each of the specific dates Daniel gives (according to the reigns of various monarchs). How do these help us trace Daniel's ministry across history? List each date and the verse in which it is found. In a third column, list the B.C. date for each of Daniel's dates. *The Seventh-day Adventist Bible Commentary* on each verse will be of help in establishing these dates. What can you learn from this exercise?

■ Further Study of the Word

1. See the list at the end of chapter 12.

CHAPTER TWELVE

Daniel's Final Message— Part 2

Daniel 11:23–12:13

Let's summarize what we learned in the preceding chapter as we examined Daniel 10:1–11:22. We said that chapter 10 comprises the introduction to that prophecy and involves the appearance of God and a conversation with an angel, probably Gabriel, to confirm the truth of this prophecy. In chapter 11, the angel messenger began to recite the prophetic history of kings and nations that were to follow after Daniel's time. That prophecy began with the kings of Persia (11:2) and then moved on to Alexander the Great of Greece (11:2). After Alexander died, his kingdom broke up into four main pieces (11:4). Daniel 8 refers to all four of these divisions of Alexander's kingdom through the symbol of four horns (8:8, 22). Daniel 11, however, concentrates especially on only two of these four. Those two are "the king of the north," whose royal residence was at Antioch in Syria (11:6), and "the king of the south," who came from Egypt (11:5). Since Judea was sandwiched between these two powers, it was passed back and forth between them. Eventually, this situation was brought to an end by Rome, which defeated both Syria and Egypt, conquering Judea at the same time that it conquered Syria (11:16). Thus Rome came to be in power in Judea in the first century A.D. when Jesus of Nazareth, "prince of the covenant," was broken, or executed, on the cross by the Roman power (11:22).

At this point in the prophecy, verse 23 takes up with a new phase of the power of Rome. That is where our study in this chapter begins.

193

■ Getting Into the Word

Daniel 11:23-45

Read Daniel 10–12 again for perspective. Then go back and read 11:23-45 more carefully before answering the following questions:

1. With these verses, we come to one of the most detailed and difficult portions of prophetic Scripture. But even though the prophetic history is complicated by the mass of details, there are at least two touch points that enable us to place the detail within the flow of history. The first is in 11:31-37. Compare those verses with 7:8-11 and 7:20-26. List the similarities between these two passages in two columns in your Daniel notebook. Then do the same, comparing Daniel 11:31-37 with the description of the same power in Daniel 8:10-12.
2. The second touchstone in 11:23-45 is found in verses 40-45 (especially verses 40 and 45). How does the information in verses 40 and 45 fit into the flow of prophetic history as described in Daniel 7?

■ Exploring the Word

Verse 23 marks a transition in the prophecy of chapter 11. Verses 1-22 have carried the action down from the time of Daniel himself to the coming of the Messiah, the "prince of the covenant." Although these verses contain a vast amount of historical detail, the interpretation is often problematical. If anything, the detail and the interpretive difficulties increase in the second section of chapter 11, verses 23-45.

In spite of these problems, however, the underlying purpose and intent of the prophecy in verses 1-22 is evident. In the first section, the action between the king of the north and the king of the south has much to do with the affairs of God's people; the struggle is essentially a spiritual one which culminates with the appearance of the Messiah and His confirming the covenant with many by His death.

Likewise, the second section of the prophecy (vss. 23-45), although framed in terms of conflicting kingdoms, concerns the spiritual struggles between God's people and His truth on the one hand, and on the other, the persecuting power that seeks to obscure God's sanctuary in heaven and the salvation that is being ministered there for us by our faithful High Priest, Jesus Christ. As we look at the details, we need to also keep in mind the grand sweep of salvation history that lies behind them.

Papal Rome, Daniel 11:23-39

By 11:22 the prophecy has reached the time of Jesus Christ under Imperial Rome in the first century A.D. The question is: Where does the prophecy go from there? It could continue with Imperial Rome for a further stretch of history. That is the way Uriah Smith treated the text in his Adventist classic, *Thoughts on Daniel*. For Smith, verses 23-30 repeated the history of the same three Caesars. Such a repetition is possibly in line with Hebrew parallelism of thought, but it is not very likely that such a repetition would occur in a consecutive, historically prophetic narrative text such as we have here in Daniel 11.

Or the text, beginning in verse 23, might skip down to the time of the Roman conquest of Jerusalem in A.D. 70, but there does not appear to be much reference to such a war and siege in these verses. The time of Constantine would make another major historical transition, with the conversion of the Roman Empire to Christianity, but Constantine does not appear to fit well in this passage either.

Having eliminated these important historical events as subjects of the prophecy in the rest of chapter 11, we are left with the time of papal Rome's rise in the sixth century A.D. If this is the subject of these verses, then the prophecy would bring us to the next segment of history that we have seen in other prophecies in Daniel—the rise of Rome's second phase, which is medieval, papal Rome as contrasted with Imperial Rome. In that case, Daniel 11 would parallel what we have found in chapters 7 and 8. Based on this understanding, this volume takes the position that Daniel 11:23-30 is dealing with the activities of Rome's second phase, papal Rome, and that the "king of the north" in these verses refers to this power.

Secular and church historians have noted that this transition from Imperial to papal Rome took place in the sixth century A.D. That was a time of the decline of the glory of Imperial Rome, but it was also a time for the rise of the power of the church as it filled the vacuum left behind by that decline. The power base of the empire had shifted to Constantinople in the east, leaving the church largely in charge in the west.

Verses 23-39 do not necessarily present the activities of the papal power in chronologically consecutive order. Rather, in this case, they are apparently arranged in topical order. The elements present in verses 23-39 can be outlined in the following fashion.

1.   Verses 23-30   actual military campaigning
2.   Verse 30   subversion of the system of salvation
3.   Verses 32-34   persecution
4.   Verses 35-39   self-exaltation

The last three of these elements are also described in Daniel 8 in terms of the activities of the little horn. The comparison may be drawn in this way:

Event	Daniel 7	Daniel 8	Daniel 11
Taking away the Daily (chap.8) Abolish the Daily (chap. 11)	---	Dan. 8:11	Dan. 11:31
persecution	Dan. 7:25	Dan. 8:10b	Dan. 11:32-34
self-exaltation	Dan. 7:8, 20, 25a	Dan. 8:10a	Dan. 11:35-39

All three chapters mention persecution and self-exaltation, but only chapters 8 and 11 mention taking away the daily. Daniel 11 also contains one element in this outline of activities—the actual military campaigning—that is not present in chapter 8. Daniel 8:9 does mention military campaigns, but these refer to the conquests of *Imperial* Rome to the east, south, and the glorious land—not to military activity by the *papal* phase of Rome. The military campaigns found in Daniel 8:9 find their corresponding parallel in 11:16, which portrays the activity of the troops of the Roman general Pompey standing in the glorious land of Judea and its capital of Jerusalem.

The Crusades (11:23-30)

Daniel 11:23-30 deals with another type of military campaign. These campaigns are conducted by the papacy, which is represented in 11:23-30 as the king of the north or in chapter 8 as the second phase of the little horn. This activity by Rome in its papal phase resembles what Imperial Rome did earlier under Pompey and Julius Caesar. But these campaigns do not take place in the sixth century A.D., the time when Rome was in the early phase of rising up from littleness. The campaigns pictured in 11:23-30 occurred considerably later when Rome had moved into its papal phase.

The classic example of this type of military activity as conducted by the papacy were the Crusades of the eleventh to the thirteenth centuries. At this time, more than at any other time in history, the papacy, the king of the north, became directly involved in warfare. This warfare was designed to win back the holy places for Christianity, but in doing so, the crusaders brought down upon themselves the wrath of Egypt, the king of the south. The last battle of the First Crusade involved forces from Egypt, and the last battle of the last Crusade involved an unsuccessful invasion of Egypt.

This pattern fits what is described in 11:23-30. The forces of the king of the north make their conquests first, and then the forces of the king of the south come on the scene of action. That is exactly what happened during the First Crusade in the eleventh century A.D. Then the last Crusade involved an actual invasion of Egypt by sea, but the forces from the north were defeated. That is also just what chapter 11 says in verses 29, 30.

Daniel 11:40-45 is the most difficult passage to interpret *prophetically* because its events still lie in the future, but 11:23-30 is the most difficult passage to interpret *historically* in terms of events that now lie in the past. It is difficult to be definite about the interpretation of 11:23-30, and we should keep this difficulty in mind when studying this passage. There are at least five different possible interpretations for these verses. For the present, we will proceed with the working hypothesis that 11:23-30 describes the Crusades carried out at the behest of the papal power in the eleventh to the thirteenth centuries. As we do so, let's see how well the historical details of those events match what is described prophetically in these verses.

There is quite a gap between the death of Jesus Christ, described in 11:22 to the time of the Crusades 1,000 years later, described in verse 23. While this gap is large, we have already seen that gaps exist in the course of the prophecy of Daniel 11. From the time of Xerxes, the last Persian king mentioned in verse 2, until the time of Alexander, the first Greek king mentioned in verse 3, a century and a half elapsed, and the prophecy makes no attempt to fill in that gap by mentioning the other later Persian kings. It simply goes from one significant figure to the next which appears on the scene of action. The same is true in 11:22, 23. It was Jesus, brought to view in verse 22 as the "prince of the covenant," who created the church that came to be the papal power referred to in verse 23. It was that church's attempt to conquer back the holy places connected with Jesus that led to the Crusades that are described beginning in verse 23.

This new section of chapter 11 (verses 23-30) begins with the making of an "agreement" or covenant (vs. 23). This is not the new covenant in Jesus' blood, for this covenant was created in deceit, according to verse 23.

"With only a few people [literally, 'a small people'] he will rise to power" (vs. 23). This could refer to the numbers of the crusaders in relation to the hordes of Islam they faced in the Middle East. Or it could refer, even more classically, to the Children's Crusade of A.D.1217-1221. "The richest provinces" (vs. 24) that are invaded by this military movement fits well as the glorious or "Beautiful Land" referred to in verse 16. Thus verse 24 would refer to the land of Judea. Verse 24 also says that this power "will achieve what neither his fathers nor his forefathers did." This does not fit very well with Imperial Rome, for each of the Caesars (Julius, Augustus, Tiberius) could only say that he was doing what his fathers had done before him. In the case of the papacy, however, the call for the Crusades was a call for something entirely new in the history of that institution. The world had never seen anything like it before.

The text of verse 24 talks about this power distributing plunder, loot, and wealth among his followers. While this could be said of many armies in many times, it was especially true of the Crusades. The motivation behind the Crusades was twofold: to obtain spiritual benefits and to obtain wealth. Knights who participated in the Crusades commonly were those who had not inherited land in Europe because they were not the eldest in their families. The Crusades were a route to riches in a way that was not an option open to them at home.

The last phrase of verse 24 requires a different translation from that given by the NIV—"he will plot the overthrow of fortresses." The phrase begins with the preposition '*al*, followed by the plural noun for "fortresses." Translators have commonly interpreted this phrase as referring to military attacks upon fortresses, but there is no verb here for such attacks. Instead, the verb which follows, in a dual emphatic form, is the verb which means "to think," "to consider," "to give attention to." In other words, these forces are going to give thought or attention to fortresses—their own fortresses! When one visits Israel and Jordan today, one can see the results of that thought. The crusader castles and fortresses that were constructed for defensive purposes during the twelfth and thirteenth centuries still dot the land. They are some of the most remarkable archaeological remains still present in the Holy Land. Some of them are in a good state of preservation. In the twentieth century, the British used the crusader fortress at Akko as a jail for political prisoners during the days of the Palestine mandate (1918 to 1948)! Verse 24 concludes by stating that this attention to and construction of fortresses would last only for a time. The crusaders' occupation of the Holy Land lasted less than two centuries, and now these fortresses stand as monuments to a long-gone era.

It is only after these initial successes that the king of the south mounts his forces and comes against the forces from the north (11:25b). The last battle of the First Crusade was fought against forces that came out of Egypt to meet the crusaders after they had conquered Jerusalem. That battle took place at Ascalon on the southwestern coast of Palestine (see 11:26). The situation is well described in the following quote from a history of the Crusades:

> On 12 August 1099 battle was joined on level ground near the Egyptian harbour-fortress of Ascalon. The Egyptians were taken by surprise while still in their camp and were completely defeated. Their commander, the vizier al-Afdal (1094-1121) fled back to Egypt. On 13 August the victorious army returned in triumph to Jerusalem. The success of the crusade was now assured. The regaining of the Holy Land was an astonishing achievement. The rejoicing in Christendom was fully justified (H. E. Mayer, 57).

Verse 27 says that two kings will sit at the same table and lie to each other, their hearts bent upon evil. In the light of this verse, it is interesting to note the political jockeying that took place after the fall of Jerusalem. The question was: Who would be king of the new crusader state there? In both the secular and the sacred realm, there was infighting. In the secular struggle, there were two candidates for king—Raymond and Godfrey. Godfrey finally obtained the job of ruler (without the title of "king") by trickery. In the sacred realm, there was also a dispute to decide who would be the patriarch of Jerusalem. Arnulf from Normandy was finally given the job, even though he was not qualified for it because he was illegitimate and not even a subdeacon. He soon solidified his position as leader of the church, however, by finding a relic—the true cross! Then there was also the question of the relationship between these two "rulers" in their dual realms of church and state.

Daniel 11:28 says that the king of the north was to return to his own country with great wealth and take action against the holy covenant. Of the crusader leaders in the First Crusade, four left for their homes in Europe, and only two remained with the minikingdom of Jerusalem. Three hundred knights and 3,000 foot soldiers remained in Jerusalem with Godfrey, while the majority returned to Europe with their leaders and their spoils. Papal control of the church in Jerusalem was evident from the fact that on three occasions the pope either suspended or deposed the patriarch there.

This was also the period in history when the papacy reached some of its greatest heights of power. As an example, Innocent III (1198-1216), having learned from the Crusades in the Middle East, next launched a Crusade against the heretical Albigenses in southern France in 1208. The fighting lasted until 1227 when Raymond of Toulouse signed the Peace of Paris in which he swore allegiance to the king and the church. Although the Albigenses were not orthodox Christians, this episode illustrates how the church dealt with dissenters.

Daniel 11:29, 30 tells of another campaign against the south by this power. According to the geographical designations employed in chapter 11 thus far, the south represents Egypt, thus we should expect a campaign directly against Egypt. In the First Crusade, the Egyptians came out of Egypt to do battle with the crusaders in Palestine (11:25b), but in the last Crusade, the ninth, the invasion took place by sea directly against Egypt. That action fits the description of verses 29, 30 when correctly understood.

The first part of verse 30 is commonly translated as the "ships of Chittim" (KJV) going *against* the king of the north. But that is not the preposition used in the original Hebrew text. When the Hebrew wants to say that one army is going *against* another, it uses the preposition '*al*. However, the text here uses *be* or *beth*, which means, "by," "in," "at," "with." Thus the ships of the Chittim, or western coastlands, did not come *against* the king of the north; they came "with" him; they were *his* ships. This is precisely the way the final Crusade attempted to invade Egypt. This Crusade was led by the devout French king Louis IX. He wintered at the end of 1248 on the island of Cyprus, but in the spring of 1249 he set sail for Egypt, invading it by the Damietta branch of the Nile. The major battle of the campaign was fought at Mansourah in the delta of Egypt in February of 1250. It was a major defeat for the crusader forces, and they had to retreat to Damietta where they surrendered to the Egyptians in April. Louis IX himself was taken prisoner and held for ransom. When he finally did leave Egypt, only 1,400 troops were left to go with him. He traveled first to Palestine but eventually returned to France where he still devoutly supported the papacy in spite of his defeat (Dan. 11:30b).

With this disaster, the last of the Crusades to the Middle East came to an end. The crusader states in Palestine lived on for a few more decades, but then they, too, were wiped out, and no more Crusades came to their aid. The French king felt that his defeat was a judgment from God. To attempt to make up for his failures, Louis tried one more campaign, this time to North Africa, not the Middle East. He invaded Tunisia in 1270, but this was an even bigger disaster than the previous defeat in Egypt. A plague struck the camp of the crusaders, and even the king died as a result. It was not an army that returned to France but a great funeral procession.

All of this crusader activity took place under the aegis of the papacy in Rome. Each Crusade was begun with a commission from the pope. Becoming a knight in the crusader army was known as "taking the cross." The ultimate aims of these Crusades were religious in nature and directed by the papacy. Soldiers could obtain indulgences by virtue of fighting in one of the Crusades. Daniel 11:23-28 gives a description of how this kind of activity began, and 11:29, 30 gives a description of how it ended. It was all under the direction of the second phase of the little horn of Daniel 8, known in this part of chapter 11 as "the king of the north."

Interestingly, this passage three times refers to time factors that seem to have been involved in these activities. These time references are not specific as in other prophecies of Daniel; rather, they are general references to time. Verse 24 says that this power was to give attention to fortresses, but "only for a time." Verse 27 says that when the two kings plot at a table, it will be fruitless, but later "an end will still come at the appointed time." That time finally did come, according to verse 29, when "at the appointed time" the king of the north invaded the king of the south for the last time and was defeated. In addition to these three references to time, verse 23 implies a time element when it talks about the events that will come "after coming to an agreement [covenant] with him." That was the covenant, agreement, or decree which launched the first of these campaigns.

Basically, the Crusades lasted for a century and a half. The crusader forces captured Jerusalem in the summer of A.D. 1099 at the conclusion of the First Crusade, and the defeat suffered by the last Crusade in the delta of Egypt occurred during the winter of A.D. 1249/1250. From 1099 to 1249 is 150 years, or five months of prophetic time. This military activity had a beginning, a duration, and an end, as the language of this passage of Daniel 11 describes. The parallel with the fifth trumpet of the book of Revelation (9:1-11) is worth noting in that the locusts (soldiers) of that prophecy were to torment men for five months. Reckoning each day for a year, according to the prophetic rule, makes the duration of the fifth trumpet 150 years. The events described in Revelation 9:1-11 are historically similar to what Daniel 11:23-30 describes.

Desecration of God's Sanctuary (11:31)

The next action of the king of the north/little horn is its activity in relation to the sanctuary. "His armed forces will rise up to desecrate the temple fortress and will abolish the daily sacrifice" (vs. 31). The text does not give the location of this temple. In fact, there is some evidence that it is talking about another temple than God's temple, for it is called "the temple fortress," a word construction that is never used in the book of Daniel for the earthly temple in Jerusalem. The words imply something greater, grander, and stronger than the earthly temple. What temple is verse 31 referring to?

According to the vertical dimension employed by the prophecy of 8:11, the temple that was attacked by this power was the temple located in heaven. The direct language parallels between 8:11 and 11:31 indicate that the "temple fortress" of 11:31 is the strong heavenly temple. This is the object of attack by the little horn/king of the north power.

The NIV uses the English verb "desecrate" in this verse to describe the action of the forces of the king of the north (papal Rome). A better translation is that they "profaned" it (Hebrew *halal*). Desecration, defilement, or uncleanness comes about in a temple when unclean and impure objects are introduced into its precincts. On the other hand, one can *profane* a temple, or God's name, from a distance. One need not be bodily present in a temple to profane it.

Daniel 8:11 says that as a result of the actions of this little horn power, the heavenly temple was "cast down" (KJV) or "brought low" (NIV) to the earth (Hebrew *shalak*), meaning that the ministry of that temple was presented to the inhabitants of earth as under the control of an earthly power. But the heavenly temple did not come down to earth literally or physically; it was only made to appear cast down in the eyes of men. So, too, with the profanation of the temple carried out by this same power in 11:31. The papal power did not need to be literally and physically present in the heavenly temple in order to profane it. By the work that the papacy carried out here on earth, it brought about that profanation. The "daily" ministry, discussed earlier in our treatment of Daniel 8, was the property and activity of the Prince in the heavenly sanctuary. But now this earthly power claims to control that ministry and that its forces (a spiritual army known as a priesthood) can dispense the merits derived from it. This was how an earthly religious power substituted its activity for the work of Christ.

After obscuring the true "daily" ministry from the eyes of mankind, this power was to set something else up in its place. Something known as "the abomination of desolation" (11:31, KJV). What does this phrase mean?

In the Old Testament, an unauthorized intrusion into the literal temple area was considered to be an abomination which had to be cleansed by ritual. Likewise, the power of the state, either local or foreign, intruding into the realm of the sacred was an abomination that resulted in defilement. Thus the abomination that makes desolate may be described as a union of the secular and the religious—

the state and the church—in which the religious aspect is defiled by its merging with the functions of the state. In the history of Christendom, such a union came about as a result of state support for the church, a situation which led to the development of the medieval papacy. It was the church's use of state secular power that led to the Crusades as described above. It was also the church's use of state power that was involved earlier in the Arian wars of the sixth century, with the result that the Arian churches and peoples were brought under the control of the Roman Church. The same combined state-church power continued on into the Inquisition of later times. That brings us to the subject of persecution, the next topic on which the prophecy focuses.

Persecution of the Saints (11:32-34)

The third activity of the king of the north/little horn power mentioned in the prophecy is persecution. Persecution of the saints is mentioned in Daniel 11:32-34, the only place in chapter 11 where such a persecution is mentioned. Based on the amount of text devoted to the topic, the prophecy seems to anticipate that this persecution will be particularly severe. Jesus makes the same point in His description of it in Matthew 24:21, 22. This same persecution is brought to view in Daniel 12:7 where the prophet is told that it will last for "a time, times and half a time." The same time period with its accompanying persecution is also mentioned in 7:25. Thus all three of these texts, 7:25; 11:32-34; and 12:7, refer to the same great persecution carried out by the papal power during the Middle Ages. In our study of Daniel 7 (see pp. 140-142), we set the demarcating dates for this persecution at A.D. 538 and A.D. 1798. That same time span can be applied to 11:32-34 and to 12:7. Of course, the severity of this persecution waxed and waned throughout the period.

Self-exaltation (11:36-39)

Verses 36-39 constitute the final passage of this section of chapter 11 and the fourth activity of the king of the north/little horn power. In these verses this power expresses its dominion and authority in a final way by exalting itself. The opening sentences of verse 36 set the tone for this passage: "The king will do as he pleases. He will exalt and magnify himself above every god and will say unheard-of things against the God of gods."

We find here two charges against this power: (1) self-exaltation and (2) blasphemy. These charges correspond to the characteristics of the little horn as revealed in both Daniel 7 and 8. Daniel 8 specifically states that the little horn will exalt itself, and chapter 7 directly implies the same. Daniel 7 refers to the blasphemy that the little horn speaks as his "great words against the most High" (vs. 25, KJV). Speaking of its self-exaltation, chapter 8 states that the little horn "grew until it reached the host of the heavens," and it "set itself up to be as great as the Prince of the host" (vss. 10, 11).

The object of all this blasphemy and self-exaltation is clearly God. Not only does this power exalt itself over all the other gods, it sets itself up as a rival to the true God Himself. The word for "god" is rarely used in Daniel 11 because much of its description is couched in political and military terms. Occasionally there are references to the king of the north taking away the gods of the south, or vice versa, but these references are not common. Here in 11:36-39, however, the word or name for "god" is used nine times, showing the distinctly religious character of this power at this point and emphasizing the type of religious conflict into which it has entered by this time in the flow of history. Historically, all this rivalry against the God of heaven was manifested by the titles which this earthly power assumed and the claims that it made for itself. The power that this power claimed over earthly potentates was sometimes demonstrated by the humility it required of earthly rulers and the use it made of such threats as excommunication and the interdict. A famous example of this humbling of earthly powers is Gregory VII's action in forcing Henry IV of Germany to do penance by standing in the snow at Canossa, Italy, for three days in A.D. 1077 before he would give him a hearing. (For other examples of this power's claims and the titles it assumed, see the discussion of Daniel 7 in chapter 5 of *Daniel 1–7* in the Bible Amplifier series.)

This self-exaltation and blasphemy mark the fourth and final activity carried out by the power of papal Rome as described in this

chapter. These can be summarized as follows:
1. Vss. 23-30   Military activity; the Crusades
2. Vs. 31   Intervention in the heavenly ministry of Christ
3. Vss. 32-35   Persecution
4. Vss. 36-39   Self-exaltation and blasphemy against God

The self-exaltation of this power culminates and brings together all of its other activities. All that has gone before is ultimately an expression of self-exaltation. This attitude, expressed at the end of this passage, opens the way to the next section of the prophecy.

The Time of the End, Daniel 11:40-45

The next-to-the-last section of the prophecy of Daniel 10–12 begins with a statement about its location in time. Daniel 11:40a says that the events which follow will occur "at the time of the end." This point in the prophecy marks the transition from all that has gone on before, beginning in the prophet's own time down to this final section of history. The distinction between the time of the end and the end of time should be noted carefully. The "time of the end" is a period of time, a segment of history in which certain events will happen. Those events are narrated in the next five verses. The "end of time" is a point in time; it is the end of human history as we know it. That point comes at the end of this section.

Modern Equivalents for the Kings of the North and South
The prophecy declares that in the time of the end, yet another conflict will occur between the king of the north and the king of the south. We have now come to a point in history long after the Seleucids of Syria and the Ptolemies of Egypt have vanished from the scene of action. So we must be dealing with new powers that have taken their places. What are these new powers that make their appearance here?

Quite a number of possibilities have been suggested, but no final answer on this question has emerged. The question was debated hotly among the Adventist pioneers and by Adventist teachers in more modern times. Perhaps the best we can say is that since these events are still future, we will recognize them when they take place before our eyes.

The last actions of the king of the north/little horn power took place in 1798, when the papal power was temporarily deposed through the capture of the pope by General Berthier (see the discussion of Daniel 7 above). Therefore, it is reasonable to assume that the time of the end began at that point. In other words, we are now living in the time of the end. We have seen the historical fulfillment of all of Daniel 11 in the rise and fall of the nations from Daniel's day up to A.D.1798. From that point onward, we may expect the fulfillment of the events prophesied in 11:40-45. Since they have not been recognized yet, they must still lie in the future. We must await that future fulfillment to understand just how these details will work out. For the present, therefore, we must be content with some estimates of which powers are involved here and how their actions and fate will work out.

One major question to consider is how much continuity exists between this passage and what has gone on before. A direct continuity would suggest that the king of the north in this final passage is the same papal power that we have seen featured prominently in verses 23-39. If the connection is not quite so direct, then some other power could be involved. This volume takes the position that the connection between this final passage and the rest of the prophecy is quite direct. Therefore, we should identify the king of the north in verses 40-45 with the papal phase of Rome—the same power that has been the central focus of the preceding section of the prophecy.

The king of the south appears briefly at the beginning of this section but then takes a back seat as a more minor actor. Earlier in this chapter, the title, "king of the south," referred to Egypt from which the Ptolemies came. But here at the end of chapter 11, the identification seems to be more spiritual than political. Thus just as the king of the north has become the papacy and is no longer a territorial king in the literal sense in which chapter 11 presents him at its beginning, so the king of the south is also a spiritual entity here in these last verses of the chapter. Although in the twentieth century, the papacy does own a small piece of territory—Vatican City—its principal influence is spiritual. That comparison leads us to the conclusion that the king of the south should be seen here more as a philosophical force than a political or territorial power.

Thus we need to ask, What characteristic of ancient Egypt makes its reappearance here at the time of the end? One characteristic ancient Egypt demonstrated toward the people of God was to reject their God, Yahweh. "Who is the Lord, that I should obey him and let Israel go? I do not know the Lord and I will not let Israel go" Pharaoh declared (Exod. 5:2). In more modern times, this "Egyptian" attitude is expressed in rationalism which in the area of religion has led to atheism or agnosticism. There was a major eruption of this kind of thought in the French Revolution, right at the time when history came to the prophetic "time of the end" in 1798. The atheism expressed in Marxist Communism is a direct descendant of the philosophy developed at the time of the French Revolution. It is interesting to note in this setting that the book of Revelation, too, appears to make just such a connection with its symbols. Revelation 11 talks about the two witnesses of God—the Law and the Prophets, or the Old and the New Testaments—who prophesied throughout the long 1260 day-years period of the Middle Ages. Then at the end of that period, a new power was to arise that would put the witnesses to death, and their slaughtered bodies would lie in the streets of the city for three and a half day-years. This fits very well with the antibiblical actions and sentiments expressed at the height of the French Revolution (1789-1793) in which the Bible was rejected in favor of the goddess of reason. However, we need not limit our understanding of the king of the south in Daniel 11:40-45 to revolutionary France. It might rather be identified as rationalistic humanism—the major philosophical upheaval the French Revolution bequeathed to the modern world. That spirit has lived on in Communism and in many other aspects of modern society. And it has been in conflict with the church. Witness the fate of the Catholic Church in Communist countries, especially those behind the previously existing Iron Curtain. As a result, for a time the Soviet Union was the most popular nominee for the end-time king of the south.

But with the collapse of Communism, there has been waning support for that idea.

We need not see the king of the south in this passage as a literal, territorial France or Russia. Rather, we can view it as embodying the same ideas on the subject of religion as presented in the philosophy of those powers. Rationalistic humanism, leading to atheism or agnosticism, would fit well the actions and attitudes of the king of the south. Revelation 11:8 provides a figurative connection between these ancient and modern attitudes by stating that the bodies of the biblical witnesses would lie "in the street of the great city, which is figuratively called Sodom and Egypt, where also their Lord was crucified." Jesus was crucified again in the philosophical terms and religious expressions of this Egyptian-like ideology that has been perpetrated by revolutionary France and Russia.

In summary, the king of the north in the time of the end probably should be connected with the preceding dominant power in the prophecy—the papacy of the Middle Ages, now in its final phase. The king of the south, modeled upon the anti-Yahwistic attitudes of ancient Egypt, fits well with the modern movement of rationalistic humanism that leads to atheism or agnosticism. In the modern world, revolutionary France and the former Soviet Union have been the special propagators of those ideas. Even though the power and position of these nations have declined somewhat, the spirit of the age which they fostered persists in many places and continues to present a major challenge to the church.

The Historical Model of the End-time Struggle

It appears that Daniel 11:40-45 utilizes an actual historical incident in Persian history as a model, or type, for the spiritual battle between good and evil that will take place in the time of the end. The example comes from the Egyptian campaign of the Persian king Cambyses in 525 B.C. Invaders of Judah and Egypt from the north had to come through Syria, which lay to the north, and thus from Judah's viewpoint, conquerors from that direction ultimately came through Syria. In order to engage the king of the south in Egypt, "the king of the North will storm out against him with chariots and cavalry and a great fleet of ships" (vs. 40a). Cambyses was approaching Egypt by both sea and land, a course that is described in these words, "He will invade many countries and sweep through them like a flood" (vs. 40b). Among these countries would be Judah. "He will also invade the Beautiful Land" (vs. 41a).

Continuing his course southward toward Egypt, Cambyses bypassed Trans-Jordan and did not attack it as he passed through Judah. As Daniel 11:41b puts it: "Many countries will fall, but Edom, Moab, and the leaders of Ammon will be delivered from his hand." Cambyses did not bother with these nations as he traveled down the coastal road to the west.

Cambyses continued on his way to Egypt and conquered it. This victory is brought to view in verse 42: "He will extend his power over many countries; Egypt will not escape. He will gain control of the treasures of gold and silver and all the riches of Egypt." But Cambyses did not plan to stop with his conquest of Egypt, for the end of verse 43 says that he was going to obtain submission from the Libyans to the west of Egypt and the Nubians to the south of Egypt (the modern Sudan).

Having gone this far, however, he was to receive dire news from the rear—from the east and the north (vs. 44). This means that the news from the east had traveled west and then had been brought down through Syria and Palestine to reach the king while he was in Egypt. Although historians don't know what this news was, it clearly upset Cambyses greatly. He set out with his forces in great anger to rectify the situation (vs. 44). As he retraced his road north, he came through Judah again. While passing through that territory, he encamped on his way. The location is given as "between the seas toward the beautiful holy mountain" (vs. 45). He did not come up to the holy mountain, Mount Zion in Jerusalem; he only pitched his tents toward it. His actual campsite location was down on the coastal plain of Sharon "between the seas and the beautiful holy mountain." His target was not Jerusalem; he was intent on returning to the north where he had come from and from whence his bad news originated. But while encamped in Judea, he was to be overtaken by his end. It would come without human intervention. It was not to be brought about by battle, and no one could help him avert this personal tragedy (vs. 45).

While Cambyses was camped in the plain of Sharon, he died as the result of a self-inflicted wound, stabbing himself in the thigh with his sword. Among modern historians, interpretations of this event differ. Some say it was a suicide attempt; others say it was an accident. Whatever the cause, Cambyses died after twenty days, and none of the troops in his mighty army could help him. Paraphrasing the words of Daniel, he came to his end, but none could help him (vs. 45). The ancients saw this as a punishment from God. Cambyses was seen as a madman by the people of his time, and one of his more mad acts was to kill the sacred Apis bull when he entered Egypt by stabbing it in the thigh. Thus when he struck himself in the same location, whether by accident or intent, this was seen as retributive justice.

The End-time Struggle

Thus all the events described in Daniel 11:40-45 took place in a literal way in the life, experience, and death of Cambyses, the Persian king. But at this point in the course of the prophecy, we are not dealing any longer with ancient times. We are dealing here with "the time of the end" (11:40). The powers involved are no longer a literal Persian king and a literal king of Egypt. They have become symbols for the powers at the time of the end. Those powers we have identified as the papacy (the king of the north) and atheism (the king of the south). In some way, the religious power of the Roman Church will gain some sort of victory over the forces of atheism before the end of time (vs. 43). But while this power is enjoying the fruits of that short-lived victory, more serious challenges will arise in the east (vs. 44), for the kings of the east will march forth, according to the book of Revelation (16:12). The book of Revelation also speaks of that final spiritual battle in literal terms, locating it at Armageddon (16:16), or "the mount of Megiddo." Megiddo is also located between the seas and the glorious holy mountain. The papacy is one of the spiritual powers that will be involved in that final spiritual battle.

The plain of Sharon is located just south of Megiddo, and that plain leads up to the mountain range of Mount Carmel, which intersects Megiddo and the plain of Sharon. It was on that literal, geographical plain of Megiddo that Cambyses was encamped when he died. It was on the mount itself where, in earlier biblical times, the contest between the true God and the false gods of Baal took place (1 Kings 18). That kind of spiritual struggle will be repeated in modern times, but it will not be a literal, physical struggle upon that geographical mountain (vs. 45). That ancient contest symbolizes the final spiritual conflict that will take place on a worldwide basis. From this final battle, Christ and His heavenly army will emerge victorious. Satan and all his hosts will be defeated in this final great spiritual battle on earth. That battle is described in Revelation 19:11-21. Revelation 16 describes only the preparations for the battle of Armageddon. Revelation 19 describes the actual battle of the great day of God Almighty, and Christ wins! By borrowing from the ancient experience of Cambyses, the course of that battle has been described. This modern Cambyses will fail, too, just as the ancient one did. At this point, the powers of earth and their kingdoms will become the kingdoms of our God and of His Christ. This brings us to the last scene of this prophecy, the one that is found in the first four verses of Daniel 12.

■ Getting Into the Word

Daniel 12

Read chapter 12 through two times before answering the following questions:

1. **Using a concordance based on the King James Version, look up the phrase "stand up." How is that phrase used throughout the book of Daniel? What does it mean historically for Michael to "stand up" in light of the way that phrase is used throughout the book of Daniel? (We need to use the KJV here because the NIV is not consistent in its translation of**

this phrase.)

2. Describe Michael's function in this chapter. Compare and contrast that function with His role in chapter 10.

3. Daniel 12 contains some of the clearest references to the doctrine of resurrection in the Old Testament. List all the evidence you can find in this chapter for the idea of resurrection.

4. What is sealed in Daniel 12:4, 9? In its context, what does the phrase "many shall run to and fro, and knowledge shall be increased" mean in 12:4?

■ Exploring the Word

The End of Time (Dan. 12:1-4)

Daniel 12:1-4 actually comprises the end of the prophecy of chapter 11. The later addition of chapter divisions has made an awkward and unnecessary break here. This section is God's answer to what the king of the north does in the time of the end, as prophesied in Daniel 11:40-45. The phrase, "at that time" (12:1), connects chapter 12 to the last of the events narrated in the prophecy of chapter 11. When the king of the north comes to his end and no one is able to assist him, that is the time when Michael stands up.

As can be seen from various places in chapter 11, "to stand up," or "to arise," refers to taking up the kingship. The Hebrew verb used in Daniel 11:2, 3, 4, 7, 16, 20, 21 means "to stand up," "arise," or "appear," and in all these instances it refers to a new king coming on the scene of action at the time that he ascends to the throne and becomes the new ruler (see also Daniel 7:24; 8:23). That is what Michael, God's representative, now does. Thus in Daniel 12:1, Michael comes on the scene of action to assume rulership in answer to what has been done in the name of all the previous kings who have arisen in chapter 11. They were earthly rulers, but now the ruler from heaven will take over, and He will make up a very different type of kingdom, one that is ruled upon the principles of righteousness.

Michael is the "great prince" (12:1) who rules over all the heavenly host and who cares for God's earthly people. As we know from Jude 9 and Revelation 12:7, Michael is Christ. He appears in many places in the Bible, in both Old and New Testaments, with various titles that express His various functions in the plan of salvation. The name Michael is used particularly in situations where there is conflict over the people of God. Michael comes to fight for them and protect them and deliver them. That is also His function here in Daniel 12:1-4. Things are going to get worse before they become better. "There will be a time of distress such as has not happened from the beginning of nations until then" (12:1). As the great controversy between Christ and Satan comes to its conclusion, Satan will exert all possible force to divert and destroy the people of God, but he will not be successful. Michael, who fights for His people, will step in to deliver them. "At that time your people—everyone whose name is found written in the book—will be delivered" (12:1).

The reference to this heavenly book is interesting. When the judgment was taken up in Daniel 7, "the court was seated, and the books were opened" (vs. 10). The reference there is in the plural—books. Here (12:1) the reference is singular. The examination of the books in the judgment of Daniel 7 has led to the roster of the names present in the book brought to view in chapter 12. This book is none other than the book referred to in Revelation 17:8 and 21:27 as the Lamb's book of Life. God does know His people, and He looks out for them with tender regard. He will deliver them out of the troublous times to come.

Two groups of people are identified in 12:2—the righteous and the wicked. The righteous who sleep in the dust will be resurrected to everlasting life. The wicked will also be resurrected, but to everlasting contempt, not to everlasting life. When they are finally destroyed in the lake of fire described by Revelation 20:14, 15, it will be seen by all that their sentence and punishment were just (Phil. 2:10, 11). Seventh-day Adventists have taken Daniel 12:2 as reference to a special resurrection that will take place just before Jesus comes. This special resurrection has been suggested because of the wicked who come up at this time also. The general resurrection of the wicked comes at the end of the millennium (Rev. 20:5-10) rather than at the second advent. But there is a special class of wicked, identified as those who pierced Him (Rev. 1:7), who will arise just before the advent (Dan. 12:2). This will be a special group who have opposed Christ personally. Along with this special class of wicked are the special class of righteous who are resurrected at the same time. This will fulfill the special blessing pronounced upon those who have died during the giving of the three angels' messages (Rev. 14:13). So the resurrection promise of this prophecy can be taken in both a special sense and a general sense.

The results are also clear. They are stated in beautiful Hebrew poetic parallelism in Daniel 12:3: "Those who are wise will shine like the brightness of the heavens, and those who lead many to righteousness, like the stars for ever and ever."

The first line of this poetic couplet refers to the intensity with which the saints will be glorified. The second line refers to the duration for which they will radiate this glory—"for ever and ever." Earlier in the prophecy, there were those earthly powers that attempted to lead many away from the covenant and righteousness (Dan. 11:32-35), but now those who were working in the opposite direction will come to the fore, and their opponents will fade into insignificance. The book of Daniel never describes the future kingdom of God in detail, as does the book of Revelation (chapters 21, 22). Here, however, one gets some inkling of the glory that will overtake the saints of the Most High when they finally enter His long-promised and long-prophesied kingdom.

The ruler of this great future kingdom is identified as Michael, for he is the one who stands up to take the kingship of that kingdom (12:1). This symbolism can be compared with Daniel 7:13, 14 where the figure who takes the kingship of that future kingdom is "one like a son of man." In our discussion of that chapter, we identified the Son of man as Jesus Christ. The book of Revelation says that there will be two rulers in that future kingdom, for the Lord God Almighty will be seated upon the throne along with the Lamb (Rev. 22:3). God the Father and God the Son will both sit on the throne. Where does that leave Michael who stands up here to take the kingship? It makes him equal to the Son of man. The ruler of that future kingdom is the Son of man, and that Son of man is Michael, according to the parallelism in the book of Daniel.

That brings up the comparison between Michael in Daniel 10:13, 21, and Michael in 12:1. They are the same individual, and Michael acts in similar ways in these two narratives. But the two narratives are set at far different times. Daniel 10 is set in the local time of Persia and deals with a local problem for the people of God at the time of the prophet. In chapter 12, we see a view of Michael at the end of time and the part that He will play in those final events. His function is similar; He was struggling for and protecting the people of God back then, and He will do the same sort of thing for the people of God at the end of time. No wonder He is given kingship over the saints for eternity, for He has struggled with them and for them during their earthly pilgrimage here and now.

It is important to note at this point that 12:4 claims that the book of Daniel would be sealed "until the time of the end." We will return to that sealing and unsealing after our discussion of verses 5-12.

Epilogue: More Prophetic Time Periods and the Sealing of the Book

Daniel 12:5-13 is an epilogue, or an appendix, to the prophecy of 11:2–12:4. What we have here is the time calibration for the body of the prophecy that has gone on before. This is a common way Daniel treats this matter elsewhere in the book. For example, the time element in Daniel 7 does not come until verse 25, even though the description of the vision is complete by verse 14. The same thing occurs in chapter 8. The vision is complete by verse 12, but the conversation between the two angels regarding the time element of the 2300 days comes in verses 13 and 14. The same sort of thing takes place here in chapters 11 and 12. The body of the prophecy is given in chapter 11, but the times that go with those events are given in chapter 12. These times are also connected by the events they describe. They are not dating new events; they are dating events that have already been described in Daniel 11.

The Three and a Half Times (1260 Days)

The setting of Daniel 12 returns to that of chapter 10. Once again God Himself is seen over the river, and He is described in some of the same terms that are used of His appearance in 10:4, 5. In addition to "the man clothed in linen, who was above the waters of the river" in 12:7, there were also two angels standing by, one on each side of the river, according to verse 5. One of them asked the being above the river, "How long will it be before these astonishing things are fulfilled?" The answer came back to him in the form of a solemn oath, for He lifted His two hands toward heaven and swore by the name of God that it would be "a time, times and half a time. When the power of the holy people has been finally broken, all these things will be fulfilled." This breaking of the power of the holy people refers to a time of persecution, and it must have been a prolonged and intense time of persecution to have worked this result. The only time of persecution that is described in any detail in the preceding chapter is the one given in 11:32-35. These three and a half times must, therefore, be connected with that persecution. The same three and a half times are also mentioned in 7:25 where they are also connected with persecution. We have a parallel equation, therefore:

Daniel 7:25   =   Daniel 11:32-35   =   Daniel 12:7

3 1/2 times of persecution = a time of intense persecution = 3 1/2 times of persecution

Daniel 11 helps us place that persecution in its historical setting. In the flow of events in chapter 11, persecution comes during what is known as the Middle Ages of the Christian Era. The three and one-half times are using time symbols in which each "time" equals a year (Dan. 4:16, 23, 25, 32; Rev. 12:6, 14; 13:5). Each prophetic year contains 360 days, having been rounded off from the irregular lunar calendar year of the Jews. Thus the book of Revelation equates the three and a half times (Rev. 12:14) with 1260 days (12:6) or forty-two months (13:5). In apocalyptic prophecies, a day of symbolic, prophetic time equals a historical year (Eze. 4:6; Num. 14:34). That means we are dealing with a historical period of 1260 years here in

Daniel 12:7. In our earlier discussion of chapter 7, we dated that period from A.D.538, when the city of Rome and the bishop of Rome were freed from pagan interference, to A.D.1798 when the bishop of Rome was deposed by the forces of France. That prophetic period is reconfirmed here in this final chapter of Daniel, so that it stands as a prophetic landmark, both in this book and also in Revelation where it is reused.

There is also an indication in Daniel 11 as to when, in general, this prophetic time period was to occur. In that chapter, the "time of the end" does not begin until verse 40. Thus, the persecution of verses 32-35 must occur before the time of the end. That locates it right in the heart of the Middle Ages, which is where this persecution, dated from 538 to A.D.1798, occurred.

The 1290 Days

The second time period mentioned in Daniel 12 is found in verse 11: "From the time that the daily sacrifice is abolished and the abomination that causes desolation is set up, there will be 1,290 days." Thus we have progressed mathematically from the 1260 days to the 1290 days. The events of this time period are also described in 11:31. Once again, therefore, we have the event described in chapter 11 and the date that is given to it presented in chapter 12. The events described in both 11:31 and 12:11 include the taking away of the "daily" (Hebrew, *tamid*) and the setting up of the "abomination that causes desolation." The same power is in view here that was present in the previously described episode of persecution. The little horn, the persecuting power of 7:25 and 8:10, reappears in chapter 11 under the title of the king of the north. In all these verses, the same power is brought to view, doing the same work.

How should the 1290 days be marked off? Because of the nature of the events that occurred in A.D.1798 when the papacy, the little horn, received its temporary "deadly wound" (Rev. 13:3, KJV) and was removed from the scene of action for a time, that date must mark the end of the 1290 days as well as of the 1260 days. It was at this time that the Medieval substitution for Christ's heavenly ministry received a serious blow through the papacy's temporary loss of power and prestige. Thus, we must extend the 1290 days backward from that date so that the 1290 days commence thirty day-years prior to the beginning of the 1260 days. A.D. 538 minus thirty years takes us to the date of A.D. 508. What significant event occurred at that time to mark the beginning of the 1290 day-years?

In Europe, one of the major events that year was the conclusion of the war between Clovis, king of the Franks (later France), and the Visigoths, whom he defeated and pushed into Spain. Clovis' other conquests covered the two previous decades, with the defeat of the Visigoths being the last of these. Then Clovis was baptized and like Constantine, he marched his troops down to the river and through the river and had the bishop pronounce them Christians. These wars of Clovis also had religious overtones, because some of the powers defeated, like the Visigoths, were Arian Christians. The Arians believed that Christ was a created being, and this view was anathema to the bishop in Rome. Thus when Clovis and the Franks defeated the Arian Visigoths and drove them into Spain, it was also a theological victory for the bishop in Rome. The relationship was cemented by the baptism of Clovis and his troops. In that way Clovis became, as it were, a new Constantine.

Two major elements come together here: (1) the blending of the political arm of the state and the religious arm of the church, and (2) the use of the arms of the state to accomplish the ends of the church. With the defeat of the Visigoths as heretical Arian Christians, the church came to use the military power of the state to enforce its dogma. In this connection, the three horns which the papal little horn plucked from the head of the beast representing Imperial Rome (Dan. 7:8) can be seen as the following three powers: the Vandals in 534, the Visigoths in 508, and the Ostrogoths in 538. These were victories for the Frankish and Roman emperors, but they were also theological victories for the bishop of Rome. The first of these horns was plucked up in 508 at the beginning of the 1290 days; the last of the three was plucked up in 538 at the beginning of the 1260 days.

Thus the setting up of the abomination of desolation of Daniel 12:11 can be seen as the union of church and state and what the church set out to accomplish through the power of the state. This had the effect of eclipsing the true ministry of Christ as our High Priest in the heavenly sanctuary (cf. 11:31; 8:11-13). The eyes of humanity had been turned from heaven to earth to focus upon an earthly religious power that now stood in place of the great High Priest in heaven. For that reason, titles such as "Vicar of the Son of God" that had been assumed by this earthly power take on great theological importance; they have obscured the truth about the plan of salvation carried on in the heavenly sanctuary. In this way the "daily," the continual heavenly ministry of Christ, was taken away by being put out of mankind's view by this earthly religious power after its consolidation of power in A.D. 508.

But this deflection of the view of mankind from the true heavenly Priest was not to last forever. It was to come to an end after 1290 years as predicted by the time prophecy in 12:11. The date for that transition came to pass with the deposing of the pope by the French troops in Rome in February of 1798. It is interesting to see in this connection that the same power that started this process of the 1290 days, the Franks, was also the power (France) that brought that process to an end at the close of the 1290 day-years. When France descended into the revolution in 1789, the papacy lost its major supporter in Europe. Not long afterward, this former supporter turned upon the institution that it had formerly supported and brought it to a temporary end.

The 1335 Days

The last time period of Daniel 12—the 1335 days in verse 12—belongs to a different realm. This time period is not related to the work of the little horn. The little horn had brought about persecution and an obscuring of the heavenly ministry of Christ, but the 1335 days have a different point of reference. A blessing is pronounced upon the persons who came to the end of this prophetic time period. This is a work of a different sort, the work of God, for He is the one who gives such blessings to mankind. What blessing was this, and when did it take place or begin?

Since we have a succession of prophetic time periods in this chapter, the 1260 days (three and a half times), the 1290 days, and the

1335 days, it is logical to view their beginning points as related to each other. The 1260 days began in A.D. 538. The beginning of the 1290 days extends thirty years prior to that time, to A.D. 508. Since the next time period to appear is the 1335 days, it is logical to correlate its beginning date with commencement of the previous time prophecy in A.D. 508. If we add the 1335 day-years to A.D. 508, we come to the year 1843. In early Adventist writings, this date was taken to represent the time of the Millerite preaching when those giving this message announced that the end of the 2300 day-years of Daniel 8:14 would come in 1843/1844 and eventually settled on October 22, 1844, as the date of fulfillment. Here in 12:12 we have a prophetic time period that came to an end in 1843. Thus the two events were very close in time.

As a matter of fact, these two prophetic time periods overlap. The last year of the 2300-year prophecy of 8:14 extended from the fall of 1843 to the fall of 1844, according to the Jewish fall-to-fall calendar, which the Jews utilized for their chronological reckoning. But we have calculated the 1260 and 1290 day-years according to the Roman calendar because that was the power that exercised dominion and authority at that time. These Roman years (Julian-Gregorian) begin in January and extend until December. This means that the last four months (October to December) of the 1335th year overlapped the first four months of the Jewish calendar that year. In other words, these two prophetic time periods end very closely together, within the same twelve-month period—the twelve months leading up to October 22, 1844. This is another way of saying that the 1335 days actually take us to the end of the 2300 days and that they should be seen as overlapping or coinciding with the 2300 days in coming to that final ending point. The great event taking place at that time was the judgment that began in heaven (Dan. 7:9, 10; 8:14a, see especially the commentary above on 8:14). According to this interpretation, the blessing then comes upon those who come to that important event in the history of salvation.

A similar blessing is found at a similar point in time in the book of Revelation. "Then I heard a voice from heaven say, 'Write: Blessed are the dead who die in the Lord from now on' " (Revelation 14:13).

The context of this blessing should be noted. It is preceded immediately by the three angels' messages. We know that these are end-time messages because they result in the second coming of Christ in Revelation 14:14-18. The first of these three end-time messages announces the judgment of God (Rev. 14:6, 7). That was the judgment that began at the end of the 2300 days according to Daniel 8:14. Daniel 12:12 pronounces a blessing upon the persons who come to that great event, and Revelation 14:13 pronounces a blessing upon the people who live and die for God during the time of that judgment. The two blessings of these two books are related to each other and are historically continuous with each other. The ultimate blessing that God's people will receive has already been described by Daniel 12:1-3; it is deliverance from the troubles of the end time by Michael and an abundant and glorious entrance into His kingdom thereafter.

Concluding Remarks

Before mentioning the final fate of Daniel in the last verse in the book, some mention of the fate of the book itself should be made. Daniel 12:4 gives final instructions to Daniel regarding the prophecy of chapter 11. Daniel is told to seal up the book until the time of the end. Thus there was a special sense in which the content of this book was not to be known or made clear until a considerable amount of time had passed from Daniel's own day. L. E. Froom's study of historical interpretations of Daniel and Revelation, *The Prophetic Faith of Our Fathers*, notes that the individual prophecies of the book of Daniel were not well understood until the time of their fulfillment had come. Thus Daniel 9 pointing to the Messiah was the first of the prophecies to be understood. However, it was not until the Middle Ages and the Reformation that the other prophecies of the book came to be understood better. The final phase of this intense study of Daniel's book came in the late eighteenth century and the first half of the nineteenth century when the fulfillment of the 1260 days came to its completion with the fall of the papacy in 1798. This event also marked the beginning of the "time of the end" in Daniel.

It was also in this period that the end of the 2300-day prophecy was noted by the Millerite movement and other students of Daniel's writings.

In the wake of the French Revolution (which looked like the beginning of the end of the world to many people), the first half of the nineteenth century was a time of intense study of the prophecies. The Albury Park Conference in England in 1826 marked one high point of that interest. The Millerite camp meetings of North America focused intensively upon those same apocalyptic prophecies of Daniel and Revelation. They were seen as having almost reached their final end. In that sense, the book of Daniel was unsealed at that very time, in the time of the end (12:4). Bits and pieces of the puzzle had been put together before, but now the prophecies of Daniel stood forth in their resplendent glory as a revelation of the foreknowledge of the true God reaching down to the time of the end.

The book closes with the promise to Daniel that he will be among those to arise at the last day to receive his part in the inheritance of God's people (12:13). That is a blessed promise that is offered to all who give their allegiance to Michael, the Son of man, God's Christ.

■ Applying the Word

Daniel 11:23–12:13

1. What do I find threatening in 12:1-4? What do I find encouraging? Why?
2. Keeping the entire book of Daniel in mind, what history and promises do I find helpful that will sustain me through the "time of trouble, such as never was since there was a nation" (KJV) "until the end of time" (NIV)?
3. In what ways has my study of the book of Daniel helped the book become "unsealed" in my mind? What steps can I take to further that process?
4. "How long?" (12:6) is the cry of Daniel's heart throughout

much of this book. It has been the great cry of hearts down through history. Is that the cry of my heart today? In what ways has my study of Daniel helped me to better understand and participate in that heart cry?

■ Researching the Word

1. Using any and all Bible study aids at your disposal, discover as much as you can about the rising or resurrection of the dead in the Old Testament. Then do the same for the New Testament. Why do you think the New Testament is clearer on this topic than the Old? How do these facts help you understand the progressive aspect of God's revelation of truth?
2. Compare 11:40-45 with the seven last plagues of Revelation 16. What correlations can you find?

■ Further Study of the Word

1. For various Adventist interpretations of Daniel 11, see U. Smith, *Thoughts on Daniel*; C. M. Maxwell, *God Cares*, vol. 1; and F. D. Nichol, ed., *Seventh-day Adventist Bible Commentary*, vol. 4.
2. For historical background on the Crusades, see H. E. Mayer, *The Crusades*.
3. For historical background on the rise of the Frankish kingdom, see Edward James, *The Franks*, especially 80-125 on Clovis.
4. For a helpful discussion on the "time of trouble" referred to in 12:1, see E. G. White, *The Great Controversy*, 613-633.
5. A helpful discussion of the Bible's teaching on the resurrection is found in S. H. Horn, et al., *Seventh-day Adventist Dictionary*, 911, 912.

CHAPTER THIRTEEN

Daniel's
Walk With God

Our study of the book of Daniel has taken us through a considerable amount of history and prophecy—often intertwined. We have looked at the history in which Daniel participated or in which he observed in the sixth century B.C. We have also looked at prophecies that started in his time and have reached from that day down to our time—and beyond.

But there is another side to the book of Daniel and his experiences that are recorded there—the personal spiritual side. What was Daniel's own spiritual relationship with God? We know that it was strong and solid, or God would not have chosen him to be a prophet. But can we say anything more about it than that? Is there anything we can learn from Daniel's own personal spiritual walk with God? I would suggest there is. When we study the progression of the revelations about God in the book and in Daniel's experience, we can see a gradual unfolding of God's purpose for the prophet. That progression in revelation and spiritual experience provides a model for our own walk with God.

■ Getting Into the Word

As you examine each of the following questions, reread the chapter(s) involved, looking for hints regarding Daniel's progressive relationship with God. Make notes in your Daniel notebook on what you find.

1. What evidence is there in chapter 1 regarding the relation-

ship between Daniel and his God? From Daniel's point of view? From God's point of view? Would you say this was an open and demonstrative relationship, or was it still undisclosed at this point in time? Give reasons for your answer.

2. According to chapter 2, how did the revelation of prophecy come? What part did Daniel play in this? What does this say about his relationship with God?

3. Compare the way in which the revelation of God came in chapter 2 with the way it came in chapter 4. What differences/similarities are there in the part Daniel played in each of the experiences?

4. Chronologically, God's revelation and relationship to Daniel in chapters 7 and 8 came before those of chapters 5 and 6. How do we know this? How did God manifest Himself to Daniel on each of these occasions?

5. In what way(s) does the mode of revelation differ in Daniel 7, 8, and 9? Is there a progression here? If so, what is it?

6. How is the final prophecy of the book of Daniel (chapters 10 to 12) introduced? What does this demonstrate about Daniel's relationship with God? How does this series of the manifestations of God progress through the book, and how does it climax?

■ Exploring the Word

Daniel 1

It must have been quite dreary trudging more than four hundred miles on foot from Jerusalem to Babylon as prisoners of Nebuchadnezzar's troops. There must have been many times along the way that Daniel and his friends asked, "Where is God in all of this? Why did this happen to us?" It would have been easy to have become discouraged and demoralized, but they didn't yield to this temptation. Even after they arrived in Babylon and were enrolled in school there, they were still willing to stand up for truth and the true God. They were still willing to make their faith manifest, regardless of the consequences. In all this, however, God was hidden from them. They did not have any direct visions or dreams at this time to encourage them along the way during their captivity and their studies in Babylon. Nevertheless, God was still with them, even though He was unseen. Three times in Daniel 1 the text says that Daniel and his companions were blessed. God blessed them with favor in the sight of the Babylonian officials who were attending them, and thus they were able to obtain the diet they preferred (vs. 9). This resulted in their appearing and performing in a manner superior to their fellow students. (Incidentally, do you think Daniel and his three friends were the only Hebrew captives enrolled in this school?)

God also blessed them with knowledge and understanding in all the material they studied (vs. 17). Finally, God gave them grace to demonstrate these qualities when they stood before the king (vs. 18). Even though God did not give them a direct revelation during this period, He still was with them, though hidden.

Daniel 2

The first major revelation of the book came during the events described in chapter 2. This revelation, however, was not given directly to Daniel or his friends. It was given to Nebuchadnezzar, the pagan king whom they served. This made matters difficult for Daniel and his friends. By now they had come to be classified with the wise men of Babylon, and since these wise men had failed to provide either the dream or its interpretation to the king, the lives of Daniel and his friends were threatened along with the other wise men. The four Hebrews went to God in prayer, and what an earnest prayer meeting it must have been! Seldom have we had to pray as if our lives depended upon it. God was gracious and gave to Daniel just the knowledge the king wanted. He and his friends and all the wise men of Babylon were saved. It should be noted here, however, that when the revelations of the book of Daniel began, the first was given directly to the king. Daniel served as the inspired wise man who interpreted the dream for the king through God's aid. As far as Daniel was concerned, the revelation was indirect. God did give him the knowledge to interpret the dream, but ultimately the vision was for the king; Daniel served as the conduit to present that knowledge to the king.

Daniel 4

Since Daniel was not part of the experience described in chapter 3, we need not comment on the mode of revelation employed there. The prophetic revelations take up again in chapter 4. There we have the same situation as in Daniel 2. The king had a dream, and Daniel ultimately came in to interpret it for the king. The king's dream was of a great tree that represented Nebuchadnezzar himself. It was cut down, representing Nebuchadnezzar's period of madness. Eventually, he was to be restored and would recognize that the God of heaven is in control of earthly affairs—even those concerning Nebuchadnezzar's kingdom and his life. Daniel's part, again, was to serve as the inspired wise man who interpreted the king's dream for him. It was a direct revelation to Nebuchadnezzar; it was indirect to Daniel. The case is directly parallel to what happened in Daniel 2. Thus far in the book, we have chapter 1 in which God was hidden but still active, and chapters 2 and 4 in which the king received the primary revelation and Daniel served as the inspired wise man who interpreted the king's dreams for him.

Daniel 7

This prophecy came to Daniel in the first year of Belshazzar, or about 550 B.C. This was sometime before the events of Daniel 5 and 6 that we can date to 539 B.C. and 538 B.C. respectively. Belshazzar was still one of the kings of the Neo-Babylonian Empire before it fell to the Persians. But in this case, the dream did not come to Belshazzar. It came directly to Daniel. It came to him exactly as the dreams had come to Nebuchadnezzar previously. Nebuchadnezzar had had dreams at night while he was lying on his bed asleep. The next morning when he awoke, he could not remember the dream; Daniel had to supply the dream itself as well as the interpretation. In this case, however, the dream came directly to Daniel as he lay asleep upon his bed. And he did not forget the content of the dream. He woke up the next morning ready to write down what he had seen in the dream. The mode of revelation was the same, a night dream, but the target recipient was different. In the two previous cases, the dream was given to the pagan king, and Daniel had to go in to the king to interpret the dream for him. Now the dream came directly to Daniel with no intermediary.

One can say that Daniel became a prophet in his own right on this occasion. Previously, he had served as an inspired wise man at court; now he stood free and independent as a prophet. The vision of chapter 7 was, in essence, his call to the office of a prophet. Another aspect of this prophetic dream was that within it, while in vision, Daniel was given an angel interpreter. He had not had such an interpreter previously. In 7:9-14, his view was lifted up to the heavenly court, and while he was watching, he "approached one of those standing there and asked him the true meaning of all this" (vs. 16). In vision, the angel spoke to him and gave him the explanation. This marks an advance in Daniel's experience over the two previous cases. Now the revelation was directed especially to Daniel himself, and he was given an angel interpreter within the night dream to interpret the symbols of the vision for him.

Daniel 8

The vision in this chapter was of a different nature. Daniel was not given a dream while lying on his bed. Instead, he was taken out of his daily activities and transported in vision to the province of Elam, east of Babylon. There he watched the rise of Persia through the symbol of the ram, followed by the rise of Greece through the symbol of the goat that came from the opposite direction. Then came the four horns and the little horn and finally the promise of the two angels who talked about the 2300 days. In this vision, Daniel was transported east to Elam, just as Ezekiel was transported west to Jerusalem. This does not mean that either of them were transported bodily; they were transported in vision.

After Daniel had seen and heard the vision of Daniel 8, an angel interpreter was sent to him. In this case, however, the angel did not appear to
him within the vision itself as had the two angels in the earlier vision
who talked to him about the 2300 days. Instead, Gabriel was sent to
him personally, bodily, and audibly. While Daniel was in a deep sleep,
having been overcome by the majesty and events of the vision, Gabriel
touched him and gave him strength so he could stand up and listen to
the angel's explanation. In this case, therefore, the mode of presentation
of the vision is becoming more and more direct. Daniel was the direct
recipient of the vision, and an angel is sent directly to him to interpret it
for him. God is coming closer and closer to Daniel as the prophet continues His faithful walk with Him.

Daniel 5

In terms of the order of the book, we need to drop back to chapter 5 in order to pick up the transition from the Babylonian kingdom to the Persian kingdom. Daniel 5 depicts the very night in which
Babylon was overthrown by the Persians and tells us what happened
in the palace at that time. A disembodied hand appeared and wrote
on the wall of the palace throne room a message for the king and the
people in attendance at the banquet. Only Daniel was able to interpret the writing. The writing on the wall signified that the kingdom
of Belshazzar, the Neo-Babylonian Empire, had come to an end and
that the Persians were going to take over.

In this case, the mode of revelation was visible to all of the participants present. They saw the hand writing and the message it wrote,
even though they could not read or understand it. This was a message sent directly from God through one of His angel servants. It
was the direct presence of an angel that put the message on the wall.
The revelation did not come through a dream or vision; it came
through a personal appearance by the angel. This is very much like
the second half of Daniel 8, where an angel came directly to Daniel
to interpret the vision for him. In chapter 5, Daniel served as the
interpreter of the writing that predicted the downfall of the kingdom that very night.

Daniel 9

In the chronological order of the book, the events of chapter 9 follow next after those of chapter 5. Daniel's prayer and Gabriel's prophecy as recorded in this chapter occurred sometime during the first year of Darius the Mede, or 538 B.C., which was also the first year after the fall of Babylon to the Persians. What happened here bears considerable similarity to both the last half of chapter 8 and the revelation in Daniel 5. In both those cases, there was a personal appearance by an angel. The same thing occurred here in chapter 9. But there are a few differences. In Daniel 8 a vision preceded the angel's interpretation. In chapter 9 there was no immediately preceding vision, although the angel began his interpretive prophecy by referring back to the vision of chapter 8. In Daniel 5, the writing of the angel was addressed to the whole audience present in the banquet hall. In chapter 9, the prophecy was directed only to Daniel himself, to be given by him to his own and later generations. Thus chapters 5, 8, and 9 all contain the same type of revelation—the personal appearance of an angel—but the circumstances were different in each case. In chapter 9 the focus comes down more directly to Daniel himself; here is a prophetic message delivered directly to Daniel orally and without any other audience present.

In Daniel 1 there was no direct disclosure of God Himself; He remained hidden, though active behind the scenes. In chapters 2 and 4, God worked indirectly through the dreams of a pagan king, which Daniel interpreted as an inspired wise man. Now in chapters 5, 8, and 9, there is the personal appearance of an angel— once with writing, once with a day vision, and once directly with oral communication. Thus we see a progression in God's mode of revelation as He comes to Daniel more and more directly and personally. But an angel is not God; he is only a servant of God. Will Daniel ever see God Himself before his prophetic ministry is finished? That great climax comes in the last prophecy of the book.

Daniel 10

Chapters 10, 11, and 12 form a unit. Chapter 10 is the introduction to the prophecy given by the angel Gabriel; chapter 11 is the body of the prophecy; and chapter 12 is the epilogue. Daniel 10 carries the date of the third year of Cyrus, or 536 B.C. Daniel was an old man by this time. He had been carried into captivity in 605 B.C., so he himself had lived out the seventy years of Jeremiah's prophecy (Jer. 25:11, 12) in Babylonian captivity. Since he was about eighteen to twenty years of age when he was taken into captivity, Daniel must have been about ninety years of age at the time this final revelation came to him. The body of the prophecy in chapter 11 was delivered orally by Gabriel to Daniel, just as he had done in chapter 9. But the introduction to the prophecy in chapter 10 is something new that has not been seen before in the book of Daniel.

At the time of this vision, Daniel was out by the Tigris River. He was praying, mourning, and fasting about the interruption in the efforts of God's people to rebuild the temple. Now as Daniel was out by the river agonizing over this situation, something dramatic happened.

> I looked up and there before me was a man dressed in linen, with a belt of the finest gold around his waist. His body was like chrysolite, his face like lightning, his eyes like flaming torches, his arms and legs like the gleam of burnished bronze, and his voice like the sound of a multitude (Daniel 10:5-7).

Daniel was overwhelmed with the majestic theophany. This was a vision, but the English word *vision* does not convey the full meaning of the original word used here. This was a *mareh* vision, or an appearance vision. It means that this Being had put in a personal appearance before the prophet. Daniel had been overwhelmed by previous visions, Daniel 8 in particular. But this appearance was far more powerful than anything he had ever received previously. This is a theophany—an appearance of God Himself.

There are two other passages in the Bible that present descriptions closely aligned with the appearance of this Being that is described here in chapter 10. Those two visions are found in Ezekiel 1 and Revelation 1. In Ezekiel 1, the prophet recognized that the Being he saw was "the appearance of the likeness of the glory of the Lord" (Eze. 1:28). In Revelation 1, John turned to see who was speaking to him and recognized that he was looking directly at his Lord, Jesus Christ. By means of these parallels, therefore, we know who appeared to Daniel when he was out by the Tigris River. On the basis of the parallel with Ezekiel 1, we know that this was God, and on the basis of the parallel with Revelation 1, we know that this particular manifestation of God was Jesus Christ. It was He who appeared to Daniel on the plain of the Tigris on that spring day in 536 B.C.

This was the same God who had been with Daniel all of the seventy years the prophet had been in Babylon. God had been working with him, working for him, inspiring him, and protecting him. He had been walking at his side all the time Daniel ministered there. Little by little, more and more, God opened Himself up to Daniel in terms of the revelations that He gave to Him. The mode of these revelations demonstrates the way in which God came closer and closer and closer to Daniel. First, there was no revelation at all. Then the revelations came through a pagan king and his night dreams; then they came through a night vision given to Daniel himself. Following that, came a day vision and an angel, Gabriel, who began appearing to Daniel and communicating the prophetic word to him. Finally, near the end of Daniel's life and prophetic ministry, God Himself appeared to Daniel and said in essence, "Here I am, Daniel. We have been walking together for these past seventy years. Now I want you to see the One you have been walking with." Daniel met his Lord personally. God had been coming closer and closer to Him until He finally revealed His personal being to Him in all His glory.

When Daniel lay down to rest in death, as the angel told him he soon would, he could do so with a smile on his face, for he had finally met his Lord personally. The next thing Daniel will know is awaking on the resurrection morning. His resurrection from the dead was also promised to him by the angel (12:13). Daniel will see that same glorious, radiant, smiling face beaming down upon him; he will listen to the Lifegiver's voice, "Awake, awake, you that sleep in the dust and arise." And Daniel will come forth to walk with his Lord anew in a walk that will take him into eternity.

Enoch's case is somewhat similar to that of Daniel's in this regard, but Enoch was translated alive, while Daniel will have to wait a bit longer for that experience. Nevertheless, their spiritual experience has parallels. Ellen White has described Enoch's walk with God in very poignant terms that could well apply to Daniel:

> For three hundred years Enoch had been seeking purity of soul, that he might be in harmony with Heaven. For three centuries he had walked with God. Day by day he had longed for a closer union; nearer and nearer had grown the communion, until God took him to Himself. He had stood at the threshold of the eternal world, only a step between him and the land of the blest; and now the portals opened, the walk with God, so long pursued on earth, continued, and he passed through the gates of the Holy City—the first from among men to enter there (*Patriarchs and Prophets*, 87).

This type of experience is not just for Enoch, and it is not just for Daniel. It is also for us today. Granted, we may not have prophetic revelations as Daniel did. However, we may have a walk with God in which we come closer and closer to Him each day. That should be the course of progress in our spiritual lives as it was for Daniel. As we come closer to God in this way, we will understand His will for our lives better. We will also learn more of His character and come to reflect it more fully. As we become more and more like Him, people will take knowledge of us, as they did of the disciples, that we have been with Jesus.

Daniel would be happy to see this taking place in our lives. When he comes up in the resurrection, Daniel will be pleased to know that his book, which God gave to him, has provided such hope and comfort and inspiration to us in the final generation of those things predicted in it. In God's eternal kingdom, we will be able to continue the walk with God that we have begun here on this earth. At the head of that great throng will be our Lord Jesus Christ, leading us onward.

■ Applying the Word

1. Even though I do not receive direct prophetic revelations as did the prophets, can my personal spiritual walk with God parallel Daniel's experience? As I review my personal experience with God, has it gotten closer, or has it been arrested? On what evidence do I base my answer?
2. Am I coming closer and closer to God in my daily spiritual walk so that when He reveals Himself in glory I will be ready to walk into the heavenly kingdom with Him? What specifics do I need to do in my personal spiritual life to enrich this experience?

■ Researching the Word

1. Study the life of other biblical prophets to see how their experience with God developed. Jeremiah is an excellent example because he gives us more of the biographical details of his life than did the other prophets.

■ Further Study of the Word

1. For an overview of Daniel's walk with God, see E. G. White, *Prophets and Kings*, chapters 39–44, but especially chapter 42.